iOS 10
by Tutorials

By the raywenderlich.com Tutorial Team

Sam Davies, Jeff Rames, & Rich Turton

iOS 10 by Tutorials

Sam Davies, Jeff Rames, & Rich Turton

Copyright ©2016 Razeware LLC.

ISBN: 978-1-942878-31-5

Dedications

"To Siri, without whom this project would have been far less frustrating, and to Pui, without whom Siri would have found itself thrown out of a window."

— *Sam Davies*

"To my wonderful wife April, for all the love and support. To my daughters Heidi and Jillian, for reminding me to take time to play."

— *Jeff Rames*

"To my wife and daughters, who had to (or is that "got to"?) spend many summer evenings without me."

— *Rich Turton*

About the authors

Sam Davies is a strange mashup of developer, writer and trainer. By day you'll find him recording videos for Razeware, writing tutorials, attending conferences and generally being a good guy. By night he's likely to be out entertaining people, armed with his trombone and killer dance moves. He'd like it very much if you were to follow him on twitter at @iwantmyrealname.

Jeff Rames is an iOS developer at AirStrip Technologies, building software that helps save lives. Originally a mainframer, he found his passion in iOS development shortly after the SDK was released and has been doing it ever since. When not working, he's spending time with his wife and daughters, watching rocket launches, or cooking with his pizza oven. Say hi to Jeff on Twitter at @jefframes.

Rich Turton Rich Turton is an iOS developer for MartianCraft, prolific Stack Overflow participant and author of a development blog, Command Shift. When he's not in front of a computer he is usually building Lego horse powered spaceships (don't ask!) with his daughters.

About the editors

Zoltán Matók is a tech editor of this book. Zoltán is an iOS and OS X developer from Hungary. While he is not working or fiddling with new stuff, he likes to read insightful articles from around the development world. https://medium.com/@quinnnorton ftw.

Morten Faarkrog is a tech editor of this book. Morten is a twenty-something Software Development student and iOS developer from Copenhagen, Denmark. He was first introduced to iOS development around the launch of Swift and has been in love with it ever since. When Morten isn't developing apps and studying, and his adorable cat isn't riding on his shoulders, he spends his time working out, reading interesting books, and diving into the world of biohacking. You can find Morten on Twitter at @mfaarkrog.

 **Chris Belanger** is the editor of this book. Chris is the Book Team Lead and Lead Editor for raywenderlich.com. If there are words to wrangle or a paragraph to ponder, he's on the case. When he kicks back, you can usually find Chris with guitar in hand, looking for the nearest beach, or exploring the lakes and rivers in his part of the world in a canoe.

 **Ray Wenderlich** is the final pass editor of this book. Ray is part of a great team - the raywenderlich.com team, a group of over 100 developers and editors from across the world. He and the rest of the team are passionate both about making apps and teaching others the techniques to make them. When Ray's not programming, he's probably playing video games, role playing games, or board games.

Table of Contents:

Introduction 11
    What you need 12
    Who this book is for 12
    What's in store 13
    How to use this book 18
    Book source code and forums 19
    PDF Version 19
    License 20
    Acknowledgments 20
    About the cover 21

Chapter 1: What's New in Swift 3 23
    The Grand Renaming 24
    Foundation value types 27
    Working with C APIs 29
    Language feature changes 31
    Where to go from here? 35

Chapter 2: Xcode 8 Debugging Improvements.............. 37
    Getting started.. 38
    Investigating the project 39
    Memory Graph debugging 40
    Thread Sanitizer... 49
    View debugging... 55
    Static analyzer enhancements 62
    Where to go from here? 63
    xcode-source-editor-extensions 65

Chapter 3: Xcode 8 Source Editor Extensions................ 65
    Getting started.. 66
    Why source editor extensions? 67
    Creating a new extension 68

Building the Asciiify extension 71
Dynamic commands 80
Where to go from here? 84

Chapter 4: Beginning Message Apps 85

Getting started 85
Creating a sticker application 88
Where to go from here? 102

Chapter 5: Intermediate Message Apps 103

Getting started 103
The Messages app view controller 104
Adding the first child view controller 105
Switching view controllers 108
Creating a message 109
Custom message content 113
Getting a second chance 119
Where to go from here? 120

Chapter 6: SiriKit 121

Getting started 122
Would you like to ride in my beautiful balloon? 122
99 (passengers in) red balloons 128
You can't handle the truth 133
Making a balloon animal, er, UI 136
Where to go from here? 139

Chapter 7: Speech Recognition 141

Getting started 142
Transcription basics 145
Audio file speech transcription 146
Transcription and locales 150
Live speech recognition 152
Usage guidelines 159
Where to go from here? 160

Chapter 8: User Notifications 161

Getting started 162
The User Notifications framework 163
Managing notifications 169
Notification content extensions 174
Notification Service app extensions 186
Where to go from here? 192

Chapter 9: Property Animators 195

Getting started 196
Timing is everything 197
Controlling your frog 199
Spring animations 201
Inspecting in-progress animations 204
Pausing and scrubbing 205
Stopping 208
Reversing 210
Multiple animators 211
View controller transitions 215
Where to go from here? 218

Chapter 10: Measurements and Units 219

Measurement and Unit 220
I want to ride my bicycle 221
Uranium Fever 223
Measure for MeasurementFormatter 226
(Custom) Dimension 228
Chain of fools 230
Turning it up to 11 231
24 Hours From Tulsa 233
Where to go from here? 236

Chapter 11: What's New with Core Data 237

Getting spudded 238

An eye to new data models 238
A stack with a peel 241
Frenched russet controllers.. 243
Digging in to the background... 246
iCloud Core Data gets mashed 251
Where to go from here? 251

Chapter 12: What's New with Photography 253

Smile, you're on camera!.. 253
Taking a photo.. 259
Making it fabulous 266
Live photos 270
Editing Live Photos 274
Where to go from here? 280

Chapter 13: What's New with Search......................... 281

Getting started.. 282
Enabling search continuation 284
Implementing search continuation....................................... 285
Core Spotlight Search API 289
Proactive suggestions for location 296
Where to go from here? 300

Chapter 14: Other iOS 10 Topics............................. 301

Getting started.. 301
Data source prefetching 303
UIPreviewInteraction 308
Haptic feedback 317
Where to go from here? 320

Conclusion 323

Introduction

Each year at WWDC, Apple introduces brand new tools and APIs for iOS developers. This year, iOS 10 and Xcode 8 has brought a lot of new goodies to play with!

First, iOS 10 brought some fun features to Messages — and also opened up the app to third party developers. First, developers can now create and sell sticker packs — simple, but sure to be popular. Second, developers can go deeper and create fully interactive message experiences. For example, you could create a simple drawing guessing game right within Messages — in fact, you'll learn how to do that in this book.

Second, iOS 10 brings a feature long wished for by developers — the ability to integrate with Siri! If your app fits into a limited number of categories, you can create a new Intents Extension to handle voice requests by users in your own apps. Regardless of your app's category, you can also use the new iOS 10 speech recognizer within your own apps.

Third, Xcode 8 represents a significant new release. It ships with Swift 3, which has a number of syntax changes that will affect all developers. In addition. Xcode comes with a number of great new debugging tools to help you diagnose memory and threading issues.

And that's just the start. iOS 10 is chock-full of new content and changes that every developer should know about. Gone are the days when every 3rd-party developer knew everything there is to know about the OS. The sheer size of iOS can make new releases seem daunting. That's why the Tutorial Team has been working really hard to extract the important parts of the new APIs, and to present this information in an easy-to-understand tutorial format. This means you can focus on what you want to be doing — building amazing apps!

Get ready for your own private tour through the amazing new features of iOS 10. By the time you're done, your iOS knowledge will be completely up-to-date and you'll be able to benefit from the amazing new opportunities in iOS 10.

Sit back, relax and prepare for some high quality tutorials!

What you need

To follow along with the tutorials in this book, you'll need the following:

- **A Mac running OS X Yosemite or later.** You'll need this to be able to install the latest version of Xcode.

- **Xcode 8.0 or later.** Xcode is the main development tool for iOS. You'll need Xcode 8.0 or later for all tasks in this book. You can download the latest version of Xcode 8 beta on Apple's developer site here: apple.co/2asi58y

- **One or more devices (iPhone, iPad, or iPod Touch) running iOS 10 or later.** Most of the chapters in the book let you run your code on the iOS 10 Simulator that comes with Xcode. However, a few chapters later in the book require one or more physical iOS devices for testing.

Once you have these items in place, you'll be able to follow along with every chapter in this book.

Who this book is for

This book is for intermediate or advanced iOS developers who already know the basics of iOS and Swift development but want to learn about the new APIs, frameworks, and changes in Xcode 8 and iOS 10.

- **If you are a complete beginner to iOS development**, we recommend you read through *The iOS Apprentice, Fifth Edition* first. Otherwise this book may be a bit too advanced for you.

- **If you are a beginner to Swift**, we recommend you read through either *The iOS Apprentice, Fifth Edition* (if you are a complete beginner to programming), or *The Swift Apprentice, Second Edition* (if you already have some programming experience) first.

If you need one of these prerequisite books, you can find them on our store here:

- www.raywenderlich.com/store

As with raywenderlich.com, all the tutorials in this book are in Swift.

What's in store

Here's a quick summary of what you'll find in each chapter:

1. Chapter 1, What's New in Swift 3: Swift 3 represents the biggest change to the language since it was first introduced. Read this chapter for a quick overview of what's new!

```
// Swift 2 definition
prepareForSegue(segue: UIStoryboardSegue, sender: AnyObject?)
// Swift 2 calling code
viewController.prepareForSegue(segue, sender: something)

// Swift 3 definition
prepare(for segue: UIStoryboardSegue, sender: Any?)
// Swift 3 calling code
viewController.prepare(for: segue, sender: something)
```

2. Chapter 2, Xcode 8 Debugging Improvements: Learn about the powerful new debugging tools in Xcode 8, including the new Thread Sanitizer and Memory Graph Debugger.

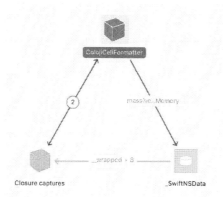

3. Chapter 3, Xcode 8 Source Editor Extensions: Learn how to integrate your own text tools into the Xcode UI by creating a fun ASCII art extension.

4. Chapter 4, Beginning Message Apps: Learn how to create your own sticker pack for Messages — with a custom user interface.

5. Chapter 5, Intermediate Message Apps: Learn how to create your own sticker pack for Messages — with a custom user interface.

6. Chapter 6, SiriKit: Learn how to integrate Siri into your app and process voice commands as you build a Uber clone for hot air balloons.

7. Chapter 7, Speech Recognition: Learn how to transcribe live or pre-recorded audio from over 50 languages and use that data in your app.

8. Chapter 8, User Notifications: Learn how to use the new iOS 10 User Notifications framework, and create Notification Content extensions and Notification Service app extensions.

9. Chapter 9, UIView Property Animator: Learn about a new way of animating in iOS 10, which allows you to easily pause, reverse, and scrub through animations part-way through.

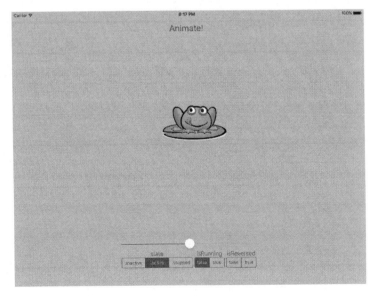

10. Chapter 10, Measurements and Units: Learn about some new Foundation classes that help you work with measurements and units in an easy and type-safe way.

```
let cycleRide = Measurement(value: 25, unit:
UnitLength.kilometers)
let swim = Measurement(value: 3, unit: UnitLength.nauticalMiles)
let marathon = Measurement(value: 26, unit: UnitLength.miles)
    + Measurement(value: 385, unit: UnitLength.yards)
```

11. Chapter 11, What's New with Core Data: Learn how the new convenience methods, classes, code generation and other new features in Core Data will make your life easier.

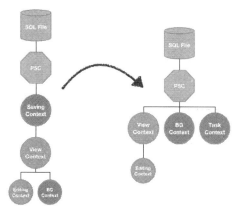

12. Chapter 12, What's New with Photography: Learn how to capture and edit live photos, and make use of other photography advancements.

13. Chapter 13, What's New with Search: Learn how to tie your app into the Core Search Spotlight API and perform deep searches using your app, and how to surface your app to respond to location-based searches as well.

App Switcher   QuickType   Maps   Siri

14. Chapter 14, Other iOS 10 Topics: Make your apps more responsive with prefetching, make custom interactions with 3D touch, and add haptic feedback to your apps.

Preview State   Commit State   Post Commit

How to use this book

This book can be read from cover to cover, but we don't recommend using it this way unless you have a lot of time and are the type of person who just "needs to know everything". (It's okay; a lot of our tutorial team is like that, too!)

Instead, we suggest a pragmatic approach — pick and choose the chapters that interest you the most, or the chapters you need immediately for your current projects. Most chapters are self-contained, so you can go through the book in a non-sequential order.

Looking for some recommendations of important chapters to start with? Here's our suggested Core Reading List:

- Chapter 1, "What's New in Swift 3"

- Chapter 2, "Xcode 8 Debugging Improvements"

- Chapter 4, "Beginning Message Apps"

- Chapter 5, "Intermediate Message Apps"

- Chapter 6, "SiriKit"

- Chapter 8, "User Notifications"

That covers the "Big 6" topics of iOS 10; from there you can dig into other topics of particular interest to you.

Book source code and forums

You can get the source code for the book here:

www.raywenderlich.com/store/ios-10-by-tutorials/source-code

You'll find all the code from the chapters, as well as solutions to the challenges for your reference.

We've also set up an official forum for the book at www.raywenderlich.com/forums. This is a great place to ask any questions you have about the book, or to submit any errors you might find.

PDF Version

We also have a PDF version of this book available, which can be handy if you want a soft copy to take with you, or you want to quickly search for a specific term within the book.

Buying the PDF version of the book also has a few extra benefits: free PDF updates each time we update the book, access to older PDF versions of the book, and you can download the PDF from anywhere, at anytime.

Visit the book store page here: raywenderlich.com/store/ios-10-by-tutorials.

License

By purchasing *iOS 10 by Tutorials*, you have the following license:

- You are allowed to use and/or modify the source code in *iOS 10 by Tutorials* in as many apps as you want, with no attribution required.

- You are allowed to use and/or modify all art, images, or designs that are included in *iOS 10 by Tutorials* in as many apps as you want, but must include this attribution line somewhere inside your app: "Artwork/images/designs: from the *iOS 10 by Tutorials* book, available at www.raywenderlich.com".

- The source code included in *iOS 10 by Tutorials* is for your own personal use only. You are NOT allowed to distribute or sell the source code in *iOS 10 by Tutorials* without prior authorization.

- This book is for your own personal use only. You are NOT allowed to sell this book without prior authorization, or distribute it to friends, co-workers, or students; they must purchase their own copy instead.

All materials provided with this book are provided on an "as is" basis, without warranty of any kind, express or implied, including but not limited to the warranties of merchantability, fitness for a particular purpose and non-infringement. In no event shall the authors or copyright holders be liable for any claim, damages or other liability, whether in an action of contract, tort or otherwise, arising from, out of or in connection with the software or the use or other dealings in the software.

All trademarks and registered trademarks appearing in this guide are the property of their respective owners.

Acknowledgments

We would like to thank many people for their assistance in making this possible:

- **Our families:** For bearing with us in this crazy time as we worked all hours of the night to get this book ready for publication!

- **Everyone at Apple:** For developing an amazing operating system and set of APIs, for constantly inspiring us to improve our apps and skills, and for making it possible for many developers to have their dream jobs!

- **And most importantly, the readers of raywenderlich.com — especially you!** Thank you so much for reading our site and purchasing this book. Your continued readership and support is what makes all of this possible!

About the cover

The clownfish, also known as the anemonefish, lives inside the sea anemone in a symbiotic arrangement. The tentacles of the anemone protect the clownfish from other predators, while the clownfish eats the parasites that would otherwise attack the anemone. It's a lot like being an iOS developer: Apple creates great environments for our apps, and iOS developers create amazing apps (and file annoying Radar bug reports) for those environments. There's nothing fishy about that! :]

Chapter 1: What's New in Swift 3

By Rich Turton

Swift 3 brings a tremendous set of changes to the language. In fact, the changes are so big, that I hope this is the biggest set of changes we'll ever see; as developers, we can't go through this kind of pain again! :]

But on the bright side, the changes do leave you with *much* nicer code. It finally feels like you're writing UIKit apps in Swift, rather than forcing a Swift peg into an Objective-C (or even just C) shaped hole.

If you take a reasonably-sized project written in Swift 2, and let Xcode migrate it to Swift 3, you're in for a shock. It's a big bang, and almost everything has changed.

The noisiest part of the upgrade is what Apple refers to as the Grand Renaming. This is a huge review of *all* of the first-party frameworks, and redefines types and method signatures to match a set of solid naming guidelines. As third-party developers, we're also encouraged to follow these naming guidelines in our own code.

On top of this, lots of Foundation **NS** types have been swallowed up by more "Swifty" value types, making them clearer to work with and more accessible to non-Apple platforms.

Some of the low-level C APIs have also been thoroughly worked over, making working with them as simple and expressive as working with native Swift types.

Finally, there have been some language-level changes to Swift itself, which will probably affect the code you've written up to now.

If you're new to Swift, congratulations and welcome — it's a great language. If you've got existing Swift code you want to keep working on, get yourself ready for a few days of grunt work. Let's get started.

The Grand Renaming

The Grand Renaming affects the methods provided by Foundation, UIKit and the other Apple frameworks. Remember that most of these frameworks are probably still written in Objective-C, and up until this point the Swift methods have looked very similar.

Here's an example from UIKit, to get a specific cell from a table view. I sneaked in to the code graveyard on a foggy night and exhumed this from the Objective-C family plot:

```
UITableViewCell *cell =
  [tableView cellForRowAtIndexPath: indexPath];
```

Take a close look at this line of code, and look to see if you can find any words that are repeated.

I count two "table views", three "cells" and two "indexPaths". Here's what this same line looks like in Swift 2:

```
let cell = tableView.cellForRowAtIndexPath(indexPath)
```

Type inference lets us drop a "table view" and a "cell", but we still have two "index paths" — because who *doesn't* call a temporary local variable holding an index path indexPath?

And finally in Swift 3:

```
let cell = tableView.cellForRowAt(indexPath)
```

Now, the only repeated word is "cell", and that's acceptable, because one of them is a value name, and the other is part of the function.

This evolution of this method name follows the three key principles guiding the Grand Renaming:

1. **Clarity at the call site**: Method calls should read as much like English sentences as possible.

2. **Assume common patterns and naming conventions**: As in the assumption that the indexPath variable would be so named.

3. **Avoid repeated words**: Allowing the "index path" to be removed from the parameter name.

You'll find that many UIKit and Foundation methods have similarly shrunk. In particular, methods that would name the type of the first argument have had that part of the name removed.

```
// Swift 2 definition
prepareForSegue(segue: UIStoryboardSegue, sender: AnyObject?)
// Swift 2 calling code
viewController.prepareForSegue(segue, sender: something)

// Swift 3 definition
prepare(for segue: UIStoryboardSegue, sender: Any?)
// Swift 3 calling code
viewController.prepare(for: segue, sender: something)
```

This highlights another important difference between Swift 2 and Swift 3. The first argument name now appears by default in the signature of a function or method, whereas in Swift 2 (and Objective-C) it was ignored by default.

```
// Function definition:
func engageFluxCapacitor(fluxCapacitor: FluxCapacitor)

// Called in Swift 2:
timeMachine.engageFluxCapacitor(fluxCapacitor)

// Called in Swift 3:
timeMachine.engageFluxCapacitor(fluxCapacitor: fluxCapacitor)
```

When you migrate a project from Swift 2 to Swift 3, Xcode will take care of all of the framework methods for you, but it might make a bit of a mess of your own code. For example, the Swift 3 updater will change the function signature above to this:

```
func engageFluxCapacitor(_ fluxCapacitor: FluxCapacitor)
```

The underscore indicates that you don't wish to use an argument label for the first argument. This is the simplest code change that will allow your project to run using Swift 3. However, the method doesn't follow the new guidelines. The type of the first argument doesn't need to form part of the method name, because you can assume that the value you pass in will have a name that makes this obvious. The correct Swift 3 signature of this method would be:

```
func engage(_ fluxCapacitor: FluxCapacitor)

// Called like this:
timeMachine.engage(fluxCapacitor)
```

When migrating your existing projects, you'll have to decide if it's worth the effort to Grandly Rename your own APIs. The bizarre and continuing lack of refactoring support for Swift in Xcode probably means that for most projects, you probably won't bother. But for new code, you really should.

In addition to the three principles above, there are some more specific guidelines to understand, regarding overloading and grammatical rules.

Overloading

If you remove the type name from the method name and don't use a label for the first argument, then you may end up in a situation where you have multiple methods with the same name, that differ only in the type of argument. You should only do this if the methods are doing semantically the same thing.

For example, if you're adding a single item or multiple items to a list, you could have two `add(_:)` methods, one which takes an array, and one which takes an individual item. That's fine because they both do the same thing, just with different types.

However, in cases where the methods perform different actions based on the type, you should use the argument label or rename the methods so that it is clear from the call site what is happening.

For example, consider a `VideoLoader` class. This class could have `VideoRequest` objects which deal with getting video data from the internet, and `VideoOutputHandler` objects which deal with playing the video.

It isn't right to have two `add(_:)` methods, one for adding requests, and one for adding output handlers, because those methods are doing completely different things. You should have an `addLoader(_:)` and `addOutput(_:)` method in this case.

Grammatical rules

The examples in this section will all be methods on a made-up struct called `WordList`, which as you may have guessed, holds a list of words.

The first rule is that you shouldn't name the first argument, unless it doesn't make sense at the call site without it. For example, to get a word at a specific index in the list:

```
// Doesn't read like a sentence
let word = wordList.word(1)

// Reads like a sentence
let word = wordList.word(at: 1)

// Function definition:
func word(at index: Int) -> String {
    ...
}
```

If a method has side effects, it should be named with a verb. Side effects are work that is done by a method that affects something other than the return value of that method. So if you had a method that sorted the word list, you'd name it:

```
// "Sort" is a verb, the sorting is in-place,
// so it is a side effect.
mutating func sortAlphabetically() {
  ...
}
```

Value types often have a non-mutating version of any of their mutating methods, which return a new instance of the type with the changes applied. In this case, you should use the **ed/ing** rule to name the method:

```
// sortED
func sortedAlphabetically() -> WordList {
  ...
}
```

When "ed" doesn't make sense, you can use "ing". Here's another mutating / non-mutating pair:

```
// Remove is a verb
mutating func removeWordsContaining(_ substring: String) {
  ...
}

// RemovING
func removingWordsContaining(_ substring: String) -> WordList {
  ...
}
```

The final grammatical rule relates to `Bool` properties. These should be prefixed with `is`:

```
var isSortedAlphabetically: Bool
```

Foundation value types

Many Foundation types have now adapted value semantics rather than reference semantics in Swift 3. What does that mean?

Value types are types that can be identified by their *value*. As the simplest example, an `Int` of 1 can be considered identical to any other `Int` of 1. When you assign a value type to another variable, the properties are copied.

```
var oneNumber = 1
var anotherNumber = oneNumber
anotherNumber += 1
// oneNumber will still be 1
```

Swift structs are all value types.

Reference types are identified by *what they are*. You might have two friends named Mic, but they are different people. When you assign a reference type to another variable, they share the reference:

```
class Person {
   var name: String
}

let person1 = Person(name: "Ray")
let person2 = person1
person2.name = "Mic"
// person1.name is also Mic
```

Swift classes are all reference types.

Value and reference types both have their advantages and disadvantages. This isn't the place to get into that argument, but the only value types available in Objective-C were structs and primitives, which had no functionality beyond holding information.

This limitation meant that anything with any functionality became a class, and was therefore a reference type. The main problem with reference types is that you have no idea who else is also holding a reference, and what they might do with it.

Immutability or mutability in Foundation types was implemented by having two separate classes, like `NSString` and `NSMutableString`. Anything that holds a mutable reference type property runs the risk of the meaning of that property being changed by something else that shares the reference. This is the source of a lot of hard-to-detect bugs, and it's why experienced Objective-C programmers do things like declare `NSString` properties as `copy`.

In Swift 3, lots of Foundation classes are now wrapped in Swift value types. You can declare immutability or mutability by using `var` or `let` declarations. This was already the case with the `String` type, but now it has gone much further. In most cases, this is indicated by a disappearing `NS` prefix: `NSDate` is now `Date`, and so on.

What's happening under the hood is quite interesting. You might be panicking about copies of objects being made all over the place and eating up all of your memory, but this doesn't happen. These value type wrappers use a mechanism called *copy on write*.

Copy on write means that the underlying reference type is shared between everything that cares about it, *until something tries to change it*. At that point, a new copy is made, just for the thing that made the changes, with the new values applied. This optimization lets you get the benefits of value and reference types at the same time :]

> **Note:** For more details on value vs. reference types in Swift, check out our free tutorial on the subject: bit.ly/2eeZuNG

Working with C APIs

If you've spent much time developing iOS apps, there are two C APIs you've probably encountered: Grand Central Dispatch (GCD) and Core Graphics. Like all C APIs, they are notable by their use of free functions (meaning, top-level functions rather than methods defined on instances or classes).

Free functions are no fun, because they are essentially all in a massive bucket. Autocomplete can do nothing to help you. To counter these problems, free functions all end up with long, wordy names that include identifying text (everything relating to a core graphics context begins with `CGContext`, for example), and you need to pass in the basic values you're working with (like the graphics context) to every single operation. This results in code that is tedious to read and tedious to write.

Here's some great news: As of Swift 3, you will no longer realize you're dealing with C!

Grand Central Dispatch

Here's how you create a dispatch queue in Swift 3:

```
let queue = DispatchQueue(
    label: "com.razeware.my-queue",
    qos: .userInitiated)
```

And here's how you add some work to it:

```
queue.async {
    print("Hello from my serial queue!")
}
```

All of the `dispatch_whatever_whatever()` functions have now been beautifully gift-wrapped in the Dispatch framework, giving you a much nicer interface for dealing with GCD. It looks like native Swift code now, making it easier to read, write, and blend in with the rest of your codebase.

A common GCD use case is to send some work off to the main queue, for example when you've completed work on a background thread and want to update the UI. That's done like this:

```
DispatchQueue.main.async {
  print("Hello from the main queue!")
}
```

Dispatching work after a delay is now much easier as well. You used to need a magic incantation involving nanoseconds, now you can do this:

```
DispatchQueue.main.asyncAfter(deadline: .now() + 5) {
  print("It's five seconds later!")
}
```

Core Graphics

Core Graphics is a very useful framework, particularly in these days of multiple scale-factor, multiple screen size support. It can often be easier to draw some of your assets in code than supply and update 15 PNG files of the same image. But the Core Graphics code is written in C, and it used to look pretty clunky. Now, it's kind of nice.

Consider transforms. When creating beautiful animations or transitions, you often want to stack up several transitions, such as a scale, a translation and a rotation. In Swift 3, you can do this:

```
let transform = CGAffineTransform.identity
  .scaledBy(x: 0.5, y: 0.5)
  .translatedBy(x: 100, y: 100)
  .rotated(by: .pi / 4)
```

If you're not doing the screaming face emoji in real life right now, then you've probably never written CGAffineTransform code before. It gets better! When dealing with a CGContext, there are a variety of things you can set on the context to affect the next lot of drawing you could do — the stroke color, shadow offset and so forth. That code now looks like this:

```
let rectangle = CGRect(x: 5, y: 5, width: 200, height: 200)

context.setFillColor(UIColor.yellow.cgColor)
context.setStrokeColor(UIColor.orange.cgColor)
context.setLineWidth(10)

context.addEllipse(in: rectangle)
context.drawPath(using: .fillStroke)
```

Just like with GCD, all of the nasty old free functions have been transformed into sensible methods.

Language feature changes

In addition to the naming style and rule changes you've learned about, there are also several changes to features in the language.

Increment operators

Increment operators are gone. No more `counter++` for you! Why is this? The main reason seems to be that they are ambiguous. What's the value of `currentCount` or `nextCount` in this sample?

```
var counter = 1
let currentCount = counter++
let nextCount = ++counter
counter++ // Expression result is unused!
```

If, like me, you can never remember which order these things happen in, now you don't have to. The most popular use of these operators was in "C-style for loops", and you'll never guess what's happened to them.

C-Style for loops

Also gone! A C-Style for-loop was written like this:

```
for var i = 0; i < 10; i++ {
    print(i)
}
```

Good riddance. Look at all those semicolons, all that cruft. Replace with:

```
for i in 0..<10 {
    print(i)
}
```

Or, if you're iterating through a collection, a `for...in` loop, which you really should have been using anyway.

Currying syntax

If you're one of the few people who actually understood the Swift currying syntax (or one of the even fewer people who actually used it) you might be upset by this one, and you've probably already followed the proposal and comments and know the new way of doing things. If you've never used it, congratulations, you don't have to unlearn anything!

That's all the main things that have gone from the language. Now, onto the new stuff, which is much more fun.

Key paths

This is a super addition to the language. Key paths and key-value coding are somewhat frowned upon because they introduce what's called "stringly typed" code, where you use literal strings to access properties. However they can be extremely useful, for example when setting up key value observers or creating predicates.

Swift 3 offers a safe, compile-time verified way to get a key path. It works like this:

```
class TimeMachine: NSObject {
  var currentYear = 2016
}

let timeMachine = TimeMachine()
timeMachine.value(forKey: #keyPath(TimeMachine.currentYear))
// gives 2016
```

This works with autocomplete as well. The #keyPath expression is converted into a String. Because of the way key-value coding works, this technique can only be used on classes, and furthermore only on those properties that are implemented using the Objective-C runtime. In practical terms, this means that any classes inheriting from NSObject are fine, and any "pure" swift classes must have the property marked as dynamic:

```
class TimeMachine {
  dynamic var currentYear = 2016
  var destinationYear = 1985
}

#keyPath(TimeMachine.currentYear) // "currentYear"
#keyPath(TimeMachine.destinationYear) // Error
```

Key-value coding doesn't work on non-NSObject classes anyway, so key paths aren't as useful for these types of objects.

Access control

Swift 2 had public, internal (the default, so you didn't see that one often) and private modifiers that controlled the visibility of your code across files and modules.

In Swift 3 the meaning of `public` and `private` have changed, and there are two new access control keywords, `open` and `fileprivate`. Here's a quick summary:

- `open`: The code is visible from anywhere, and `open` classes can be subclassed from anywhere.

- `public`: The code is visible from anywhere, but classes can only be subclassed within the same module.

- `internal`: The code is visible from anywhere within the module

- `fileprivate`: The code is visible from anywhere within the file.

- `private`: The code is only visible from within the enclosing declaration.

The single largest impact this will have on your code is that anything you'd marked as `private`, but accessed within an extension in the same file, will now not compile until you change the declaration:

```
class PotatoListViewController: UIViewController {
  private var potatoes: [Potato]
  ...
}


extension PotatoListViewController: PotatoSelectionDelegate {
  func didDelete(_ potato: Potato) {
    potatoes.remove(potato)
  }
}
```

In the example above, `potatoes` is not accessible in the extension. If the variable is declared as `fileprivate` instead, then it will be accessible. This redefinition of an existing, commonly used keyword, coupled with the fact that extensions are encouraged as a way of dividing up functionality within a file, means that when you migrate to Swift 3 you will spend a lot of time correcting access control issues like this.

The difference between `open` and `public` is mainly of interest to framework developers. The use of `open` indicates that you have explicitly considered and encouraged inheritance of the classes included in your framework. So far, all UIKit and Foundation classes are `open`.

The remainder of this section talks about changes to existing language features.

Enums

An enum case is an instance, and instances should begin with lower case letters. That's now a standard, and all of the framework enums have been amended to match.

```
// Swift 2
label.textAlignment = .Center
// Swift 3
label.textAlignment = .center
```

There's also an inconsistency with enums that has been removed. There used to be a little quirk whereby you didn't need to use a leading period when dealing with a case *inside* the definition of an enum:

```
// Swift 2
enum Size {
  case Big
  case Little
  case Tiny

  var isSmall: Bool {
    switch self {
      case Big: return false
      case .Little: return true
      case .Tiny: return false
    }
  }
}

let size = Size.Big
switch size {
  case Big: // Illegal
  case .Little: ...
  case .Tiny: ...
}
```

Note that `Big` doesn't have a leading period. Inside an enum, this was optional, outside it was not. Now, you have to use the leading period. Also, as per the previous change, it would be `.big`.

Closures

Closures are objects; you can store them as properties. Closure are objects; you can pass them as function parameters. Closures also retain anything that is captured within them.

These three statements mean that there can be interesting memory management issues when dealing with closures that are passed as function parameters.

If you pass a closure to a function, how do you know what that function is going to do with it? Will the closure be executed before the function call returns, or will it be stored somewhere to be executed later?

In Swift 2, the default assumption was that closures passed as parameters were *escaping*, that is to say, they could be stored away and executed later after the function had returned. The majority of UIKit methods that take closures (like the animations parameter of a UIView animation method) are escaping, which is why you have to use `self` inside them all the time. If a function guaranteed that a closure was discarded after the function had returned, you could mark it as `@noescape` and the compiler could make sensible decisions about it.

In Swift 3, that assumption has reversed. Now, all closures passed in to functions are assumed to be non-escaping unless explicitly marked otherwise. This has meant a lot of work on the UIKit and Foundation end, and if you've written code which takes a completion block and stores it away somewhere, you'll need to add the `@escaping` notation to it:

```
func doSomethingWith(_ this: Thing, then: @escaping (Thing) ->
()) {
   self.completion = then
   ... do stuff in the background ...
}
```

The migrator should either fix this for you, or offer it as a change. It tries to detect if additional references to the closure are made within the function body.

This also means that you don't have to put `self` in closure bodies by default anymore:

```
func doSomething(_ then: () -> ()) {
    // do something
    then()
}

// Swift 2
doSomething {
    self.finished = true
}

// Swift 3
doSomething {
    finished = true
}
```

Where to go from here?

I hope this chapter gave you a quick introduction to what's new in Swift 3 and helps make your code migration a little bit easier.

The most important aspect of all of this is the Grand Renaming. There is a full and detailed explanation of the naming guidelines at https://swift.org/documentation/api-design-guidelines/.

This is really worth reading, so that you ensure that your future code follows these guidelines.

Swift is an open source language! To review proposed and implemented changes to Swift, or to submit your own, visit https://github.com/apple/swift-evolution. All of the changes discussed in this chapter are discussed in far greater detail on that repo.

Chapter 2: Xcode 8 Debugging Improvements

By Jeff Rames

Xcode 8 adds some powerful updates to your debugging toolbox. Race conditions and memory leaks — some of the most challenging issues to diagnose when developing an app — can now be automatically identified in the Issue navigator with runtime tools. The already excellent View Debugger has also gained some polish and makes runtime debugging of constraints easier than ever.

This chapter will cover three major debugging improvements in Xcode 8:

- The **View Debugger** lets you visualize your layouts and see constraint definitions at runtime. Although this has been around since Xcode 6, Xcode 8 introduces some handy new warnings for constraint conflicts and other great convenience features.

- The **Thread Sanitizer** is an all new runtime tool in Xcode 8 that alerts you to threading issues — most notably, potential race conditions.

- The **Memory Graph Debugger** is also brand new to Xcode 8. It provides visualization of your app's memory graph at a point in time and flags leaks in the Issue navigator.

In this chapter, you'll be playing the role of a senior developer at Nothin' But Emojis LLC, where you spend your days cranking out mind-blowing emoji-related products for iOS. Today you're assisting the boss' nephew — Ray Nooberlich — with a highly anticipated product named Coloji that lets users view curated colors and emojis.

Ray is a bit new; arguably, too new to be the primary resource on such an important project. As you help him get the app up and running, you'll find these new tools invaluable for debugging the tricky runtime issues he throws your way.

If you've not used the View Debugger before, you may want to brush up with *View Debugging in Xcode 6* at <u>raywenderlich.com/98356</u>. The other tools are brand new, so just bring your desire to crush bugs!

Getting started

The design specifications for Coloji indicate a master-detail interface. The master is a table view with cells displaying colojis, which consist of colors and emojis. The detail view for color colojis shows the selected color in full screen. For emojis, it shows a large view of the emoji centered in the view.

Below is a preview of what the finished project will look like:

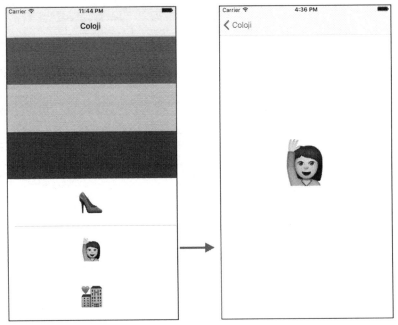

The problem is that it will be a while before you get any code in good shape from Ray Nooberlich. He means well, and he's trying — but, I mean, look at the picture below. This could easily be the featured image for the "Newbie" entry on Wikipedia:

Here's a rundown of the issues you'll face, and which tools you'll use to solve them:

1. **Memory leak.** First, the memory footprint of Coloji continues to grow during use. You'll use the new Memory Graph Debugger to clean this up.

2. **View bug.** Next, the table view cells don't load anymore. You'll use the View Debugger to figure out why.

3. **Auto Layout Constraint bug.** Then you'll encounter a mysteriously absent emoji detail view. You'll use the run time constraint debugger to flush out this bug.

4. **Race condition.** Finally, a race condition has reared its ugly head. You'll use Thread Sanitizer to hunt it down and fix it for good.

Investigating the project

Imagine you've just received a pull request from Ray with what he hopes is the completed project. Open **Coloji.xcodeproj** in the **memory-debugger-starter** folder and take a look at what he pushed. Here are some notes on the most important pieces of the project:

- **ColojiTableViewController.swift** manages the table view, whose data source is loaded with colors and emojis in `loadData()`. The data source is managed by `colojiStore` defined in **ColojiDataStore.swift**.

- **Coloji.swift** contains code used to configure the cells, which are defined and constructed in **ColojiTableViewCell.swift**. It also generates the data source objects.

- **ColojiViewController.swift** controls the detail view, which displays the color or emoji.

Build and run, scroll around a bit, and drill through to some detail views. You might occasionally notice a cell's content change to a different coloji briefly when you select it, which implies there might be duplicate labels present on a cell:

Because this would have impacts on memory usage, you'll start by checking out the Memory Report as you use the app.

With the project still running, open the Debug navigator and select **Memory** to display the Memory Report. Note the memory in use by Coloji under the **Usage Comparison** view. In Coloji, start scrolling the table view up and down, and you'll see the memory usage growing.

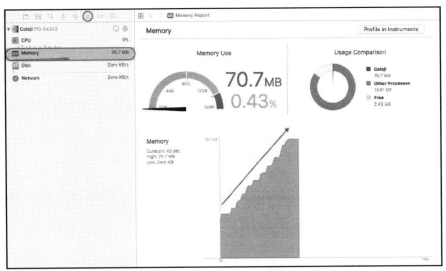

Some of this could definitely be duplicate labels — but the rate at which it's climbing implies there might be more going on. Right now, you're going with the suspicion of duplicate labels and a likely memory leak. What a perfect opportunity to check out Memory Graph Debugging!

Memory Graph debugging

In the past, your best bets for tracking unnecessary allocations and leaks were the Allocations or Leaks instruments. They can still be useful, but they are resource-intensive and require a lot of manual analysis.

The Memory Graph Debugger has taken a lot of the work out of finding leaks and memory usage problems. It does this without the learning curve of Instruments.

When you trigger the Memory Graph Debugger, you're able to view and filter objects in the heap in the Debug navigator. This brings your attention to objects you didn't expect to see — for instance, duplicate labels.

Additionally, knowing what objects currently exist is the first step in identifying a leak. If you see something there that shouldn't be, you'll know to dig deeper.

After you find an object that shouldn't exist, the next step is to understand how it came into being. When you select an object in the navigator, it will reveal a root analysis graph that shows that object's relation to all associated objects. This provides you with a picture of what references are keeping your object around.

Below is an example of a root analysis graph focused on the `ColojiDataStore`. Among other things, you can easily see that `ColojiTableViewController` retains the `ColojiDataStore` via a reference named `colojiStore`. This matches up with what you may have seen when reviewing the source.

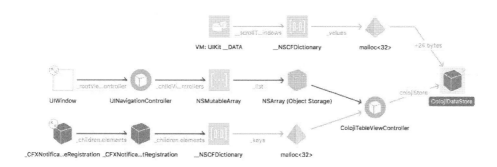

On top of this, the tool also flags occurrences of potential leaks and displays them in a manner similar to compiler warnings. The warnings can take you straight to the associated memory graph as well as a backtrace. Finding leaks has never been this easy!

Finding the leak

It's time to look at the Memory Graph Debugger to see what's causing the growing memory usage in Coloji.

Build and run if you aren't already, and scroll the table view around a bit. Then, select the **Debug Memory Graph** button on the Debug bar.

First, check out the Debug navigator where you'll see a list of all objects in the heap, by object type.

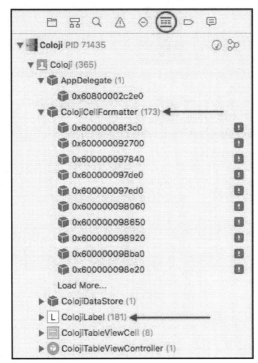

In this example, you see 173 instances of ColojiCellFormatter and 181 instances of ColojiLabel in the heap. The number you'll see will vary based on how much you scrolled the table, but anything over the number of visible cells on your table view is a red flag. The ColojiCellFormatter should only exist while the cell is being configured, and there should only be one ColojiLabel per visible cell.

The duplicate ColojiLabel instances are likely the reason you saw an unrelated cell appear under the one you selected. Seeing all these occurrences lends support to your theory that labels were placed on top of older ones, rather than being reused. You'll dig into that further in just a moment — there's something even *more* interesting going on here.

You should see a purple warning label to the right of each ColojiCellFormatter instance memory address. To investigate the warning, select the warning icon in the activity viewer in the workspace toolbar.

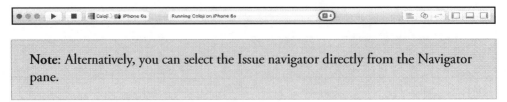

> **Note:** Alternatively, you can select the Issue navigator directly from the Navigator pane.

This will take you to the Issue navigator, where a few memory leaks are flagged with multiple instances. Be sure that you have **Runtime** issues selected in the toggle if they weren't already.

Select one of the instances of a `ColojiCellFormatter` leak:

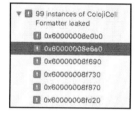

Then and you'll see a graph appear in the editor. This graph illustrates a retain cycle, where the `ColojiCellFormatter` references `Closure captures` (a closure) and the closure has a reference to the `ColojiCellFormatter`.

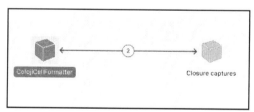

The graphs may vary slightly among instances, but all will show the core retain cycle. In some cases, you may see a triangle-like graph:

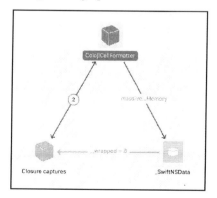

Ultimately, the point of interest is the arrow pointing both ways, including a retain in both directions.

The next step is to get to the code in question. Select **Closure captures** from the graph and open the Memory Inspector in the Utilities pane.

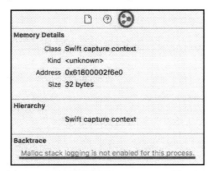

The backtrace would be a lot more helpful if it was actually there. It's turned off by default because it does add some notable overhead and might conflict with other tools. You only want it on when you're actively using it.

Fortunately, it's easy to enable malloc stack logging. Select **Coloji** from your schemes and then click **Edit Scheme**:

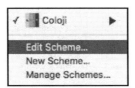

In the scheme editor, select the Run action on the left, then the Diagnostics tab at the top. Under Logging, check **Malloc Stack** and then choose **Live Allocations Only**: this requires fewer resources and still retains the logging you need while in the Memory Debugger. Now select **Close**.

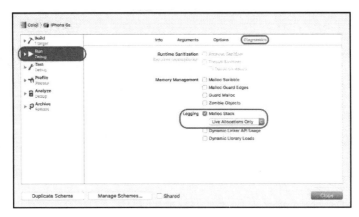

Build and run again, scroll the table a bit, and enter the Memory Debugger. As before, go to the Issue navigator and select one of the `ColojiCellFormatter` leaks.

In the graph, select **Closure captures**, and this time you should see a backtrace in the Memory Inspector. The source code you don't have access to will be dimmed and inactive, and only a few lines will appear as active. Hover over the line where `tableView(_:cellForRowAt:)` is called and click the **jump indicator** that appears.

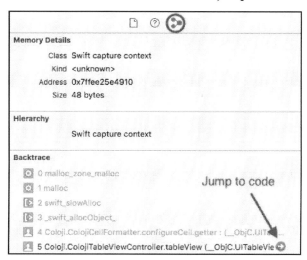

This brings you to the following line in **ColojiTableViewController.swift**:

```
cellFormatter.configureCell(cell)
```

There's nothing obviously wrong here. A `ColojiCellFormatter` is defined on the prior line, and this line uses it to configure the current cell. **Command-click** on `configureCell` and you'll be taken to the following lazy property declaration:

```
lazy var configureCell: (UITableViewCell) -> () = {
  cell in
  if let colojiCell = cell as? ColojiTableViewCell {
    colojiCell.coloji = self.coloji
  }
}
```

`configureCell` is initialized with a closure which should make your retain cycle senses tingle. You'll notice a strong reference to self (`self.coloji`) in the closure. This means `ColojiCellFormatter` retains a reference to `configureCell` and vice versa — a classic retain cycle which leads to the type of leak the Memory Debugger pointed you to.

To fix it, change the line reading `cell in` to the following:

```
[unowned self] cell in
```

You've specified an unowned reference to self via the capture list, removing the strong reference to `ColojiCellFormatter`. This breaks the retain cycle.

Build and run, restart the Memory Debugger, and navigate back to the Issue navigator to confirm the leak warnings are gone.

You just identified and tracked down a leak with just a few clicks. Feels pretty good, doesn't it?

Improving memory usage

The leaks are gone, but you still have that peculiar issue with random labels appearing behind any cells you select. You probably recall seeing many instances of `ColojiLabel` hanging around in the heap, while you'd only expect one per visible cell. The exact number of instances depends on how many times you've loaded cells, but note the 44 labels in the example heap below:

Build and run, and start the Memory Debugger if it's not already running.

Select a few instances of `ColojiLabel` from the Debug navigator, and you'll see varying graphs as the state of objects associated with each instance change over time.

In all cases, however, you should see the `ColojiLabel` is tied to a
`ColojiTableViewCell`:

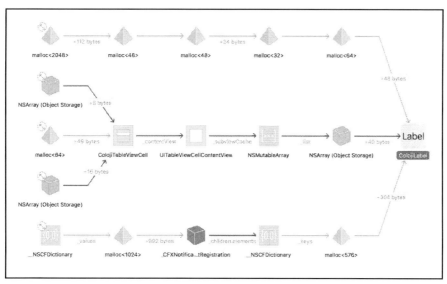

Select a `ColojiTableViewCell` on the graph, and you'll see its memory address in the
Memory Inspector (it can also be found in bread crumbs above the graph):

If you select a few different `ColojiLabel` graphs from the Debug navigator and verify
the address of the associated `ColojiTableViewCell`, you'll eventually notice some
overlap. This further confirms the theory that duplicate labels are being placed on each
cell.

On the graph, select the **ColojiLabel** and then select the top active line in the backtrace:

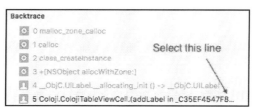

This should take you to `addLabel(_:)` in **ColojiTableViewCell.swift**, where you create
the `ColojiLabel`.

The contents of the method looks like this:

```
let label = ColojiLabel()
label.coloji = coloji
label.translatesAutoresizingMaskIntoConstraints = false
contentView.addSubview(label)
NSLayoutConstraint.activate(
  [label.leadingAnchor.constraint(equalTo:
    contentView.leadingAnchor),
   label.bottomAnchor.constraint(equalTo:
    contentView.bottomAnchor),
   label.trailingAnchor.constraint(equalTo:
    contentView.trailingAnchor),
   label.topAnchor.constraint(equalTo:
    contentView.topAnchor)
  ])
```

This creates a new `ColojiLabel`, provides it with the passed-in `coloji` for formatting, and places it in the cell's `contentView`. The problem is that this code is called every time a cell is passed a coloji. The end result is that *every single time* a new cell appears, this code creates a brand-new label and places it on the cell — just as you suspected!

The solution is to create a single `ColojiLabel` per cell and update its contents when the cell is reused. First, add the following property to the top of `ColojiTableViewCell`:

```
private let label = ColojiLabel()
```

Here you initialize a label that will be retained by the cell and updated when content changes.

Next, modify the contents of `addLabel(_:)` to match the following:

```
label.coloji = coloji
if label.superview == .none {
  label.translatesAutoresizingMaskIntoConstraints = false
  contentView.addSubview(label)
  NSLayoutConstraint.activate([
    label.leadingAnchor.constraint(equalTo:
      contentView.leadingAnchor),
    label.bottomAnchor.constraint(equalTo:
      contentView.bottomAnchor),
    label.trailingAnchor.constraint(equalTo:
      contentView.trailingAnchor),
    label.topAnchor.constraint(equalTo:
      contentView.topAnchor)
    ])
}
```

Rather than initializing a new label every time here, you use the `label` property instead, and simply update its displayed coloji. To avoid the label being added to the cell repeatedly, you wrap that bit of code in a check that ensures it only adds the label the first time through.

Build and run, scroll the table a bit, and tap a few cells. You should no longer see a flicker of some other `ColojiLabel` when a cell is selected.

Enter the Memory Debugger and return to the Debug navigator. Now you'll only see one `ColojiLabel` on the heap per cell, confirming this bug has been exterminated!

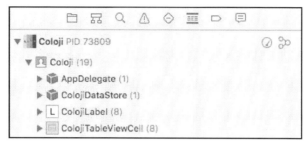

Now that you've found the bug, you walk Ray through the changes, trusting he'll get it right in the next push. What could possibly go wrong?

Thread Sanitizer

Well, something went wrong. Open **Coloji.xcodeproj** in the **thread-sanitizer-starter** folder to see what Ray sent over after fixing the memory issues.

Build and run, and while the memory issues were resolved, you're now seeing something new. There's missing data, and you're only seeing a random sample of cells. Each time you run, different cells may appear, but here's a look at one attempt:

Only three cells loaded, and they appear to be a random selection. Open **ColojiTableViewController.swift** and take a look up top at the properties that drive the data source:

```
let colors: [UIColor] =
[.gray, .green, .yellow, .brown, .cyan, .purple]
let emoji = [" ", " ", " ", " ", " ", " "]
```

It seems the latest run displayed the second-to-last color and the last two emojis. That doesn't make much sense. Now is a good time to check what Ray did to the code that loads the data. Take a look at `loadData()` in the extension and you'll see it contains the following:

```
// 1
let group = DispatchGroup()

// 2
for color in colors {
  queue.async(
    group: group,
    qos: .background,
    flags: DispatchWorkItemFlags(),
    execute: {
      let coloji = createColoji(color)
      self.colojiStore.append(coloji)
  })
}

for emoji in emoji {
  queue.async(
    group: group,
    qos: .background,
    flags: DispatchWorkItemFlags(),
    execute: {
      let coloji = createColoji(emoji)
      self.colojiStore.append(coloji)
  })
}

// 3
group.notify(queue: DispatchQueue.main) {
  self.tableView.reloadData()
}
```

The code above does the following:

1. `group` is a dispatch group created to manage the order of tasks added to it.

2. For each color and emoji in the arrays you just reviewed, this code kicks off an asynchronous operation on a `background` thread. Inside, the operation creates a

`coloji` from the color or emoji and then appends it to the store. These are all queued up together in the same `group` so that they can complete together.

3. The `notify` kicks off when all the asynchronous `group` operations complete. When this is done, the table reloads to display the new colojis.

It looks like Ray was trying to improve efficiency by letting the coloji data store operations run concurrently. Concurrent code, coupled with random results, is a strong indicator a race condition is at play.

Fortunately, the new Thread Sanitizer makes it easy to track down race conditions. Like the Memory Graph and View Debuggers, it provides runtime feedback right in the Issue navigator.

Here's an example of what it looks like (note this will not appear for you yet):

One of the toughest bugs to squash in development has been refined down to a single warning in the Issue navigator! This tool will surely save a lot of headaches.

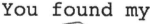

It's important to note that Thread Sanitizer only works in the simulator. This is contrary to how you've probably debugged race conditions in the past, where the device has usually been the better choice. Threading issues often behave differently on devices than they do in the simulator due to processor timing and speed differences.

However, the sanitizer can detect races even when they don't occur on a given run, as long as the operations involved in the race kick off. Thread Sanitizer does this by monitoring how competing threads access data. If Thread Sanitizer sees the opportunity for a race condition, it flags a warning.

Using Thread Sanitizer is as simple as turning it on, running your app in the simulator and exercising the code where a race might exist. For this reason, it works well alongside unit testing, and ideally, should be run on a regular basis.

In this section, you're focusing on race conditions as they are the most common use case for Thread Sanitizer. But the tool can do much more, such as flag thread leaks, the use of uninitiated mutexes and unlocks happening on the wrong thread.

Detecting thread conflicts

There's basically only one step to use Thread Sanitizer: enable it.

Edit the **Coloji** scheme, select the Run action and select the Diagnostics tab. If **Malloc Stack** is still checked from your Memory Debugging, uncheck it as it can't be enabled while running the Thread Sanitizer. Now check **Thread Sanitizer** and then select **Close**.

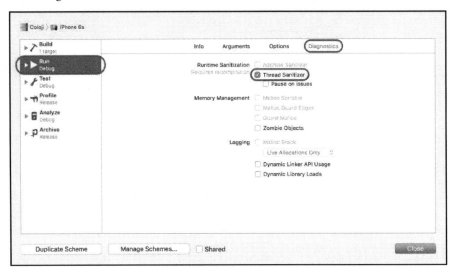

> **Note:** You can also check **Pause on issues** under Thread Sanitizer to have execution pause each time a race is detected. Although you won't do this in this chapter, this will break on the problem line and display a message describing the issue.

Build and run. As soon as the table view loads, Thread Sanitizer will start notifying you of threading issues via the workspace toolbar and the Issue navigator. You'll also see logging in the console spitting out detail on the issues. It looks like DEFCON 1 here!

> **Note:** In this tutorial, you'll use the Issue navigator to hunt down issues. The console provides similar info, but isn't quite as user friendly. However, it is handy if you want to save some logging on an issue.

Open the Issue navigator, ensure you have **Runtime** selected, and you should see a number of data races on display.

The following image focuses on a single data race. In it, you can see a read operation on thread 6 is at odds with a write on thread 12. Each of these operations shows a stack trace, where you'll see they conflicted on a line within `append()` inside `ColojiDataStore`:

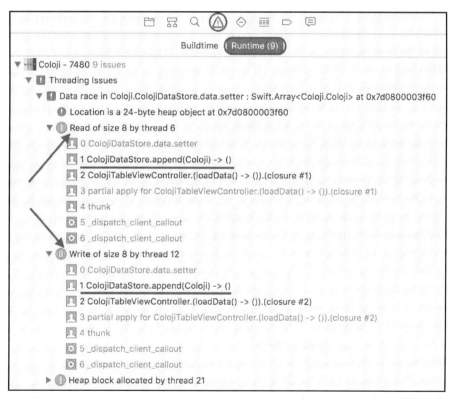

Select `ColojiDataStore.append(Coloji) -> ()` in either trace, and you'll be taken straight to the problematic code in the editor:

```
data = data + [coloji]
```

`data` is an array of `Coloji` objects. The above line appends a new `coloji` to the array. It's not thread-safe since there is nothing to prevent two threads from attempting this read/write operation at the same time. That's why Thread Sanitizer identified a situation where one thread was reading at the same time another was writing.

A simple solution to this to create a `DispatchQueue` and use it to execute operations on this data serially.

Still in **ColojiDataStore.swift**, add the following property at the top of `ColojiDataStore`:

```
let dataAccessQueue = DispatchQueue(label:
"com.raywenderlich.coloji.datastore")
```

You'll use the serial queue `dataAccessQueue` to control access to the data store array. The label is simply a unique string used to identify this queue.

Now, replace the three methods in this class with the following:

```
func colojiAt(_ index: Int) -> Coloji {
  return dataAccessQueue.sync {
    return data[index]
  }
}

func append(_ coloji: Coloji) {
  dataAccessQueue.async {
    self.data = self.data + [coloji]
  }
}

var count: Int {
  return dataAccessQueue.sync {
    return data.count
  }
}
```

You've wrapped each data access call in a queue operation to ensure no operation can happen concurrently. Note that `colojiAt(_:)` and `count` are run synchronously, because the caller is waiting on them to return data. `append(_:)` is done asynchronously, because it doesn't need to return anything.

Build and run, and you should see all your colojis appear.

The order can vary since your data requests run asynchronously, but all the cells make it to the data source. Looks like you may have solved the issue.

To further confirm you've solved the race conditions, take a look at the Issue navigator where you should see no issues:

Congratulations — you chased down a race condition by simply checking a box! Now it's just a matter of sending a politely-worded feedback report to Ray, and surely, *surely* that will be the end of Ray's issues.

View debugging

According to your Apple Watch, your pulse has climbed to 120 beats per minute after seeing the next pull request from Ray. Open **Coloji.xcodeproj** in the **view-debugging-starter** folder to see how Ray made out with his race condition fixes.

Build and run, then navigate around a bit. It's tough to tell if the threading issue was fixed because the cells are now completely blank! There are functional color detail views, but the emojis are way at the top, obstructed by the navigation bar. Sigh.

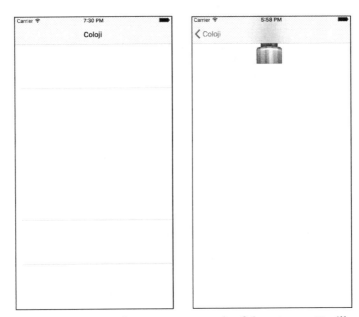

The View Debugger is a great tool to investigate each of these issues. You'll start with the blank cells.

Prior versions of the View Debugger already displayed run time constraints of your views in the Size Inspector. The biggest improvement in the View Debugger under Xcode 8 is that you can now see constraint warnings, similar to those you see at design time in Interface Builder. Below is an example of such a warning in the Size Inspector:

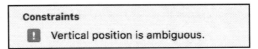

Because the table view constraints in Coloji are all set in code, the only way you could view constraint warnings before Xcode 8 was via difficult-to-discern console output. These new visual constraint warnings will make debugging constraint issues in Coloji much easier.

There are plenty more subtle enhancements as well. In the Debug navigator, you can now filter the view hierarchy by memory address, class name or even super class name. From the Object Inspector, you can jump straight to a view class. Debug snapshots are also much faster — 70% faster, according to Apple.

It's time to try out a few of these new features as you determine what happened to the cell content and emoji detail view.

Debugging the cell

First, open **ColojiTableViewCell.swift** to see how the layout of the cell is defined.

You'll see a setter for the `coloji` property that calls `addLabel(_:)`, passing the newly set coloji. `addLabel(_:)` sets the cell's `ColojiLabel` with the given coloji. If the label is not already on the cell's `contentView`, this code places it there and positions it with Auto Layout.

In this same file, you can see the definition of `ColojiLabel` which is a UILabel subclass. When it gets set, as `addLabel(_:)` does, it uses the provided coloji either to color its background or to set its text with the emoji.

Since you don't see the `ColojiLabel`, the only view that should be in the cell's content view, that's a good place to focus your questions. Is the label actually in the content view? If so, what size is it and where does it sit within the content view?

Build and run, and stay on the blank table view. Now select the **Debug View Hierarchy** button in the Debug bar.

In the Debug navigator, enter **ColojiLabel** in the filter. This will show the view hierarchy leading to each label. Here you're able to confirm that the `ColojiLabel` is inside the content view (`UITableViewCellContentView`) of the cell (`ColojiTableViewCell`).

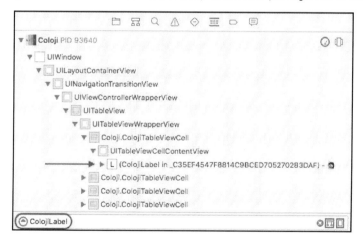

> **Note:** You can also try filtering for **UILabel**, and you'll see all the `ColojiLabel` as well as the UILabel in the navigation bar. The ability to filter by parent class is a very useful new feature for complex layouts.

Select any of the labels, and take a look at the Size Inspector. In the Constraints section, you'll see all the currently active constraints for the label. Looking over the constraints, you'll notice immediately that something looks wrong:

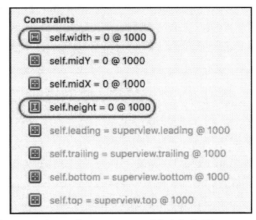

A 0 height and width certainly explains an invisible label! It's time to investigate what has gone wrong with the code that sets the constraints.

With a `ColojiLabel` still selected, switch to the Object Inspector in the Utilities pane. For public classes, an annotation will be present next to the **Class Name** allowing you to jump directly to the source. Because ColojiLabel is private, you won't see it.

Back in the debug navigator, move up the label's hierarchy a bit until you get to the public **ColojiTableViewCell**, which happens to reside in the same file as the label. In the Object Inspector, you'll now be able to click the annotation to jump right to the source for this class.

Now inside **ColojiTableViewCell.swift**, find `addLabel(_:)` where the `label` is added to the `contentView` and constrained to its parent. It looks like this:

```
label.coloji = coloji
if label.superview == .none {
  contentView.addSubview(label)
  NSLayoutConstraint.activate([
    label.leadingAnchor.constraint(equalTo:
      contentView.leadingAnchor),
    label.bottomAnchor.constraint(equalTo:
      contentView.bottomAnchor),
    label.trailingAnchor.constraint(equalTo:
```

```
        contentView.trailingAnchor),
      label.topAnchor.constraint(equalTo:
        contentView.topAnchor)
    ])
}
```

There aren't any constraints here that set the height or width of the `label` that explain what you're seeing at runtime.

But, something else may have caught your eye. Auto Layout is being used, yet this is missing the vital setting to prevent autoresizing masks from being converted into constraints. The zeroed label size is exactly the type of behavior you might hit in such a case, so it seems you've found your culprit.

Add the following line, right after the `if label.superview == .none` line:

```
label.translatesAutoresizingMaskIntoConstraints = false
```

This prevents autoresizing masks from converting into constraints that you don't expect.

Build and run, check out the table view, and you'll see you're back in business.

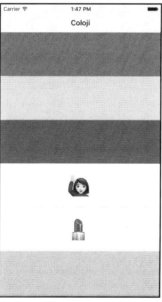

Unfortunately, this still hasn't solved your issue with emoji detail views. Take another look, and you'll see they appear to be centered horizontally, but not vertically.

Runtime constraint debugging

Missing constraints at runtime are View Debugger's time to really shine. With an emoji detail view presented, select Debug View Hierarchy again. Once the debugger renders, select the Issue navigator and **Runtime** toggle and you'll see something like this:

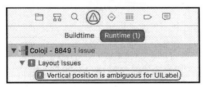

Select the warning and then go to the Size Inspector to see a little more information about the vertical layout. You'll see the same things as you do at design time in Interface Builder, but now you can see them at runtime!

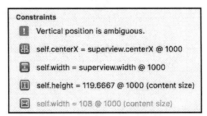

It's pretty easy to see why the vertical layout is ambiguous. The height of the label is defined, but it has no y-position.

Open **ColojiViewController.swift** and find the `layoutFor(_:)` that accepts an emoji String. This is where the label constraints are defined. Modify the array passed to `NSLayoutConstraint.activate` so that the call looks like this:

```
NSLayoutConstraint.activate([
    emojiLabel.centerXAnchor.constraint(equalTo:
  view.centerXAnchor),
    emojiLabel.widthAnchor.constraint(equalTo: view.widthAnchor),
    emojiLabel.centerYAnchor.constraint(equalTo:
  view.centerYAnchor)
    ])
```

You've added a constraint that equates the `centerYAnchor` of the `emojiLabel` with that of the `view`. With this and the height derived via the label's intrinsic content size, you now have a full set of vertical constraints.

Build and run, select an emoji from the table, and the emoji will now be centered on the detail view.

In the past, it was difficult to debug runtime issues if you created or modified your constraints programmatically. You had to dig through frequently-confusing console logs and go over your constraint code with a fine-toothed comb. Layout issue warnings in the View Debugger have changed all this, bringing the ease of design time constraint warnings to runtime.

Having fixed these last couple of issues, it's just a simple matter of sending the feedback to Ray and getting Coloji out the door. The good news is, Ray (hopefully) has learned a lot throughout this ordeal. Who knows — maybe someday *Ray* will be the one helping others learn how to build apps! :]

Static analyzer enhancements

Xcode 8 drastically enhances your ability to debug runtime issues. But it doesn't stop there — the trusty **static analyzer** has gained a few tricks of its own. But before you get too excited, remember the static analyzer only works with C, C++ and Objective-C.

If you're working with legacy code, the static analyzer does have some goodies to offer. Besides identifying logic and memory management flaws, it can now assist with solving localization issues and instance cleanup. It can also flag nullability violations.

To use the static analyzer, select **Product\Analyze** with a project open in Xcode. If there are any issues, a static analyzer icon will be displayed in the activity viewer. Clicking the icon will bring you to the Issue navigator, where you can see more information about the problem.

Localizability will notify you whenever a non-localized string is set on a user-facing control in a localized app. Consider the situation where you have a method that accepts an `NSString` and uses it to populate a `UILabel`. If the method caller provided a non-localized string, the static analyzer will flag it and visually indicate the flow of the problem data so you can resolve it.

```objc
18  - (void)viewDidLoad {
19      [super viewDidLoad];
20
21      NSString *notLocalizedString = @"What language am I?!";   // 1. Non-localized string literal here
22      [self configureLabelWithString:notLocalizedString];       // 2. Calling 'configureLabelWithString:'
23  }
24
25
26  -(void)configureLabelWithString:(NSString*)localizedString {  // 3. Entered call from 'viewDidLoad'
27      self.label.text = localizedString;                         // 4. User-facing text should use localized string macro
28  }
```

Instance Cleanup adds some new warnings around manual retain-release. The mere mention of this probably sends shudders down your spine! But if you occasionally have to suffer through some legacy code without ARC, know that there are some new checks centered around `dealloc`.

Finally, nullability checking finds logical issues in code that contains nullability annotations. This is especially useful for applications that mix Objective-C and Swift. For example, it flags cases where a method with a `_Nonnull` return type has a path that would return `nil`.

While not quite as exciting as new runtime tools, it's great to see continued improvement in the static analyzer. You can get more detail and some demos of these tools in the WWDC videos referenced in the next section.

Where to go from here?

In this chapter, you learned about several great new additions and enhancements to Xcode's debugging tools. The Memory Graph Debugger and Thread Sanitizer have the potential to save countless developer hours and make difficult problems much easier to debug. That old dog, View Debugger, also learned some new tricks including runtime constraint warnings.

This chapter provided a basic introduction to what these tools can do and how to use them. You now know enough to take them for a spin and fit them into your debugging workflow. For more detail on each, check out these WWDC videos:

- Thread Sanitizer and Static Analysis—apple.co/2aCtz6t
- Visual Debugging with Xcode—apple.co/2as1vVu

Chapter 3: Xcode 8 Source Editor Extensions

By Jeff Rames

New in Xcode 8, Apple has provided the first official way to extend the capabilities of Xcode: source editor extensions. As the name implies, they rely on the extension architecture that has gained increasing prevalence on Apple's platforms recently.

The scope is limited to performing operations on text. This means you cannot customize Xcode's UI or modify settings — your interface is via menu items, and only text passes between Xcode and the extension.

> **Note:** There's no official word, but there *is* plenty of chatter about Apple's plans to expand editor extension capabilities based on community demand. Make sure to file a Radar if there is an Xcode extension you're trying to build that isn't possible with a source extension.

Many developers will prefer to use editor extensions created by others. If you don't have the itch, and don't have any needs requiring a custom extension, feel free to skip ahead to the next chapter.

In this chapter, you'll build an extension called **Asciiify**, based on an existing macOS application that takes text input and outputs an ASCII art version of that text:

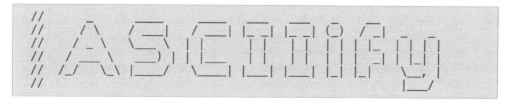

Getting started

Open **Asciiify.xcodeproj** in the starter project folder.

Before you can build and run, you need to set up signing with your team information.

Select the **Asciiify** project from the navigator and then the **Asciiify** target. From the **General** tab, select your team name from the **Team** dropdown:

Build and run the **Asciiify** scheme and type some text into the top text field. Your asciiified output will show up in the label below.

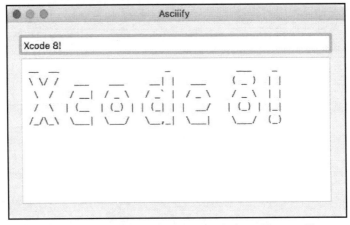

Take a look around the source, which includes some helper files you'll use to build the source editor extension:

• The **Figlet** group consists of **FigletRenderer.swift**, a Swift wrapper around a JavaScript FIGlet implementation by Scott González. A FIGlet is a program that makes ASCII art representations of text. You'll use this, but you don't need to know how it works in detail.

- **Main.storyboard** contains a simple view with a text field and label. This view is for the macOS app, not your extension. However, it will help demonstrate what the library does.

- **AsciiTransformer.swift** transforms `String` input to a FIGlet and is used by the Asciiify macOS app.

Why source editor extensions?

Your goal is to take this functionality and build it into Xcode itself. But before you begin, you might be wondering why source code extensions are useful at all, considering the community has been able to develop Xcode plugins without an official method provided by Apple for some time.

Xcode 8 source editor extensions bring several benefits:

- They are fully asynchronous and run under their own process, minimizing any performance impacts to the IDE.

- Using an officially supported interface, they're also less likely to break with each Xcode release.

- Finally, the extension model provides a clean interface to Xcode that makes it quite easy to generate tools.

It's true that Xcode plugins have been available with fewer restrictions for some time, thanks to the developer community and the package manager Alcatraz. These community extensions are able to modify Xcode's UI and behavior anywhere — not just within a single source file. However, these rely on private frameworks, introduce security and stability risks, and depend on frequent updates to keep them working.

Xcode 8 uses runtime library validation to improve security. With this change, the time for updating plugins has come to an end, as the mechanism they used to run under in Xcode is now closed off. It's a brave new world: for better or worse, developers will be working within Apple's ecosystem to create new tools.

The new source extensions are fairly limited compared to Xcode plugins of old — but here are a few ideas of what you *can* do:

- Generate a documentation block for a method containing all parameters and the return type based on its signature

- Convert non localized `String` definitions within a file to the localized version

- Convert color and image definitions to the new color and image literals in Xcode 8 (demoed in the WWDC session on source editor extensions)

- Create comment MARKs above an extension block using the name of a protocol it extends

- Generate a print statement with debugging info on a highlighted property

- Clean up whitespace formatting of a file; for instance, you might enforce a single line between each method by deleting or adding lines to the file

You'll likely come up with a half dozen more off the top of your head. Even with their limitations, source editor extensions have a lot of utility. Some will be more general in scope, and some may be very specific to your codebase or standards.

While this is a book about iOS 10, keep in mind that source editor extensions are actually macOS applications. That being said, you'll be working primarily with Foundation, so even if this is your first foray into macOS, there aren't any pre-requisites.

Creating a new extension

Back to your goal: to implement this same asciiification within Xcode's source editor. To do this, you'll create a source editor extension that leverages the Figlet framework in the same way this macOS application does.

Navigate to **File\New\Target** and under the **macOS** tab select **Xcode Source Editor Extension**.

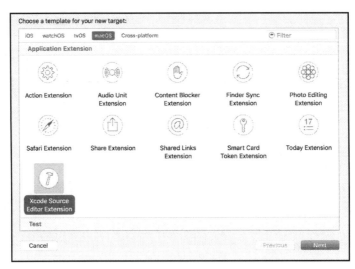

Click **Next**, use **AsciiifyComment** for the Project Name, ensure Swift is selected and click **Finish**.

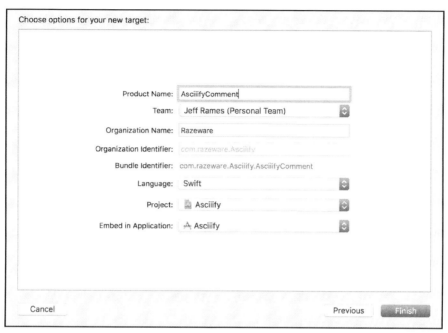

If prompted to activate the AsciiifyComment scheme, click **Activate**. This will be used when building the extension.

You'll now notice a new target and a new group in the navigator, both named **AsciiifyComment**. Expand the new group and take a look at what the template has provided:

- **SourceEditorExtension.swift** contains an NSObject that conforms to the `XCSourceEditorExtension` protocol. The protocol defines an optional method, `extensionDidFinishLaunching()`, which is called upon initial launch allowing you to do any required setup. `commandDefinitions` is an optional property that can be used to provide an array of objects that define commands the extension can accept.

- **SourceEditorCommand.swift** defines an object that conforms to the `XCSourceEditorCommand` protocol which consists of one required method—`perform(with:completionHandler:)`. The method is called when a user invokes the extension by selecting a menu item. This is where you'll asciiify the passed text.

- The **Info.plist** of an extension has several important keys under `NSExtension` that point to the classes covered above, as well as providing a name for the command. You'll dig into this shortly.

Select the AsciiifyComment build scheme, then build and run. When prompted to choose an app to run, select Xcode (version 8 or above) and then click **Run**. A version of Xcode will launch with a dark icon, activity viewer, and splash screen icon:

This instance of Xcode is meant for testing your extensions. Once launched, create a new playground, as all you'll be doing is adding comments. Make sure that the new playground is open in the test instance of Xcode, not the original version of Xcode.

With the cursor in your test playground, navigate to **Editor\Asciiify Comment\Source Editor Command**. Clicking the command does nothing at present:

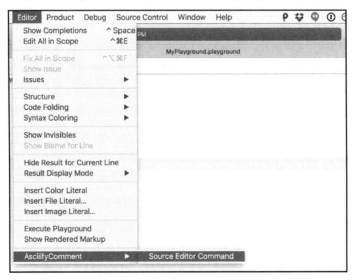

Time to implement some functionality!

Building the Asciiify extension

You probably already noticed some low hanging fruit — the name **Source Editor Extension** in the menu item doesn't explain what it's going to do.

Open **Info.plist** in the AsciiifyComment group and expand the `NSExtension` dictionary. Now expand `NSExtensionAttributes` which contains an array of command definitions with the key `XCSourceEditorCommandDefinitions`.

For the first array item, change the value for key `XCSourceEditorCommandName` to be **Asciiify Comment**:

Take a moment to check out the other keys found in the **Item 0** dictionary that help Xcode determine what code to execute for a given command.
`XCSourceEditorCommandIdentifier` is a unique ID Xcode will use to look up this command in the dictionary. `XCSourceEditorCommandClassName` then points to the source editor command class responsible for performing this command.

Build and run the extension, open your test playground from earlier, and you'll now be able to navigate to **Editor\Asciiify Comment\Asciiify Comment**:

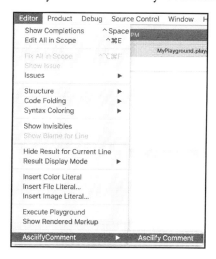

Now the name looks the way you'd expect, but it still doesn't do anything. Your next step will be to implement the functionality, but first you need to learn a bit more about the data model used by source editor extensions.

Exploring the command invocation

Selecting a menu command associated with your extension will call `perform(with:completionHandler:)` in the `SourceEditorCommand` implementation. In addition to the completion handler, it's passed an `XCSourceEditorCommandInvocation`.

This class contains the text buffer and everything you need to identify the selections. Here's a quick overview of its properties:

- **commandIdentifier** is a unique identifier for the invoked command, used to determine what processing should be done. The identifier comes from the `XCSourceEditorCommandIdentifier` key in the command definition found in **Info.plist**.

- **buffer** is of type `XCSourceTextBuffer` and is a mutable representation of the buffer and its properties to act upon. You'll get into more detail about its makeup below.

- **cancellationHandler** is invoked by Xcode when the user cancels the extension command. Cancellation can be done via a banner that appears within Xcode during processing by a source editor extension. Extensions block other operations, including typing in the IDE itself, to avoid merge issues.

> **Note**: The cancellation handler brings up an important point: Your extensions need to be fast, because they block the main UI thread. Any type of network activity or processor-intensive operations should be done at launch whenever possible.

The `buffer` is the most interesting item in the `XCSourceEditorCommandInvocation`, as it contains the data to act upon. Here's an overview of the `XCSourceTextBuffer` class' notable properties:

- **lines** is an array of `String` objects in the buffer, with each item representing a single line from the buffer. A line consists of the characters between two line breaks.

- **selections** is an array of `XCSourceTextRange` objects that identify start and end positions in the text buffer. Generally a single item will be present, representing the user's selection or cursor position in absence of selection. Multiple selections are also possible with macOS using *Shift+Command*, and are supported here.

It's also important to understand XCSourceTextPosition, the class used to represent the start and end of selections. XCSourceTextPosition uses a zero-based coordinate system and defines column and line indexes to represent buffer position.

The diagram below illustrates the relation between a buffer, its lines and selections.

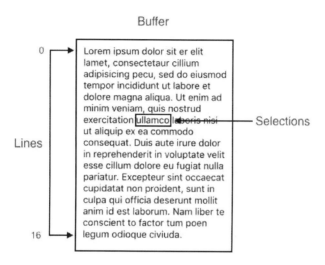

Now that you have a better understanding of the model involved, it's time to dive in and handle a request.

Build the editor command

Open **SourceEditorCommand.swift** and add the following to the top with the other imports:

```
import Figlet
```

This is the framework used to create FIGlet representations of text.

Just inside the SourceEditorCommand class, add the following:

```
let figlet = FigletRenderer()
```

FigletRenderer is the primary controller involved in rendering FIGlets. You'll call this in the extension. Now replace the body of perform(with:completionHandler:) with the following:

```
let buffer = invocation.buffer
```

```
// 1
buffer.selections.forEach({ selection in
  guard let selection = selection as? XCSourceTextRange,
    selection.start.line == selection.end.line else { return }

  // 2
  let line = buffer.lines[selection.start.line] as! String
  let startIndex = line.characters.index(
    line.startIndex, offsetBy: selection.start.column)
  let endIndex = line.characters.index(
    line.startIndex, offsetBy: selection.end.column)

  // 3
  let selectedText = line.substring(
    with: startIndex..<line.index(after: endIndex))
  // TODO: asciiify the text
})
// 4
completionHandler(.none)
```

This code does some validation and then examines
`XCSourceEditorCommandInvocation` to get the selected `String` and its location in the
buffer. Here's how this happens:

1. You test each `selection` in the buffer to determine if it exists on a single line.
   `XCSourceTextRange` contains a `start` and end position, and this code confirms
   those positions are on the same line. This is necessary as FIGlets aren't designed to
   wrap.

2. Because the selection is only a single line, you find it in the `buffer.lines` array
   using the selection's `start` line position. You derive the `startIndex` and `endIndex`
   of the selected text within the buffer using the index of the start of the line offset by
   the start and end `column` properties, respectively.

3. You then set `selectedText` to the selected `String` by using
   `substring(with:aRange:)` and the selection start and end index. A `TODO` is here to
   pass the resulting `String` to the FIGlet framework to generate the new content.

4. The `completionHandler()` must be called to signify completion of processing for
   this invocation.

Now that you've the selected text, it's time to feed it to the FIGlet renderer and update
the text buffer with the results. Still in `perform(with:completionHandler:)`,
replace `// TODO: asciiify the text` with the following:

```
// 1
if let asciiified = figlet.render(input: selectedText) {
  // 2
  let newLines = asciiified.components(separatedBy: "\n")
```

```
  let startLine = selection.start.line
  // 3
  buffer.lines.removeObject(at: startLine)
  buffer.lines.insert(
    newLines,
    at: IndexSet(startLine ..< startLine + newLines.count))
}
```

Here's a detailed look at what this does:

1. The FIGlet renderer method `render(input:)` takes the `selectedText` you obtained earlier and returns its ASCII art version.

2. Using the newline character as a separator, this code breaks the resulting `String` into the array `newLines`. It then sets `startLine` to the first line of the `selection`. Because you've guarded against multi-line selections, the first line is the only line.

3. This removes the originally selected line from the `buffer`, replacing it with those in `newLines`. The insertion range for `newLines` is from the original selection's `startLine` through the number of lines being inserted.

Build and run, attach to Xcode and open the Playground from earlier. Select a piece of text and then select **Editor\Asciiify Comment\Asciiify Comment** to kick off the extension. And then you'll see...

Sigh. This probably looks quite familiar if you've used Xcode more than once or twice.

In the report window that appears, scroll until you see **Application Specific Information** followed by a backtrace.

For once it's not Xcode being flaky. It's you!

Xcode is crashing due to a an `NSSelectionArray` — an internal class associated with selection ranges — that contains no ranges. By the time you call the completion handler in `perform(with:completionHandler:)`, `buffer.selections` is empty. Without a selection or insertion point in the buffer, Xcode doesn't know where to put the cursor when it regains control. Whoops!

Take a look at the code you just added. When the extension kicks off, the buffer selection is whatever you had selected. But near the end of `perform(with:completionHandler:)`, you call `removeObject(at:)` on the selected line — thus removing the selection from the buffer.

For the sake of simplicity, you're going to get around this by inserting the cursor at a known position: the start of the buffer.

Still in **SourceEditorCommand.swift**, add the following to `perform(with:completionHandler:)`, just above the completion handler at the end of the method:

```
let insertionPosition = XCSourceTextPosition(line: 0, column: 0)
let selection = XCSourceTextRange(
  start: insertionPosition,
  end: insertionPosition)
buffer.selections.setArray([selection])
```

Here you create an `XCSourceTextPosition` at the first line and column of the buffer. The position is used to create an `XCSourceTextRange` where the start and end are equal — which means you're inserting the cursor without doing any selection. You wrap `selection` in an array and set it to the buffer `selections`.

Build and run, and launch the extension as you've done before. This time, you'll see your asciiified text! As expected, the cursor appears at the start of the file.

Adding some polish

Congrats! You officially have a working source editor extension. But while the asciiified text isn't going to revolutionize the way you code, there are some things you could do to make it a bit more useful.

While the FIGlet you created looks glorious, it won't compile as code. Since you are working on a *source* editor, it makes sense to output these decorative items as comments.

In **SourceEditorCommand.swift**, find the following line in perform(with:completionHandler:):

```
let newLines = asciiified.components(separatedBy: "\n")
```

Replace that line with the following:

```
let newLines = asciiified.components(separatedBy: "\n")
  .map { "// \($0)" }
```

You've added a `map` to the existing `String` operation. The map simply appends `//` and a space to the start of each line, thus changing your FIGlet into a comment.

Build and run and test the extension again. This time, you'll see the FIGlet is commented:

That's definitely better, but not perfect. It's a little jarring to have some text selected, then have the cursor hop to the start of the file after the extension returns. It would be a lot nicer to have the replaced text selected when the call returns.

Add the following property to the top of perform(with:completionHandler:):

```
var newSelections = [XCSourceTextRange]()
```

This will be used to save the position of the FIGlet you create so you can select it in the buffer before returning.

Add the following code to the bottom of the body of if let asciiified:

```
// 1
let startPosition = XCSourceTextPosition(
  line: startLine,
  column: 0)

// 2
var endLine = startLine
if newLines.count > 0 {
  endLine = startLine + newLines.count - 1
}
// 3
var endColumn = 0
if let lastLine = newLines.last {
  endColumn = lastLine.characters.count
}
// 4
let endPosition = XCSourceTextPosition(
  line: endLine,
  column: endColumn)

// 5
let selection = XCSourceTextRange(
  start: startPosition,
  end: endPosition)
newSelections.append(selection)
```

This code sets a selection range around the newly inserted FIGlet. Here's how:

1. The selection startPosition is the first column of the originally selected line — the same place you inserted the new text.

2. You calculate the line number for the last inserted line by adding the newly inserted lines to the start line and subtracting one so the start line isn't double counted. If no lines were added, the startLine is used as the endLine.

3. You then determine the last column to select by looking at the last of the newLines and counting its characters. This results in a selection point at the end of the new insertion.

4. endPosition is an XCSourceTextPosition created with the newly calculated endLine and endColumn.

5. Finally, you use the calculated positions to create an XCSourceTextRange covering the area you want selected after the extension returns. To handle the possibility of multiple selections, you save each range to the array newSelections.

Once you've created all the FIGlets, you can set the selections in the buffer.

Look just above the call to to `completionHandler()` and replace the code below:

```
let insertionPosition = XCSourceTextPosition(line: 0, column: 0)
let selection = XCSourceTextRange(
  start: bufferStartPosition,
  end: bufferStartPosition)
buffer.selections.setArray([selection])
```

...with the following:

```
if newSelections.count > 0 {
  buffer.selections.setArray(newSelections)
} else {
  let insertionPosition = XCSourceTextPosition(line: 0, column:
0)
  let selection = XCSourceTextRange(
    start: insertionPosition,
    end: insertionPosition)
  buffer.selections.setArray([selection])
}
```

If `newSelections` contains any ranges, it's used to set the buffer's `selections`. Now Xcode will select the newly inserted text when the buffer is returned.

If nothing was inserted, there is no selection. In that case, this code falls back to the old method of setting an insertion at the top of the file.

Build and run, select some text in the editor, and launch the extension. This time, you'll see the new text ends up selected:

You're probably going to be asciiifying with reckless abandon from now on, and navigating to the menu item is going to cut into productivity. Fortunately, you can map a key binding for your extension once it's installed.

In Xcode, navigate to **Xcode\Preferences**. Select the **Key Bindings** tab and filter for **Asciiify Comment** to find your new command. Double click the **Key** field and hold down **Control+Option+Command+A** (or anything available you prefer) to assign a hotkey.

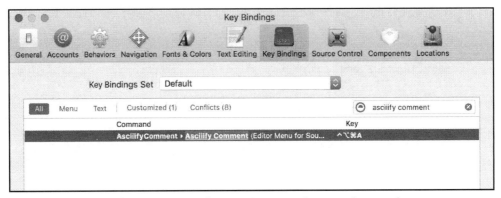

Now build and run the extension, select some text in the test editor and type **Control+Option+Command+A** to trigger Asciiify.

Now that triggering your extension is this easy, you only have one thing left to do:

Dynamic commands

What you've built works well to asciiify text, but it doesn't fully leverage the FIGlet library. The library is capable of creating FIGlets with a number of different fonts, whereas your extension doesn't offer the user a choice.

You could go through and add each supported font to the extension `Info.plist`, but that isn't very flexible and it's manually intensive. If you wanted the extension to download new fonts, for instance, you'd have no way to dynamically add them to the menu, and you'd have to update the extension.

Fortunately, source editor extensions allow an alternate, dynamic means to define menu items. The `XCSourceEditorExtension` protocol defines an optional property `commandDefinitions` that provides the same information about each command as the **Info.plist**.

commandDefinitions is an array of dictionaries, with each dictionary representing a single command. The dictionary keys are defined in a struct XCSourceEditorCommandDefinitionKey and represent the command name, associated source editor class, and a unique identifier. They map directly to keys provided in the **Info.plist** here:

Item 0	⊘⊖	Dictionary ◇ (3 items)	
XCSourceEditorCommandClassName	String	$(PRODUCT_MODULE_NAME).SourceEditorCommand	
XCSourceEditorCommandIdentifier	String	$(PRODUCT_BUNDLE_IDENTIFIER).SourceEditorCommand	
XCSourceEditorCommandName	String	Asciiify Comment	

You'll implement this property and use it to pull available fonts from the FIGlet library.

Open **SourceEditorExtension.swift** and delete the commented template code inside SourceEditorExtension.

Add the following import above the class:

```
import Figlet
```

You'll use the Figlet library to pull over a list of available fonts.

Now add the following property definition to SourceEditorExtension:

```
var commandDefinitions: [[XCSourceEditorCommandDefinitionKey:
Any]] {
  // 1
  let className = SourceEditorCommand.className()
  let bundleIdentifier = Bundle(for: type(of:
self)).bundleIdentifier!
  // 2
  return FigletRenderer.topFonts.map {
    fontName in
    let identifier = [bundleIdentifier,
fontName].joined(separator: ".")
    return [
      // 3
      .nameKey: "Font: \(fontName)",
      .classNameKey: className,
      .identifierKey: identifier
    ]
  }
}
```

You've implemented the commandDefinitions property covered above. Here's what the code does:

1. className contains the String representation of the SourceEditorCommand class responsible for processing the commands to be defined here. bundleIdentifier is a String containing the name of the bundle this extension resides in, which will be part of the unique identifier for the commands.

2. FigletRenderer has a topFonts property containing the names of fonts the extension can use. This maps each fontName to the required dictionary. Before returning the dictionary, the identifier for a given font command is created by joining the bundleIdentifier and fontName.

3. You set each of the three required keys here. The nameKey value will appear in the menu item, and consists of the word Font followed by the fontName. The class name and identifier use values derived in earlier steps.

> **Note:** You may have noticed another optional method defined in the template of SourceEditorExtension. extensionDidFinishLaunching() is called as soon as the extension is launched by Xcode and provides an opportunity to prepare prior to a request. Asciiify, for instance, might take this opportunity to download new fonts.

Now that the command definition contains a font name, you need to use it on the receiving end.

Open **SourceEditorCommand.swift** and add the following method to SourceEditorCommand:

```
private func font(from commandIdentifier: String) -> String {
  let bundleIdentifier = Bundle(for: type(of:
self)).bundleIdentifier!
    .components(separatedBy: ".")
  let command = commandIdentifier.components(separatedBy: ".")

  if command.count == bundleIdentifier.count + 1 {
    return command.last!
  } else {
    return "standard"
  }
}
```

This accepts a String representing the command identifier which you formatted in the dynamic command creation as {Bundle Identifier}.{Font Name}. The method first obtains arrays representing the period delimited components of the bundleIdentifier and the incoming commandIdentifier.

It then checks that the count of items in the command array is one more than the count for those in bundleIdentifier. This enables a check to see that the commandIdentifier consists only of the bundle identifier followed by a command name. In this case, the command name would be the font name.

If the count comparison determines a command name is present, the final array element is the font name and it gets returned. If it isn't, the code falls back to returning "standard", which is the default font name.

Now add the following property to the top of perform(with:completionHandler:):

```
let selectedFont = font(from: invocation.commandIdentifier)
```

This uses the new font(from:) method to set selectedFont with the font name to be processed.

Now find where you set asciiified using figlet.render(input:). Replace the render(input:) call with the following:

```
figlet.render(input: selectedText, withFont: selectedFont)
```

This now uses render(input:withFont:), which accepts a font name String as its second argument. This uses selectedFont to render the text with the chosen font.

Build and run, and navigate to the **AsciiifyComment** menu once again. This time, you'll see several new menu options, courtesy of commandDefinitions!

The extension previously used the **Standard** font. Select something different this time to confirm your new commands do indeed pass a different parameter to the FIGlet library.

```
 5  //
 6  //      ___         __     __
 7  //     / _ \ ___   __ \  / _ \ (_< / /
 8  //    /_/   \__//_/_/\_/  /__/(_)
 9  //
10  //
11
```

> **Note**: Of course, because you've replaced the **Asciiify Comment** command with the new dynamic commands, your key binding no longer works. If you like, you can add new key bindings for each of the new Asciiify commands.

Where to go from here?

In a short amount of time, you've created a functional source editor extension. In the process, you learned everything you need to know to implement your own idea for a source editor extension.

While it is disappointing to lose the progress made in the thriving plugin community, exciting times are ahead. The simplicity of source editor extensions make Xcode extension development much more accessible to the masses. Creating extensions for your own refactoring efforts, or to address standards on your product, can be done quickly.

The landscape extensions will continue to change as Apple opens up more Xcode functionality to developers. It's up to the community to adopt and leverage source editor extensions while also pleading the case for more Xcode extension points to fill any voids.

For more insight into source editor extensions, see the 2016 WWDC session on the topic here: apple.co/2byNQd6

Chapter 4: Beginning Message Apps

By Rich Turton

iOS 10 brought some fun features to iMessage – and also opened up the app to third party developers. This means you can create and sell things to use in iMessage such as applications and sticker packs, and unlike other extension points, Messages apps don't need to have a "standard" iOS app to work.

In this chapter, you'll learn how to make a sticker app, which is a great introduction to the Messages framework. You'll build the sticker pack to start. Next, you'll make a Messages app to provide stickers using some built-in classes. Finally, you'll create a custom sticker app using a collection view.

Ready to get sticky? :]

Getting started

Sticker packs are the simplest possible iMessage application you can make. So simple, in fact, that you don't need to write any code! Create a new Xcode project and choose the **iOS\Application\Sticker Pack Application** template:

Name the project **RWPeeps**, click **Next**, and then **Create**.

The project will likely be one of the simplest Xcode projects you've ever seen! It only contains one thing – a specialized asset catalog named **Stickers.xcstickers**. Within the asset catalog is a place for the app icon and a folder named **Sticker Pack**:

The resources for this chapter contains a folder called **RWPeepsImages**. Drag images from that folder into the **Sticker Pack** folder:

You're done! No, seriously – you're done.

Build and run your "app", and you'll see that Xcode now offers you a choice of host applications to run. Select **Messages**, since that's what your sticker pack is designed for:

The iOS simulator now contains a working Messages app, where you can view both sides of a conversation. This lets you test and develop Messages apps with ease.

Once the simulator has launched and Messages opens, you'll see an app button at the bottom of the screen:

Tap the button and wait a second or so; it seems to take some time for the simulator to launch your app. You'll see your stickers are ready to go! Tap any sticker to send it, or tap and hold to "peel" it off and attach to another message:

You can use the back button in the navigation bar to switch to the other side of the conversation.

There are a few rules around sticker pack applications:

- The sticker images must be PNG, APNG, GIF or JPEG format, and less than 500KB in size.

- Messages will display all the stickers in a pack at the same size.

- You can choose either small (100x100), medium (136x136) or large (206x206) for the size of your sticker pack.

- You should supply the images at **3x** resolution *only*.

Once you have recovered from the dizzying excitement of static sticker packs, you're ready to move on to a sticker *application*!

Creating a sticker application

Sticker apps offer way more functionality beyond sticker packs; instead of relying on a static set of images, you can add custom UI and control the stickers available at runtime.

Next you're going to make a mouth-watering sticker app called **Stickerlicious**, so you can send yummy treats to your friends via iMessage. You'll learn how to create stickers dynamically from code, and you'll also learn how to filter and divide these stickers to help your users quickly find the stickers they're looking for.

Close your **RWPeeps** project if you still have it open, and create a new project in Xcode. Choose the **iOS\Application\iMessage Application** template:

Name the project **Stickerlicious** and make sure the language is **Swift**. Click **Next**, and then **Create**.

This is another new application template. Here's a quick tour of what you get in the template:

- An application target, named **Stickerlicious** – this is necessary because message applications are actually *extensions* of standard applications, much like Today extensions. However, with Messages extensions, the parent app doesn't have to do anything and doesn't appear on the home screen. You can safely ignore the application.

- A Messages extension, named **MessagesExtension**. This is what actually runs inside Messages, and is where you'll do all your work.

- Of additional interest inside the Messages extension are a storyboard, an asset catalog, and **MessagesViewController.swift**, which is a subclass of `MSMessagesAppViewController`.

- **Messages.framework**, which contains all of the message-related classes you will need.

All Messages apps live inside a `MSMessagesAppViewController` subclass. `MSMessagesAppViewController` contains several properties and methods of interest when building more complex message apps, but for a dynamic sticker pack, you can ignore all of them.

> **Note:** For more information on `MSMessagesAppViewController`, see Chapter 6, "Intermediate Message Apps".

For now, open **MessagesViewController.swift** and delete all of the template methods, leaving you with an empty class declaration.

The sticker browser view controller

The Messages framework contains a pair of classes, `MSStickerBrowserView` and `MSStickerBrowserViewController`, which you can use to display your stickers. Think of them as a pair, like `UITableView` and `UITableViewController`, or `UICollectionView` and `UICollectionViewController`.

`MSMessagesAppViewController` has to be the root view controller of your Messages extension, so to add a sticker browser, you have to embed it as a child view controller.

Open **MainInterface.storyboard** and delete the "Hello World" label from the **Messages View Controller** scene.

In the object library, find a **Container View** and drag it into the scene. With the view selected, add constraints to pin it to all edges of the scene, not relative to the margins:

When the frames are updated, the container view will fill the scene.

Before you can assign a class to the embedded view controller, you need to create it. Make a new file and choose the **iOS\Source\Swift File** template. Name the file **CandyStickerBrowserViewController.swift**.

Delete the contents of the file and replace them with the following:

```
import Messages

class CandyStickerBrowserViewController:
MSStickerBrowserViewController {

}
```

Switch back to **MainInterface.storyboard** and select the embedded view controller. In the Identity Inspector, change the class to CandyStickerBrowserViewController.

Return to **CandyStickerBrowserViewController.swift**. Add the following property to hold the stickers you are going to display:

```
var stickers = [MSSticker]()
```

MSSticker is the model object representing a Messages Sticker.

Add the following constant above the class declaration to hold an array of image names:

```
let stickerNames = ["CandyCane", "Caramel", "ChocolateBar",
  "ChocolateChip", "DarkChocolate", "GummiBear",
  "JawBreaker", "Lollipop", "SourCandy"]
```

These names all correspond to images that have been supplied for you in the starter materials for this chapter. Find the **candy** folder and drag it into the **MessagesExtension** group in Xcode:

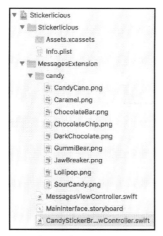

Add the following extension to **CandyStickerBrowserViewController.swift**, below the class declaration:

```
extension CandyStickerBrowserViewController {

  func loadStickers() {
    stickers = stickerNames.map({ name in
      let url = Bundle.main.url(forResource: name,
        withExtension: "png")!
      return try! MSSticker(
        contentsOfFileURL: url,
        localizedDescription: name)
    })
  }

}
```

This method creates an array of `MSSticker` elements by converting the names supplied in `stickerNames` to URLs. In your own apps, you could create stickers from packaged resources, or files that you have downloaded.

In the main class body, override `viewDidLoad()` as follows and call your new method:

```
override func viewDidLoad() {
  super.viewDidLoad()
  loadStickers()
  stickerBrowserView.backgroundColor = #colorLiteral(
    red:  0.9490196078, green: 0.7568627451,
    blue: 0.8196078431, alpha: 1)
}
```

In this method you also set a sweet pink color for the background.

The last step is to set up the data source methods for the sticker browser view. This should be a familiar task if you've ever written a table view or collection view data source.

The protocol `MSStickerBrowserViewDataSource` has two methods; implement them both by adding the following extension:

```
//MARK: MSStickerBrowserViewDataSource
extension CandyStickerBrowserViewController {
  override func numberOfStickers(in stickerBrowserView:
    MSStickerBrowserView) -> Int {
    return stickers.count
  }

  override func stickerBrowserView(_ stickerBrowserView:
    MSStickerBrowserView, stickerAt index: Int) -> MSSticker {
    return stickers[index]
  }
}
```

These methods are much simpler than table or collection view data sources; you have a number of stickers, and a sticker for a particular index.

Build and run on the iPhone 6S simulator, and choose to launch into the Messages app. Tap the **Apps** button and you'll need to scroll all the way to the right to find your new app. Wait a moment for the simulator to launch your app, and eventually you'll see the following:

That's nice, but so far you've only made something that looks *exactly* like a sticker pack application – just one that took more work!

Don't fret; in the next section you're going to add some additional UI and dynamic features to your app.

Adding dynamic stickers

You're about to introduce a special **Chocoholic** mode for those *special* times when only pictures of chocolate will do for ruining – er, sorry – *enhancing* your iMessage chats. Chocoholic mode will dynamically update the available stickers before your sugar-crazed eyes.

To start, open **MainInterface.storyboard**. Select the container view and use the resizing handle to drag down the top of the view by about 70 points to give yourself some room to work:

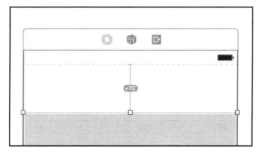

Select the top orange constraint and delete it. Drag a switch and a label into the space you've created, and set the label's text to **Chocoholic Mode**.

Select the label and the switch, then use the **Stack** button to embed them in a horizontal stack view:

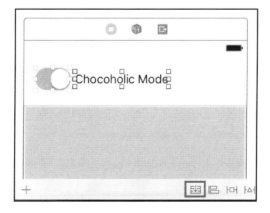

With the stack view selected, change the **Spacing** in the Attributes Inspector to **5**. Using the **Pin** menu, add constraints from the stack view to its top, leading and bottom neighbors:

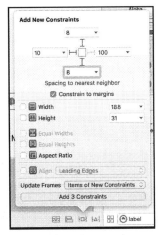

Select the switch and set its value to **Off** in the Attributes Inspector. Open the Assistant editor, and make sure it's displaying **MessagesViewController.swift**. Control-drag from the switch into the `MessagesViewController` class to create a new action, called **handleChocoholicChanged** with a sender type of **UISwitch**.

You're done with Interface Builder for now, so you can open **MessagesViewController.swift** in the main editor if you'd like some more elbow room.

Add the following new **Chocoholicable** protocol to the file:

```
protocol Chocoholicable {
  func setChocoholic(_ chocoholic: Bool)
}
```

Update the action method you just created above:

```
@IBAction func handleChocoholicChanged(_ sender: UISwitch) {
  childViewControllers.forEach({ vc in
    guard let vc = vc as? Chocoholicable else { return }
    vc.setChocoholic(sender.isOn)
  })
}
```

This will pass the chocoholic mode down to any child view controller that is `Chocoholicable`. There aren't any at present, so switch to **CandyStickerBrowserViewController.swift** to make it so.

First, update the declaration of `loadStickers()`:

```
func loadStickers(_ chocoholic: Bool = false) {
```

This lets you pass in the chocoholic mode, with a default value of `false` so the existing call from `viewDidLoad()` remains unaffected.

Next, replace the whole function body with this code:

```
stickers = stickerNames.filter( { name in
  return chocoholic ? name.contains("Chocolate") : true
}).map({ name in
  let url = Bundle.main.url(forResource: name,
    withExtension: "png")!
  return try! MSSticker(contentsOfFileURL: url,
    localizedDescription: name)
})
```

This will filter the names to only show chocolate-containing stickers if chocoholic mode is on.

Finally, add the following extension to make `CandyStickerBroswerViewController` conform to `Chocoholicable`:

```
extension CandyStickerBrowserViewController: Chocoholicable {
  func setChocoholic(_ chocoholic: Bool) {
    loadStickers(chocoholic)
    stickerBrowserView.reloadData()
  }
}
```

Build and run; now you can fulfill all your sticky, chocolatey messaging needs:

Creating a custom sticker browser

MSStickerBrowserView offers you little scope for customization. To really take control of your sticker app, you'll work with MSStickerView. This is the view that powers MSStickerBrowserView, and you can use it on its own as well.

It gives you all the sticker functionality – displaying and scaling the stickers, tapping to add to the message, drag and drop – with no extra code. All you need to do is put it on the screen and give it an MSSticker.

In this final part of the chapter you will replace the MSStickerBrowserViewController subclass with a UICollectionViewController subclass which will allow you to divide the stickers up into labelled sections.

In **MainInterface.storyboard**, select the **Candy Sticker Browser** scene and delete it. Drag in a **UICollectionViewController**, then Control-drag from the container view to the collection view controller and choose the **Embed** segue.

Select the **Collection View** in the collection view controller, open the Attributes Inspector and check the **Accessories\Section Header** checkbox.

Open the Size Inspector, and set **Header Size\Height** to **25**. Set the **Min Spacing** and **Section Insets** values to **0**.

Drag a label into the section header, using the guides to position it in the center. With the **Align** button at the bottom of the storyboard, add constraints to pin it to the horizontal and vertical centers of the view:

Drag in a **Visual Effect View with Blur** from the object library onto the section header. Using the **Pin** button at the bottom of the storyboard, add constraints to pin the view to all sides of the section header, with zero spacing.

Before continuing, make sure the **Label** is displayed *on top of* the **Visual Effect View**. If not, open the document outline on the left of Interface Builder and place it below the Visual Effect View.

Drag in a plain `UIView` to the collection view cell and, using the same technique, pin it to all edges of the cell. Select the view, and using the Identity Inspector, change the class to **MSStickerView**.

Now you need to create custom subclasses for the section header, collection view cells and view controller.

For the header, create a new file and choose **iOS\Source\Cocoa Touch Class**. Name the class **SectionHeader** and make it a subclass of **UICollectionReusableView**.

For the cell, create a new file and choose **iOS\Source\Cocoa Touch Class** again. Name the class **StickerCollectionViewCell** and make it a subclass of **UICollectionViewCell**.

Add the following `import` statement to the top of **StickerCollectionViewCell.swift**:

```
import Messages
```

`MSStickerView` is part of the Messages framework. Since you'll be making an outlet to one of these, the cell needs to know what that class is.

The final new class to create is the view controller. Create a new file and choose **iOS\Source\Cocoa Touch Class** again, name the class **StickerCollectionViewController** and make it a subclass of **UICollectionViewController**.

Replace the templated contents with the following:

```
import UIKit
import Messages

class StickerCollectionViewController:
UICollectionViewController {
}
```

Switch back to **MainInterface.storyboard** to connect everything up.

First, choose the collection view controller and use the Identity Inspector to set the class to **StickerCollectionViewController**.

Choose the section header (labeled Collection Reusable View in the Document Outline), change its class to **SectionHeader**, and use the Attributes Inspector to set the reuse identifier to **SectionHeader**.

Choose the cell, change its class to **StickerCollectionViewCell**, and set the reuse identifier to **StickerCollectionViewCell**.

Open the Assistant editor, make sure **StickerCollectionViewCell.swift** is displayed, and create a new outlet from the `MSStickerView` inside the cell to the collection view cell subclass. Name it **stickerView**.

Now switch the Assistant editor to **SectionHeader.swift** and create a new outlet from the label in the section header to the `SectionHeader` class file. Name it `label`.

Check the document outline in the storyboard to make sure you haven't missed anything:

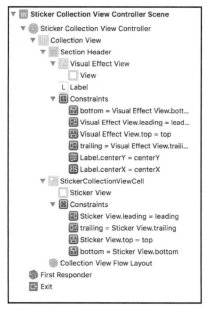

Close the Assistant editor and switch to **StickerCollectionViewController.swift**.

The stickers will be grouped in this view controller using a dictionary instead of an array. Add the following code above the class declaration:

```
let stickerNameGroups: [String: [String]] = [
  "Crunchy":   ["CandyCane","JawBreaker","Lollipop"],
  "Chewy":     ["Caramel","GummiBear","SourCandy"],
  "Chocolate": ["ChocolateBar","ChocolateChip","DarkChocolate"]
]
```

Dictionaries aren't great data objects, because you need to remember keys and values.

To help with this, still above the class declaration, define the following new struct which will form the basis of your model:

```
struct StickerGroup {
  let name: String
```

```
   let members: [MSSticker]
}
```

Inside the `StickerCollectionViewController` class, add a property to hold the model:

```
var stickerGroups = [StickerGroup]()
```

Just as you did with the sticker browser view controller subclass, you'll need to implement the `loadStickers` method. Add it in an extension as follows:

```
extension StickerCollectionViewController {
  // 1
  func loadStickers(_ chocoholic: Bool = false) {
    // 2
    stickerGroups = stickerNameGroups.filter({ (name, _) in
      // 3
      return chocoholic ? name == "Chocolate" : true
    }).map { (name, stickerNames) in
      // 4
      let stickers: [MSSticker] = stickerNames.map { name in
        let url = Bundle.main.url(forResource: name,
          withExtension: "png")!
        return try! MSSticker(contentsOfFileURL: url,
          localizedDescription: name)
      }
      // 5
      return StickerGroup(name: name, members: stickers)
    }
    // 6
    stickerGroups.sort(by: { $0.name < $1.name })
  }
}
```

This is quite similar to the previous `loadStickers` method. Here's a breakdown:

1. This takes a chocoholic mode with a default value.

2. Filtering on a dictionary takes a tuple of the key and value. For filtering we can ignore the value; ergo, the presence of "_".

3. The filtering now takes place on the group name, rather than on a substring of the sticker name.

4. There is an additional mapping step to turn the array of names from the dictionary into an array of stickers.

5. You then convert each dictionary entry to a `StickerGroup` struct.

6. Finally, you sort the array of sticker groups by name, since dictionaries don't have a guaranteed ordering.

Modify `viewDidLoad()` to call your new method and set up a few things:

```
override func viewDidLoad() {
  super.viewDidLoad()
  loadStickers()
  if let layout = collectionView?.collectionViewLayout as?
    UICollectionViewFlowLayout {
    layout.sectionHeadersPinToVisibleBounds = true
  }
  collectionView?.backgroundColor = #colorLiteral(
    red:  0.9490196078, green: 0.7568627451,
    blue: 0.8196078431, alpha: 1)
}
```

This uses the nice new feature of `UICollectionViewFlowLayout`, which gives you sticky section headers.

You may have noticed that the sticker browser view you used before managed to fit three columns onto an iPhone 6 in portrait, despite the stickers being 136 points across and the iPhone 6 only being 375 points across. You're going to perform a similar trick and make sure you get *at least* three columns of stickers.

Add the following extension:

```
// MARK: UICollectionViewDelegateFlowLayout
extension StickerCollectionViewController {
  func collectionView(_ collectionView: UICollectionView,
    layout collectionViewLayout: UICollectionViewLayout,
    sizeForItemAtIndexPath indexPath: NSIndexPath) -> CGSize {
    let edge = min(collectionView.bounds.width / 3, 136)
    return CGSize(width: edge, height: edge)
  }
}
```

This sets the cells to a square shape with an edge of 136 points *or* a third of the screen width, whichever is least.

The collection view datasource methods are next. Add the following extension:

```
extension StickerCollectionViewController {
  override func numberOfSections(
    in collectionView: UICollectionView) -> Int {
    return stickerGroups.count
  }

  override func collectionView(_ collectionView:
    UICollectionView,
```

```
    numberOfItemsInSection section: Int) -> Int {
    return stickerGroups[section].members.count
  }
}
```

The two `.count` methods are simple, thanks to the `StickerGroup` struct you're using as a model object.

The cell configuration method is also straightforward. Add the following code to the extension you just created:

```
override func collectionView(_ collectionView: UICollectionView,
  cellForItemAt indexPath: IndexPath) -> UICollectionViewCell {
  let cell = collectionView.dequeueReusableCell(
    withReuseIdentifier: "StickerCollectionViewCell",
    for: indexPath) as! StickerCollectionViewCell

  let sticker =
    stickerGroups[indexPath.section].members[indexPath.row]
  cell.stickerView.sticker = sticker

  return cell
}
```

This gets the correct sticker for the section and item and passes it to the sticker view in the cell. That's all you need to get a working sticker view.

Add the final method for the data source extension to populate the section header:

```
override func collectionView(_ collectionView: UICollectionView,
  viewForSupplementaryElementOfKind kind: String,
  at indexPath: IndexPath) -> UICollectionReusableView {
  guard kind == UICollectionElementKindSectionHeader else {
    fatalError()
  }

  let header = collectionView.dequeueReusableSupplementaryView(
    ofKind: kind, withReuseIdentifier: "SectionHeader",
    for: indexPath) as! SectionHeader
  header.label.text = stickerGroups[indexPath.section].name
  return header
}
```

You're almost done. The last thing to add is to make the view controller `Chocoholicable`. Add the following extension, which will look almost identical to the one you used for the sticker browser view controller:

```
extension StickerCollectionViewController: Chocoholicable {
  func setChocoholic(_ chocoholic: Bool) {
    loadStickers(chocoholic)
```

```
    collectionView?.reloadData()
  }
}
```

Build and run; your candy neatly separates into sections, so you know just what you're going to get. Perhaps Forrest Gump should have used a collection view? :]

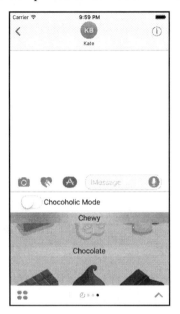

Where to go from here?

Congratulations! At this point, you know how to make a basic sticker pack ("Look ma, no code!") and how to create a custom user interface for your stickers.

There's much more you can do with Messages beyond sticker packs. In the next chapter, you'll learn how to create custom messages. Specifically, you'll create a cool drawing and guessing game you can play right within Messages!

Chapter 5: Intermediate Message Apps

By Rich Turton

In the previous chapter, you saw how to build apps containing custom stickers for use in Messages. Stickers are great, but you can do far more than that.

In this chapter, you're going to learn how to send fully custom, updatable messages. This will allow you to build a game called **WenderPic**, where one player tries to draw something with a limited supply of ink, and their opponent tries to guess what it is. Drawings and guesses all travel via iMessage.

Ready to channel your inner Picasso?

Getting started

Open the **WenderPic** starter project provided with the materials for this chapter. There's quite a lot already present in the project, but none of it really has to do with Messages. That's where you come in.

Here's a quick tour of the project:

- Just like in the previous chapter, what you're building is a **MessagesExtension**, and not a "full" app like you're used to. The code for the extension is inside the **MessagesExtension** group.

- The **Models** group contains the model object for the game, **WenderPicGame**.

- The **Controllers** group contains the three view controllers used to play the game; **SummaryViewController**, which shows the title of the game and a start button; **DrawingViewController**, which handles the drawing; and **GuessesViewController**, which lets you enter a guess.

- **MainInterface.storyboard** shows the root messages view controller and the UI for the three game controllers. You'll build code to add these as child view controllers.

In this chapter, the root messages view controller will do a lot more work than it did in the previous one, so let's start with an overview of that.

The Messages app view controller

You briefly encountered `MSMessagesAppViewController` in the previous chapter; it's a `UIViewController` subclass, but the Messages framework calls several interesting functions on it.

There are life cycle functions, similar to `viewDidLoad(_:)`, `viewWillAppear(_:)`, and its brethren:

- `willBecomeActive(with:)`: Called when your Messages app is activated. As you'll learn later, the current conversation is passed in here.

- `didResignActive(with:)`: Called when the user is done with your app, either because they switched conversations, switched to another app, or left the Messages app.

There are functions relating to the current conversation:

- `didReceive(_: conversation:)`: Called when a message *that was generated by your extension* is received. It's important to note that your extension does *not* get told about every message your user receives — only those relevant to your extension.

- `didStartSending(_: conversation:)` and `didCancelSending(_: conversation:)`: Called when the user hits send for one of your messages, or cancels sending.

Finally, there are functions relating to presentation-style transitions. Messages apps can have two presentation styles; **Compact**, where the app fills the space normally taken by the keyboard, or **Expanded**, where the app fills the entire screen. `willTransition(to:)` and `didTransition(to:)` are called when the presentation style changes.

The idea of the `MSMessagesAppViewController` is to act as the root of the rest of your Messages extension, so it can handle all the things above. Typically, the interface for your app is handled in separate view controllers which are added as children – this is what you'll be doing in the next part.

Adding the first child view controller

You'll add all of the game view controllers mentioned above as children of MessagesViewController. Adding a child view controller involves quite a lot of boilerplate, so you'll add a utility function to avoid duplicating yourself thrice.

Open **MessagesViewController.swift** and add the following extension:

```swift
// MARK: Child View Controllers
extension MessagesViewController {
  func switchTo(viewController controller: UIViewController) {
    // Remove any existing child view controller
    for child in childViewControllers {
      child.willMove(toParentViewController: .none)
      child.view.removeFromSuperview()
      child.removeFromParentViewController()
    }

    // Add the new child view controller
    addChildViewController(controller)

    controller.view.translatesAutoresizingMaskIntoConstraints =
false
    view.addSubview(controller.view)

    NSLayoutConstraint.activate([
      controller.view.leftAnchor.constraint(equalTo:
view.leftAnchor),
      controller.view.rightAnchor.constraint(equalTo:
view.rightAnchor),
      controller.view.topAnchor.constraint(equalTo:
topLayoutGuide.bottomAnchor),
      controller.view.bottomAnchor.constraint(equalTo:
view.bottomAnchor)
      ])

    controller.didMove(toParentViewController: self)
  }
}
```

First, you remove any existing child view controllers, then you add the controller passed in by the function. Finally, you pin its view to all edges of the messages view controller's view.

The first view controller the user will see is the SummaryViewController – a controller with the title of the game and a "new game" button.

Add the following utility function to the extension to create a new
SummaryViewController:

```
func instantiateSummaryViewController(game: WenderPicGame?) ->
  UIViewController {
  guard let controller = storyboard?.instantiateViewController(
    withIdentifier: "summaryVC") as? SummaryViewController
    else {
      fatalError("Unable to instantiate a summary view
controller")
    }

  controller.game = game
  return controller
}
```

This function creates and configures a new instance of a SummaryViewController from
the Storyboard.

The decision for which of the three game view controllers you will show at any point is
based on a combination of the current conversation and the current presentation style.
The following function, which you will flesh out further as the project progresses, makes
that decision. For now, you'll just show the SummaryViewController.

Add the following code to the extension:

```
func presentViewController(
    forConversation conversation: MSConversation,
    withPresentationStyle style: MSMessagesAppPresentationStyle) {

    let controller: UIViewController

    // TODO: Create the right view controller here
    controller = instantiateSummaryViewController(game: nil)
    switchTo(viewController: controller)
}
```

The final piece is to call this function at just the right time. Add the following code to
willBecomeActive(with:):

```
presentViewController(forConversation: conversation,
    withPresentationStyle: presentationStyle)
```

Build and run, and attach to the Messages app as you did in the previous chapter. You
should see the summary view controller appear.

Tapping the "New Game" button does nothing yet. You'll fix this next.

Switch back to Xcode and open **MessagesViewController.swift**. The summary view controller has a delegate, which you need to set. Make `MessagesViewController` conform to `SummaryViewControllerDelegate` by adding the following extension:

```
extension MessagesViewController: SummaryViewControllerDelegate
{
  func handleSummaryTap(forGame game: WenderPicGame?) {
    requestPresentationStyle(.expanded)
  }
}
```

You want the app to change to the expanded presentation style when you tap the button on the summary view controller so that you can do full-screen drawing.

Set the summary view controller's delegate by adding the following line to `instantiateSummaryViewController(game:)`, above the `return` statement:

```
controller.delegate = self
```

Build and run again, and tap the button; the app transitions to the expanded size!

Nice, but that's only half of what you want. In the next part you'll switch to the drawing view controller as well.

Switching view controllers

When the user taps to start a new game, the app transitions to the expanded presentation style. You want to create a new `WenderPicGame` and show the drawing view controller. To do this, you need to call the utility function which chooses and presents the view controller whenever a change in the presentation style occurs.

Open **MessagesViewController.swift** and add the following code to `willTransition(to:)`:

```
if let conversation = activeConversation {
  presentViewController(
    forConversation: conversation,
    withPresentationStyle: presentationStyle)
}
```

`activeConversation` is an optional property of `MSMessagesAppViewController`.

Inside your extension where you work with the child view controllers, add a utility function to the to make a new `DrawingViewController`:

```
func instantiateDrawingViewController(game: WenderPicGame?) ->
  UIViewController {
  guard let controller = storyboard?.instantiateViewController(
    withIdentifier: "drawingVC") as? DrawingViewController
    else {
      fatalError("Unable to instantiate a drawing view
controller")
    }

  controller.game = game
  return controller
}
```

This is almost identical to the function that creates the `SummaryViewController`, and only differs in the type of controller it returns.

Move to `presentViewController(forConversation: withPresentationStyle:)`. Find the `TODO:` comment you added earlier, and replace it, along with the line where you create the `SummaryViewController`, with the following:

```
switch style {
case .compact:
```

```
    controller = instantiateSummaryViewController(game: nil)
  case .expanded:
    let newGame = WenderPicGame.newGame(drawerId:
      conversation.localParticipantIdentifier)
    controller = instantiateDrawingViewController(game: newGame)
  }
```

Instead of always creating the `SummaryViewController`, you are now switching on the presentation style. When the app is compact, the summary controller will be shown; when expanded, you'll see the drawing controller instead.

You create a new `WenderPicGame` using a UUID which represents the person doing the drawing. This UUID is available as a property on `MSConversation` and is consistent as long as the user keeps your app installed and enabled. This will let the app track the progress of a game between two participants.

Build and run, and tap the new game button, then let your artistic side go wild!

When you've run out of ink, hit the **Done** button...and nothing happens. You need to pack up your image in a message and send it to your friend. You'll solve this in the next part.

Creating a message

The Messages framework has these model classes: a **Conversation**, a **Message**, and a **Session**. Here's a brief overview of each one.

Conversation

`MSConversation` represents the back-and-forth stream of messages visible in the Messages app. This is the view that has the speech bubbles when you are texting.

You don't have full access to the conversation, which is understandable given the privacy implications. However, you *can* access the following properties:

- `localParticipantIdentifier`: A UUID representing the user of the device — i.e. the person who is sending messages from your extension. You used this when creating a new game earlier.

- `remoteParticipantIdentifiers`: An array of UUIDs representing the recipient(s) of any sent messages.

- `selectedMessage`: An optional property representing the selected message, *if* the selected message was generated by your extension.

A conversation also has functions to add attachments, messages, text or stickers to the input field. Sending is still at the discretion of the user. This is similar to the way `MFMessageComposeViewController` works – your app can populate a message and have it all set up and ready to go, but the user still has control over the actual *sending* of the message. This way, nothing will be sent without the user's content.

Message

`MSMessage` represents an interactive message. These are unique to, and only accessible by, your Messages app. If someone receives a message created by your extension, and they don't have it installed, they'll be prompted to install it. The most important properties of a message, which must be set before the message is sent, are the `layout` and the `URL`.

The `layout` is a separate class which controls how the message appears in the conversation. You don't get to fully customize the layout, you simply set whichever of its properties (image, caption and so on) are appropriate for your message.

The `URL` is your opportunity to send any custom data along with the message. You can include key-value pairs using `NSURLQueryItem`. You'll see these in action later.

Session

`MSSession` is used when a message is intended to be updated as the conversation progresses, rather than creating new entries in the conversation each time. If you create a message and associate it with a session, it will be shown normally. If you send *another* message with the same session, the previous message will be moved down to the bottom of the conversation and be updated with the new information.

Imagine playing a game of Tic-Tac-Toe over Messages. With no sessions, the transcript would be a series of board images as the game progressed. With sessions, however, you'd only have one board image, with the latest positions appearing as each player made their move.

You can decide for yourself if sessions make sense for your messaging app.

Sending a message

With that bit of theory covered, it's time to apply what you've learned. To recap the current state of the app, you can draw a picture, but not send it to your friend.

In **MessagesViewController.swift**, add the following function in a new extension:

```
extension MessagesViewController {
  func composeMessage(with game: WenderPicGame,
  caption: String, session: MSSession? = .none) -> MSMessage {
    //1
    let layout = MSMessageTemplateLayout()
    //2
    layout.image = game.currentDrawing
    //3
    layout.caption = caption
    //4
    let message = MSMessage(session: session ?? MSSession())
    message.layout = layout

    return message
  }
}
```

Here's the play-by-play:

1. `MSMessageTemplateLayout` is currently the only available message layout class, so you have to use it. This could very well change in future versions of the Messages framework.

2. The `DrawingViewController` updates the game with the current state of the image. You use this image for the layout, so it will be part of the message.

3. The caption is text that appears under the image.

4. You create a new message with either the existing session, or if one doesn't exist, a new session.

The `DrawingViewController`, like the `SummaryViewController`, has a delegate which is called when the user taps the done button. Add the following extension to **MessagesViewController.swift**:

```
extension MessagesViewController: DrawingViewControllerDelegate
{
  func handleDrawingComplete(game: WenderPicGame?) {
    defer { dismiss() }
    guard
      let conversation = activeConversation,
```

```
      let game = game
   else { return }

   let message = composeMessage(with: game, caption: "Guess my
WenderPic!", session: conversation.selectedMessage?.session!)

   conversation.insert(message) { (error) in
      if let error = error {
        print(error)
      }
    }
  }
}
```

This function uses the theory covered earlier. You get the current conversation and insert a custom message into it. Finally, you dismiss the drawing view.

Next, update `instantiateDrawingViewController(game:)` so that the delegate is set:

```
controller.delegate = self
```

Build and run, create another artistic, ink-limited masterpiece and tap the done button – your message is ready to send!

The appearance of the message, with the image and caption, are defined by the layout object. You don't get any control over the appearance – but you don't have to do any work either. We'll call it a draw. :]

Tap the send button and the message will go to the other fake contact in the simulator.

Tap the back button, switch to the other side of the conversation, and you'll see what the recipient would see. Tap the message and you'll see a drawing controller for a new game.

What's going on here? When the user taps the message, the extension transitions to the expanded presentation style. At the moment, that action simply starts a new game. In the next section, you'll add some data to the message so you can pass the game state back and forth between participants. This will let the recipient of a WenderPic send their guess back to the artist.

Custom message content

In the discussion of MSMessage earlier, you learned that the URL property was your opportunity to add custom data to a message. You're going to do that now so that there's enough data in the message to recreate the WenderPicGame at the receiving end.

> **Note:** Messages apps are not yet available on macOS. The URL property has a second job - if your message is opened on a Mac, it will open the URL. We're not covering that in this chapter as it would involve you setting up a server that could handle the games.

To include data in a URL you'll need to use URLQueryItem. This struct represents a single key-value pair in a URL's query section – this is the part of the URL you'd see as ? key=value&otherKey=otherValue.

Open **WenderPicGame.swift** and add the following extension:

```
// MARK: Encoding / Decoding
extension WenderPicGame {
  var queryItems: [URLQueryItem] {
    var items = [URLQueryItem]()

    items.append(URLQueryItem(name: "word", value: word))
    items.append(URLQueryItem(name: "guesses", value:
      guesses.joined(separator: "::-::")))
    items.append(URLQueryItem(name: "drawerId", value:
      drawerId.uuidString))
    items.append(URLQueryItem(name: "gameState", value:
      gameState.rawValue))
    items.append(URLQueryItem(name: "gameId", value:
      gameId.uuidString))
    return items
  }
}
```

This puts all the important bits from the game into an array of query items: the word that the drawing is supposed to be, the person who drew it, any guesses that have been made, the current state of the game and the game's unique ID. You haven't made any guesses yet, but you will shortly.

Switch to **MessagesViewController.swift** and find the composeMessage(with: caption: session:). Add the following code before the return statement:

```
var components = URLComponents()
components.queryItems = game.queryItems
message.url = components.url
```

You might not think that you can create a valid URL just by using query components, but you can! The above code creates a URL that looks like this:

```
?word=dog&drawerId=D5E356A9-0B6A-4441-AB6C-08D24DB255B2
```

> **Note:** The image that's been drawn can't be sent as part of the URL - it's too big. It can't be retreived from the layout object at the receiving end either, because that's only available to the sender of the message. For your own apps you'd have to implement some form of web storage to make the image available to both sides. Because that's outside the scope of this tutorial, you're going to cheat slightly and store the drawn image in user defaults. You'll use the gameId property to do this. For the simulated conversation, the user defaults object is shared between both sides of the conversation - this trick won't work on devices!

Find handleDrawingComplete(game:) and add the following after the line where you create the message:

```
if let drawing = game.currentDrawing {
  DrawingStore.store(image: drawing, forUUID: game.gameId)
}
```

DrawingStore is the wrapper for user defaults mentioned in the note - in your own app you'd have a call to a web service here to store the image.

Now that you're sending some custom content with your message, it's time to receive it at the other end of the conversation. Remember that at the moment, when the user receives and taps a message, they simply see the drawing controller reappear. Instead, your app *should* attempt to recreate the game from the selected message and decide what to do based on that attempt.

First, you need to create a custom initializer for `WenderPicGame` that accepts some query items. Switch to **WenderPicGame.swift** and add the following inside the encoding / decoding extension:

```swift
init?(queryItems: [URLQueryItem]) {
  var word: String?
  var guesses = [String]()
  var drawerId: UUID?
  var gameId: UUID?

  for item in queryItems {
    guard let value = item.value else { continue }

    switch item.name {
    case "word":
      word = value
    case "guesses":
      guesses = value.components(separatedBy: "::–::")
    case "drawerId":
      drawerId = UUID(uuidString: value)
    case "gameState":
      self.gameState = GameState(rawValue: value)!
    case "gameId":
      gameId = UUID(uuidString: value)
    default:
      continue
    }
  }

  guard
    let decodedWord = word,
    let decodedDrawerId = drawerId,
    let decodedGameId = gameId
  else {
    return nil
  }

  self.word = decodedWord
  self.guesses = guesses
  self.currentDrawing = DrawingStore.image(forUUID:
decodedGameId)
  self.drawerId = decodedDrawerId
  self.gameId = decodedGameId
}
```

This failable initializer will return a valid game if the mandatory properties – `word`, `drawerId` and `gameId` – can be extracted from the query items. It attempts to get an image from the `DrawingStore` - remember that this is just using user defaults, and wouldn't work for a normal application.

For convenience, add the below initializer that takes a `MSMessage`, extracts the query items from it, and passes it to the previously defined initializer:

```
init?(message: MSMessage?) {
  guard
    let messageURL = message?.url,
    let urlComponents = URLComponents(url: messageURL,
resolvingAgainstBaseURL: false),
    let queryItems = urlComponents.queryItems
  else {
    return nil
  }
  self.init(queryItems: queryItems)
}
```

Now you have the ability to reconstruct a game from a message. If the user receives a drawing from their friend, they would want to see the `GuessViewController` when they tap it.

Switch to **MessagesViewController.swift** and add the following function to create the `GuessViewController` in the extension where you define the functions for dealing with child view controllers:

```
func instantiateGuessViewController(game: WenderPicGame?) ->
  UIViewController {
  guard let controller = storyboard?.instantiateViewController(
    withIdentifier: "guessVC") as? GuessViewController
    else {
      fatalError("Unable to instantiate a guess view
controller")
    }

  controller.game = game
  return controller
}
```

Now find the `switch` statement inside `presentViewController(forConversation withPresentationStyle:)`. Replace the lines after `case .expanded:` with the following:

```
if let game = WenderPicGame(message:
conversation.selectedMessage) {
  controller = instantiateGuessViewController(game: game)
} else {
  let newGame = WenderPicGame.newGame(
    drawerId: conversation.localParticipantIdentifier)
  controller = instantiateDrawingViewController(game: newGame)
}
```

Remember that the expanded style is requested when the user taps the new game button or taps a received message. If the user has tapped a message, then the conversation would have a selected message, so therefore you'll be able to create a game and show the GuessViewController.

Build and run your app; create a sketch, switch to the other conversation view and tap the message:

In what should be a familiar pattern by now, you can enter a guess, but nothing will happen. The GuessViewController has a delegate property, and you need to set it up in the MessagesViewController.

Add the following extension to **MessagesViewController.swift** to conform to the GuessViewControllerDelegate:

```swift
extension MessagesViewController: GuessViewControllerDelegate {
  func handleGuessSubmission(forGame game: WenderPicGame, guess:
String) {
    defer { dismiss() }
    guard let conversation = activeConversation else { return }

    //1
    let prefix = game.check(guess: guess) ? "👍" : "👎"
    //2
    let guesser = "$\(conversation.localParticipantIdentifier)"

    //3
    let caption = "\(prefix) \(guesser) guessed \(guess)"

    //4
    let message = composeMessage(with: game,
      caption: caption,
      session: conversation.selectedMessage?.session)
```

```
conversation.insert(message) { (error) in
  if let error = error {
    print(error)
  }
}
}
}
```

Here's the play-by-play:

1. check(guess:) sees if the guess is right, so we get a thumbs up or down to add to the message

2. If you use any of the message participant UUIDs in a message like this, prefixed with $, then they get auto-expanded into the contact's name. This allows you to personalise your custom messages without affecting the user's privacy.

3. You stitch everything together into the caption for the message

4. You create and send the message using the same convenience method as before.

> **Note:** The local participant identifier is the same for all sides of the conversation when running on a simulator, so the UUID might not convert to the correct text.

Change instantiateGuessViewController(game:) to set the delegate property:

```
controller.delegate = self
```

Build and run again, bang out a sketch, switch sides, make a guess, and you'll see your guess return to the artist:

Getting a second chance

You'll have noticed that you get a very limited supply of ink in this game. This means it's unlikely your opponent would guess your first attempt – unless you're Henri Matisse.

In the case of an incorrect guess, it would be a good idea to add some more ink to give your opponent another chance. At present, if you can recreate a game from the message, you show the `GuessViewController`. You're going to change this so that an incorrect guess lets the artist draw more.

Find `presentViewController(forConversation withPresentationStyle:)` in **MessagesViewController.swift**. Change the code where a game has been created from the message to match the following:

```
if let game = WenderPicGame(message:
conversation.selectedMessage) {
  switch game.gameState {
  case .guess:
    controller = instantiateDrawingViewController(game: game)
  case .challenge:
    controller = instantiateGuessViewController(game: game)
  }
} else {
```

> **Note:** Comparing `drawerId` with the `localParticipantIdentifer` is another option, but as noted before this does not currently work correctly in the simulator.

This will show the `DrawingViewController` if the game is a guess, or the guess controller if the game is a challenge. The game state is updated by each view controller when the player submits a drawing or guess. Build and run, send a drawing, make a guess, switch back to the original conversation and tap on the guess – and now you're able to further refine your pièce de resistance:

Congratulations! You've successfully built a collaborative messaging app, which lets you pass custom information back and forward between two participants.

Where to go from here?

Messages apps are an exciting new area for iOS. This is your chance to get involved from day one!

To learn more about the Messages framework check out the full documentation at https://developer.apple.com/reference/messages.

Chapter 6: SiriKit

By Rich Turton

Since Siri was introduced in iOS 5, people have been asking when they'd be able to use it in their apps. Just five short years later, here it is. Er, well, sort of. And only for some types of apps.

It turns out that integrating natural language processing into an app is quite a tricky problem to solve. You can't just take whatever text Siri has decoded from the user's speech, pass it as a string to the app and presto — you're done! Well, you *could*, but imagine the number of possible ways your users around the world could talk to your app. Would you *really* want to write that code?

Think about the times you've used Siri. There's usually a little conversation that happens between you and Siri; sometimes that conversation goes well, and sometimes it doesn't. Either way, there's a lot of first-party support work happening behind the scenes.

Before you start this chapter, some warnings: if you've ever been frustrated with Siri, how would you feel having to use Siri for *every build and run*? Then imagine that debugging was incredibly hard because you're running in an app extension, and because Siri times out if you pause the debugger for too long. Also, imagine you have to build using a device, because Siri isn't available on the simulator.

If that hasn't scared you off, then:

"It's time to get started."

I'm not sure I understand.

"Start the chapter."

OK, here's what I found on the web:

I'm just getting you warmed up. You'll be seeing that sort of thing a lot.

Getting started

SiriKit works using a set of *domains*, which represent related areas of functionality, such as Messaging.

Within each domain is a set of *intents*, which represent the specific tasks that the user can achieve using Siri. For example, within the Messaging domain, there are intents for sending a message, searching for messages and setting attributes on a message.

Each intent is represented by an `INIntent` subclass, and has associated with it a handler protocol and a specific `INIntentResponse` subclass for you to talk back to SiriKit.

Language processing in your app boils down to SiriKit deciding which intent and app the user is asking for, and your code checking that what the user is asking makes sense or can be done, and then doing it.

> **Note:** For a full list of the available domains and intents, check out the Intents Domains section in the SiriKit programming guide at: apple.co/2d2yUb8

Would you like to ride in my beautiful balloon?

The sample project for this chapter is **WenderLoon**, a ride-booking app like no other. The members of the Razeware team are floating above London in hot air balloons, waiting to (eventually) pick up passengers and take them to... well, wherever the wind is blowing. It's not the most practical way to get around, but the journey is very relaxing. Unless Mic is driving. :]

Open up the sample project. Before you can start, you'll need to amend the bundle identifier of the project so that Xcode can sort out your provisioning profiles. Using Siri needs entitlements, and you need to run it on a device, which means you need your own bundle ID.

Select the **WenderLoon** project in the project navigator, then select the **WenderLoon** target. Change the **Bundle identifier** from `com.razeware.WenderLoon` to something unique; I'd suggest replacing `razeware` with something random.

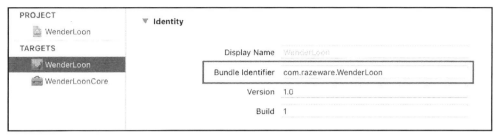

In the **Signing** section choose a development team.

Select the **WenderLoonCore** framework target and change the bundle identifier and select a development team there as well.

Connect a device running iOS 10 and build and run to confirm that everything is working:

You'll see some balloons drifting somewhere over London. The app doesn't do very much else — in fact, you'll be doing the rest of your work in an extension.

Add a new target using the plus button at the bottom of the target list, or by choosing **File\New\Target....**

Choose the **iOS/Application Extension/Intents Extension** template.

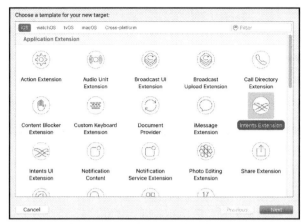

On the next screen, enter **RideRequestExtension** for the product name. Don't check the **Include UI Extension** box. If you're prompted to activate a new scheme, say yes.

A new target and group have been added to your project. Find **IntentHandler.swift** in the **RideRequestExtension** group and replace the entire contents of the file with this:

```
import Intents

class IntentHandler: INExtension {

}
```

Like a lot of Apple template code, there's a blizzard of nonsense in there that stops you from really understanding each piece. `INExtension` is the entry point for an Intents extension. It only has one job, which is to provide a handler object for the intent or intents that your app supports.

As mentioned earlier, each intent has an associated handler protocol which defines the methods needed for dealing with that particular intent.

Select the **RideRequestExtension** scheme then add a new file using **File\NewFile....** Choose the **Swift File** template, name the file **RideRequestHandler.swift** and make sure it is in the **RideRequestExtension** group and **RideRequestExtension** target.

Add the following code to the new file:

```
import Intents

class RideRequestHandler:
  NSObject, INRequestRideIntentHandling {

}
```

INRequestRideIntentHandling is the protocol for handling the — you've guessed it — ride request intent. It only has one required method.

Add the following code:

```
func handle(requestRide intent: INRequestRideIntent,
            completion: @escaping (INRequestRideIntentResponse)
-> Void) {
  let response = INRequestRideIntentResponse(
    code: .failureRequiringAppLaunchNoServiceInArea,
    userActivity: .none)
  completion(response)
}
```

This method fires when the user gets to the point where they are ready to book the ride. That's a little ahead of where the rest of your code is, so at the moment it just returns a response with a failure code.

Switch back to **IntentHandler.swift** and add the following method:

```
override func handler(for intent: INIntent) -> Any? {
  if intent is INRequestRideIntent {
    return RideRequestHandler()
  }
  return .none
}
```

Here, you're returning your new request handler object if the intent is of the correct type. The only type of intent you'll be dealing with is the INRequestRideIntent. This has to be declared in another place as well, so that Siri knows it can direct requests to your app.

Open **Info.plist** inside the **RideRequestExtension** group and find the **NSExtension** dictionary. Inside there is an **NSExtensionAttributes** dictionary which contains an **IntentsSupported** array. The template is for a messages extension, which means the array contains some messaging intents which you don't support.

Delete those intents and add in an **INRequestRideIntent** line:

Bundle Version		String	
▼ NSExtension	⇕	Dictionary	(3 items)
▼ NSExtensionAttributes		Dictionary	(2 items)
▶ IntentsRestrictedWhileLocked		Array	(0 items)
▼ IntentsSupported		Array	(1 item)
Item 0		String	INRequestRideIntent
NSExtensionPointIdentifier		String	com.apple.intents-service
NSExtensionPrincipalClass		String	$(PRODUCT_MODULE_NAME).IntentHandler

There are a few more hoops to jump through before you can use Siri. First, you need to ask the user's permission. Open **AppDelegate.swift** in the main **WenderLoon** group, and you'll see a stub method called `requestAuthorisation()`.

At the top of the file, import the `Intents` framework:

```
import Intents
```

Then replace the `//TODO` comment with this code:

```
INPreferences.requestSiriAuthorization { status in
  if status == .authorized {
    print("Hey, Siri!")
  } else {
    print("Nay, Siri!")
  }
}
```

Permission requests now come with usage strings which are displayed to the user when the dialog displays. Open **Info.plist** from the **WenderLoon** group and find the **Privacy - Location...** entry.

Add a new entry there, for **Privacy - Siri Usage Description** (it should autocomplete) and enter a usage string:

Application requires iPhone environment		Boolean	YES
Privacy - Location When In Use Usage Descri...	⬍ ⊖ ⊕	String	WenderLoon wants to see where you are
Privacy - Siri Usage Description	⬍	String	WenderLoon wants you to be able to book rides using Siri
Launch screen interface file base name	⬍	String	LaunchScreen

Finally, you need to add the Siri entitlement to the app. Select the project, then the **WenderLoon** target, then the **Capabilities** tab. Switch on Siri:

Here's a summary of the steps required to add Siri to your app:

- Add an Intents extension
- Create appropriate handler objects
- Return the handler objects in your `INExtension` subclass
- Declare the supported intents in the Info.plist of the extension
- Request the user's permission to use Siri

- Add a Siri usage description to the app's Info.plist

- Add the Siri entitlement to the app

After all that, select the **WenderLoon** scheme (not the extension) and build and run. You'll get asked to enable Siri:

After all that effort, you really want to make sure you tap **OK**. If all works well, you should see "Hey, Siri!" printed in the console.

Now the real fun begins. Back in Xcode, change to the **RideRequestExtension** scheme. Build and run, and choose **Siri** from the list of applications. Siri will start on your device and you can start having the first of many fun conversations.

Try saying "Book a ride using WenderLoon from Heathrow airport", and if Siri can understand you, you should see something like the following:

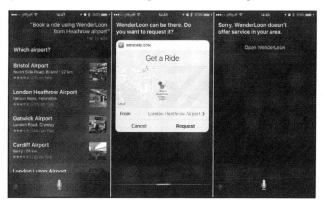

That's the basic setup complete. Remember, at the moment you're always returning a response saying that there's no service in the area, which is what you can see above. In the next sections you'll work through the detail of handling an intent properly.

99 (passengers in) red balloons

Handling an intent is a three-stage process. The first stage is called **Resolution**. In this stage, your extension has to confirm that all of the information it needs about the intent is present. If there is information missing, Siri can ask the user additional questions.

The information varies depending on the particular intent. For the ride request intent, there are the following parameters:

- Pickup location

- Drop-off location

- Party size

- Ride option

- Payment method

> **Note:** If your app isn't interested in some of the parameters, such as if you only accept Apple Pay for payments, then you can ignore them.

Each parameter comes with a related method in the handler protocol. Remember that you're using the `INRequestRideIntentHandling` for handling intents in this app. That protocol has methods for resolving each of the parameters above. Each one receives a ride request intent as a parameter and has a completion block, which you call when you've processed the intent. The completion block takes an `INIntentResolutionResult` subclass as a parameter.

The resolution result tells Siri what to do next, or if everything is OK, it moves on to the next parameter.

That all sounds a little abstract, so here's a diagram:

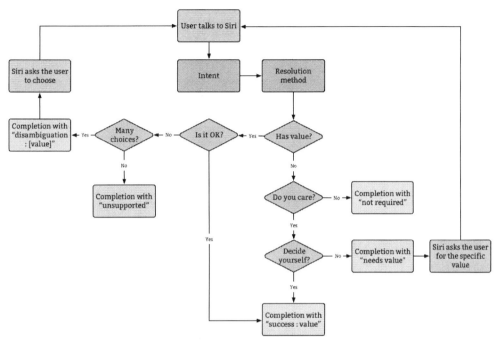

Open **RideRequestHandler.swift** and add the following method:

```swift
func resolvePickupLocation(forRequestRide intent:
INRequestRideIntent, with completion: @escaping
(INPlacemarkResolutionResult) -> Void) {
  if let pickup = intent.pickupLocation {
    completion(.success(with: pickup))
  } else {
    completion(.needsValue())
  }
}
```

This method resolves the pickup location. The completion block takes a
`INPlacemarkResolutionResult` parameter, which is the specific subclass for dealing
with location values in the Intents framework. Here you accept any pickup location that
arrives with the intent. If there is no pickup location, you tell Siri that a value is required.

Build and run the app, and ask Siri to book you a ride using WenderLoon, giving no
extra information.

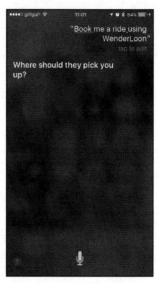

You supplied no pickup information in the original intent, so the resolution method tells Siri to ask for more data. If you then say a location, the resolution method is called again. The resolution method will get called multiple times until you end up with a success or a failure.

However, **the handler object is initialized from scratch for each separate interaction with Siri.** A different instance of `RideRequestHandler` deals with each interaction, which means you cannot use any state information on the handler when dealing with intents.

Back in Xcode, add another resolution method, this time for the drop-off location:

```
func resolveDropOffLocation(forRequestRide intent:
INRequestRideIntent, with completion: @escaping
(INPlacemarkResolutionResult) -> Void) {
  if let dropOff = intent.dropOffLocation {
    completion(.success(with: dropOff))
  } else {
    completion(.notRequired())
  }
}
```

Here you're allowing a ride with no drop-off location to go ahead. This is actually quite sensible, considering you have absolutely no control over where a hot air balloon will take you. If you build and run, Siri will use a drop-off location that you supply, but it won't try and fill in the gaps if there isn't one present.

As well as simply accepting any value that's passed in as an intent parameter, you can also perform a bit of business logic in there. In many cases, this will involve the same logic used in the main app. Apple recommends that you put code such as this in a separate framework that can be shared between your extension and the main app.

That's why the sample project contains the WenderLoonCore framework. Bring that framework into the extension by adding the following statement to the top of **RideRequestHandler.swift**:

```
import WenderLoonCore
```

Then add the following property and initializer to `RideRequestHandler`:

```
let simulator: WenderLoonSimulator

init(simulator: WenderLoonSimulator) {
  self.simulator = simulator
  super.init()
}
```

`WenderLoonSimulator` is an object which contains the business logic for the app. Open **IntentHandler.swift** and add the following to the top of the file:

```
import WenderLoonCore

let simulator = WenderLoonSimulator(renderer: nil)
```

Then replace the line where the request handler is created (it will have an error on it) with the following:

```
return RideRequestHandler(simulator: simulator)
```

Now your request handler will be able to access the business logic from the rest of the app.

Back in **RideRequestHandler.swift**, add the following method for resolving the number of passengers:

```
func resolvePartySize(forRequestRide intent:
INRequestRideIntent, with completion: @escaping
(INIntegerResolutionResult) -> Void) {
  switch intent.partySize {
  case .none:
    completion(.needsValue())
  case let .some(p) where simulator.checkNumberOfPassengers(p):
    completion(.success(with: p))
  default:
    completion(.unsupported())
  }
}
```

This will ask for a number of passengers if the intent doesn't already contain that information. If the number of passengers is known, it is validated against the rules held in the `WenderLoonSimulator` object. The maximum number of passengers is four. Build and run and see what happens with different party sizes:

You've seen that the resolution stage works by dealing with a single parameter at a time. In the next stage, you can handle the final intent with all of the parameters resolved.

The **Confirmation** stage of intent handling happens after all of the parameters have been resolved. As with resolution, there are delegate methods specific to each intent. The delegate method has a similar signature to the resolution methods, but there is only one per intent.

Add the following to **RideRequestHandler.swift**:

```swift
func confirm(requestRide intent: INRequestRideIntent,
  completion: @escaping (INRequestRideIntentResponse) -> Void) {
  let responseCode: INRequestRideIntentResponseCode
  if let location = intent.pickupLocation?.location,
    simulator.pickupWithinRange(location) {
    responseCode = .ready
  } else {
    responseCode = .failureRequiringAppLaunchNoServiceInArea
  }
  let response = INRequestRideIntentResponse(code: responseCode,
userActivity: nil)
  completion(response)
}
```

Here you use a method from the simulator to check that the pickup location is in range. If not, you fail with the "no service in area" response code.

Sure, you could have performed this check when resolving the pickup location. But then you wouldn't have seen any implementation at all! :] You can also use this method to ensure that you had connectivity to your services, so the booking could go ahead. This method is called just before the confirmation dialog is shown to the user.

Try to book a ride with a pickup location more than 50 km away from London, and you'll receive an error telling you there is no service in the area.

> **Note**: If you don't live near London, edit WenderLoonCore > WenderLoonSimulator.swift > `pickupWithinRange(_:)` and add a few more zeros to the radius.

You've dealt with the first two phases of a Siri interaction: resolution and confirmation. The final phase is where you actually take that intent and convert it into something actionable.

You can't handle the truth

You implemented a handler way back in the first section of the chapter. All it did was return a failure code, saying there was no service in the area. Now, you're armed with a fully populated intent so you can perform more useful work.

After the user has seen the confirmation dialog and has requested the ride, Siri shows another dialog with the details of the ride that has been booked. The details of this dialog will differ between the different intents, but in each case you must supply certain relevant details. Each intent actually has its own data model subset, so you need to translate the relevant part of your app's data model to the standardized models used by the Intents framework.

Switch schemes to the **WenderLoonCore** framework, add a new Swift file to the **Extensions** group and name it **IntentsModels.swift**. Replace the contents with the following:

```
import Intents

// 1
public extension UIImage {
  public var inImage: INImage {
    return INImage(imageData: UIImagePNGRepresentation(self)!)
```

```
    }
  }

  // 2
  public extension Driver {
    public var rideIntentDriver: INRideDriver {
      return INRideDriver(
        personHandle: INPersonHandle(value: name, type: .unknown),
        nameComponents: .none,
        displayName: name,
        image: picture.inImage,
        rating: rating.toString,
        phoneNumber: .none)
    }
  }
```

Here's what each method does:

1. The Intents framework, for some reason, uses its own image class `INImage`. This `UIImage` extension gives you a handy way to create an `INImage`.

2. `INRideDriver` represents a driver in the Intents framework. Here you pass across the relevant values from the `Driver` object in use in the rest of the app.

Unfortunately there's no `INBalloon`. The Intents framework has a boring old `INRideVehicle` instead. Add this extension to create one:

```
public extension Balloon {
  public var rideIntentVehicle: INRideVehicle {
    let vehicle = INRideVehicle()
    vehicle.location = location
    vehicle.manufacturer = "Hot Air Balloon"
    vehicle.registrationPlate = "B4LL 00N"
    vehicle.mapAnnotationImage = image.inImage
    return vehicle
  }
}
```

This creates a vehicle based on the balloon's properties.

With that bit of model work in place you can build the framework (press Command-B to do that) then switch back to the ride request extension scheme.

Open **RideRequestHandler.swift** and replace the implementation of `handle(intent:completion:)` with the following:

```
// 1
guard let pickup = intent.pickupLocation?.location else {
  let response = INRequestRideIntentResponse(code: .failure,
    userActivity: .none)
```

```
    completion(response)
    return
}

// 2
let dropoff = intent.dropOffLocation?.location ??
  pickup.randomPointWithin(radius: 10_000)

// 3
let response: INRequestRideIntentResponse
// 4
if let balloon = simulator.requestRide(pickup: pickup, dropoff:
dropoff) {
  // 5
  let status = INRideStatus()
  status.rideIdentifier = balloon.driver.name
  status.phase = .confirmed
  status.vehicle = balloon.rideIntentVehicle
  status.driver = balloon.driver.rideIntentDriver
  status.estimatedPickupDate = balloon.etaAtNextDestination
  status.pickupLocation = intent.pickupLocation
  status.dropOffLocation = intent.dropOffLocation

  response = INRequestRideIntentResponse(code: .success,
userActivity: .none)
  response.rideStatus = status
} else {
  response =
INRequestRideIntentResponse(code: .failureRequiringAppLaunchNoSe
rviceInArea, userActivity: .none)
}

completion(response)
```

Here's the breakdown:

1. Theoretically, it should be impossible to reach this method without having resolved a pickup location, but hey, Siri...

2. We've decided to embrace the randomness of hot air balloons by not forcing a dropoff location, but the balloon simulator still needs somewhere to drift to.

3. The `INRequestRideIntentResponse` object will encapsulate all of the information concerning the ride.

4. This method checks that a balloon is available and within range, and returns it if so. This means the ride booking can go ahead. If not, you return a failure.

5. `INRideStatus` contains information about the ride itself. You populate this object with the Intents versions of the app's model classes. Then, you attach the ride status to the response object and return it.

> **Note:** The values being used here aren't what you should use in an actual ride booking app. The identifier should be something like a UUID, you'd need to be more specific about the dropoff location, and you'd need to implement the actual booking for your actual drivers :]

Build and run; book a ride for three passengers, pickup somewhere in London, then confirm the request. You'll see the final screen:

Hmmm. That's quite lovely, but it isn't very balloon-ish. In the final part, you'll create custom UI for this stage!

Making a balloon animal, er, UI

To make your own UI for Siri, you need to add *another* extension to the app. Go to **File\New\Target...** and choose the **Intents UI Extension** template from the **Application Extension** group.

Enter **LoonUIExtension** for the **Product Name** and click **Finish**. Activate the scheme if you are prompted to do so. You'll see a new group in the project navigator, **LoonUIExtension**.

A UI extension consists of a view controller, a storyboard and an Info.plist file. Open the **Info.plist** file and, the same as you did with the Intents extension, change the

NSExtension/NSExtensionAttributes/IntentsSupported array to contain
INRequestRideIntent.

Each Intents UI extension must only contain one view controller, but that view
controller can support multiple intents.

Open **MainInterface.storyboard**. You're going to do some quick and dirty interface
builder work here, since the actual layout isn't super-important.

Drag in an image view, pin it to the top, left and bottom edges of the container and set
width to 0.25x the container width. Set the view mode to **Aspect Fit**.

Drag in a second image view and pin it to the top, right and bottom edges of the
container and set the same width constraint and view mode.

Drag in a label, pin it to the horizontal and vertical center of the view controller and set
the font to System Thin 20.0 and the text to **WenderLoon**.

Drag in another label, positioned the standard distance underneath the first. Set the text
to **subtitle**. Add a constraint for the vertical spacing to the original label and another to
pin it to the horizontal center.

Make the background an attractive blue color.

This is what you're aiming for:

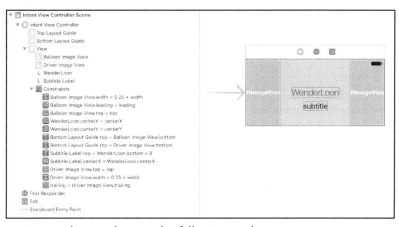

Open the assistant editor and create the following outlets:

• The left image view, called **balloonImageView**

• The right image view, called **driverImageView**

• The subtitle label, called **subtitleLabel**

In **IntentViewController.swift**, import the core app framework:

```
import WenderLoonCore
```

You configure the view controller in the `configure(with: context: completion:)` method. Replace the template code with this:

```
// 1
guard let response = interaction.intentResponse as?
INRequestRideIntentResponse
  else {
    driverImageView.image = nil
    balloonImageView.image = nil
    subtitleLabel.text = ""
    completion?(self.desiredSize)
    return
}

// 2
if let driver = response.rideStatus?.driver {
  let name = driver.displayName
  driverImageView.image =
WenderLoonSimulator.imageForDriver(name: name)
  balloonImageView.image =
WenderLoonSimulator.imageForBallon(driverName: name)
  subtitleLabel.text = "\(name) will arrive soon!"
} else {
// 3
  driverImageView.image = nil
  balloonImageView.image = nil
  subtitleLabel.text = "Preparing..."
}

// 4
completion?(self.desiredSize)
```

Here's the breakdown:

1. You could receive any of the listed intents that your extension handles at this point, so you must check which type you're actually getting. This extension only handles a single intent.

2. The extension will be called twice. Once for the confirmation dialog and once for the final handled dialog. When the request has been handled, a driver will have been assigned, so you can create the appropriate UI.

3. If the booking is at the confirmation stage, you don't have as much to present.

4. Finally, you call the completion block that has been passed in. You can vary the size of your view controller and pass in a calculated size. However, the size must be

between the maximum and minimum allowed sizes specified by the
`extensionContext` property. `desiredSize` is a calculated variable added as part of
the template that simply gives you the largest allowed size.

Build and run and request a valid ride. Your new UI appears in the Siri interface at the
confirmation and handle stages:

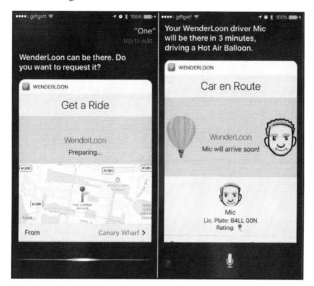

Notice that your new stuff is sandwiched in between all of the existing Siri stuff. There
isn't a huge amount you can do about that. If your view controller implements the
`INUIHostedViewSiriProviding` protocol then you can tell Siri not to display maps
(which would turn off the map in the confirm step), messages (which only affects
extensions in the Messages domain) or payment transactions.

Where to go from here?

This chapter has been all about ride booking, but the principles should cover all of the
different intents and domains. Take a look at the documentation to find out what's
possible for your app. If your app isn't covered by the existing domains and intents, try
mapping out the intents, parameters, responses and model objects and file a radar.
Maybe your app can add Siri next year!

If you've followed along with this chapter, you might also want to take a trip to the
Apple store to replace the devices you smashed in a fit of rage when Siri didn't
understand you. You've been warned! :]

Chapter 7: Speech Recognition

By Jeff Rames

iOS 10's new Speech Recognition API lets your app transcribe live or pre-recorded audio. It leverages the same speech recognition engine used by Siri and Keyboard Dictation, but provides much more control and improved access.

The engine is fast and accurate and can currently interpret over 50 languages and dialects. It even adapts results to the user using information about their contacts, installed apps, media and various other pieces of data.

Audio fed to a recognizer is transcribed in near real time, and results are provided incrementally. This lets you react to voice input very quickly, regardless of context, unlike Keyboard Dictation, which is tied to a specific input object.

Speech Recognizer creates some truly amazing possibilities in your apps. For example, you could create an app that takes a photo when you say "cheese". You could also create an app that could automatically transcribe audio from Simpsons episodes so you could search for your favorite lines.

In this chapter, you'll build an app called Gangstribe that will transcribe some pretty hardcore (hilarious) gangster rap recordings using speech recognition. It will also get users in the mood to record their own rap hits with a live audio transcriber that draws emojis on their faces based on what they say. :]

The section on live recordings will use AVAudioEngine. If you haven't used AVAudioEngine before, you may want to familiarize yourself with that framework first. The 2014 WWDC session *AVAudioEngine in Practice* is a great intro to this, and can be found at apple.co/28tATc1. This session video explains many of the systems and terminology we'll use in this chapter.

The Speech Recognition framework doesn't work in the simulator, so be sure to use a real device with iOS 10 for this chapter.

Getting started

Open **Gangstribe.xcodeproj** in the starter project folder for this chapter. Select the project file, the **Gangstribe** target and then the **General** tab. Choose your development team from the drop-down.

Connect an iOS 10 device and select it as your run destination in Xcode. Build and run and you'll see the bones of the app.

From the master controller, you can select a song. The detail controller will then let you play the audio file, recited by none other than our very own DJ Sammy D!

The transcribe button is not currently operational, but you'll use this later to kick off a transcription of the selected recording.

Tap **Face Replace** on the right of the navigation bar to preview the live transcription feature. You'll be prompted for permission to access the camera; accept this, as you'll need it for this feature.

Currently if you select an emoji with your face in frame, it will place the emoji on your face. Later, you'll trigger this action with speech.

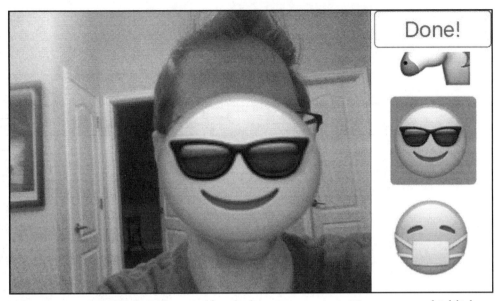

Take a moment to familiarize yourself with the starter project. Here are some highlights of classes and groups you'll work with during this chapter:

- **MasterViewController.swift**: Displays the list of recordings in a table view. The recording model object is defined in **Recording.swift** along with the seeded song data.

- **RecordingViewController.swift**: Plays the pre-recorded audio selected in the master controller. You'll code the currently stubbed out `handleTranscribeButtonTapped(_:)` to have it kick off file transcription.

- **LiveTranscribeViewController.swift**: Handles the Face Replace view, which leverages the code included in the **FaceReplace** folder. It currently displays live video and a collection view of emojis, attaching the selected emoji to any face in the live view. This is where you'll add code to record and transcribe audio.

- **FaceReplace**: Contains a library provided by Rich Turton that places emojis over faces in live video. It uses Core Image's CIDetector — but you don't need to understand how this works for this tutorial. However, if you'd like to learn more, you can read about CIDetector here: apple.co/1Tx2uCN.

You'll start this chapter by making the transcribe button work for pre-recorded audio. It will then feed the audio file to Speech Recognizer and present the results in a label under the player.

The latter half of the chapter will focus on the Face Replace feature. You'll set up an audio engine for recording, tap into that input, and transcribe the audio as it arrives. You'll display the live transcription and ultimately use it to trigger placing emojis over the user's face.

You can't just dive right in and start voice commanding unicorns onto your face though; you'll need to understand a few basics first.

Transcription basics

There are four primary actors involved in a speech transcription:

1. **SFSpeechRecognizer** is the primary controller in the framework. Its most important job is to generate recognition tasks and return results. It also handles authorization and configures locales.

2. **SFSpeechRecognitionRequest** is the base class for recognition requests. Its job is to point the `SFSpeechRecognizer` to an audio source from which transcription should occur. There are two concrete types: **SFSpeechURLRecognitionRequest**, for reading from a file, and **SFSpeechAudioBufferRecognitionRequest** for reading from a buffer.

3. **SFSpeechRecognitionTask** objects are created when a request is kicked off by the recognizer. They are used to track progress of a transcription or cancel it.

4. **SFSpeechRecognitionResult** objects contain the transcription of a chunk of the audio. Each result typically corresponds to a single word.

Here's how these objects interact during a basic Speech Recognizer transcription:

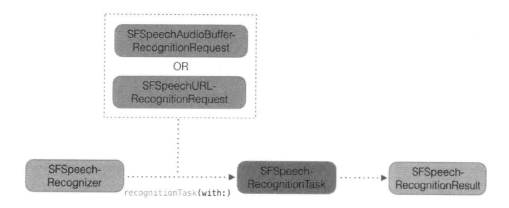

The code required to complete a transcription is quite simple. Given an audio file at `url`, the following code transcribes the file and prints the results:

```
let request = SFSpeechURLRecognitionRequest(url: url)
SFSpeechRecognizer()?.recognitionTask(with: request) { (result,
_) in
  if let transcription = result?.bestTranscription {
```

```
      print("\(transcription.formattedString)")
    }
  }
```

SFSpeechRecognizer kicks off a SFSpeechRecognitionTask for the
SFSpeechURLRecognitionRequest using
recognitionTask(with:resultHandler:). It returns partial results as they arrive via
the resultHandler. This code prints the formatted string value of the
bestTranscription, which is a cumulative transcription result adjusted at each
iteration.

You'll start by implementing a file transcription very similar to this.

Audio file speech transcription

Before you start reading and sending chunks of the user's audio off to a remote server, it
would be polite to ask permission. In fact, considering their commitment to user privacy,
it should come as no surprise that Apple requires this! :]

You'll kick off the the authorization process when the user taps the **Transcribe** button in
the detail controller.

Open **RecordingViewController.swift** and add the following to the import statements
at the top:

```
import Speech
```

This imports the Speech Recognition API.

Add the following to handleTranscribeButtonTapped(_:):

```
SFSpeechRecognizer.requestAuthorization {
  [unowned self] (authStatus) in
  switch authStatus {
  case .authorized:
    if let recording = self.recording {
      //TODO: Kick off the transcription
    }
  case .denied:
    print("Speech recognition authorization denied")
  case .restricted:
    print("Not available on this device")
  case .notDetermined:
    print("Not determined")
  }
}
```

You call the `SFSpeechRecognizer` type method `requestAuthorization(_:)` to prompt the user for authorization and handle their response in a completion closure.

In the closure, you look at the `authStatus` and print error messages for all of the exception cases. For `authorized`, you unwrap the selected recording for later transcription.

Next, you have to provide a usage description displayed when permission is requested. Open **Info.plist** and add the key `Privacy — Speech Recognition Usage Description` providing the String value `I want to write down everything you say`:

Key		Type	Value
▼ Information Property List		Dictionary	(16 items)
Localization native development region	↕	String	en
Executable file	↕	String	$(EXECUTABLE_NAME)
Bundle identifier	↕	String	$(PRODUCT_BUNDLE_IDENTIFIER)
InfoDictionary version	↕	String	6.0
Bundle name	↕	String	$(PRODUCT_NAME)
Bundle OS Type code	↕	String	APPL
Bundle versions string, short	↕	String	1.0
Bundle version	↕	String	1
Application requires iPhone environment	↕	Boolean	YES
Privacy - Speech Recognition Usage Description	↕ ○ ⊖	String	↕ I want to write down everything you say

Build and run, select a song from the master controller, and tap **Transcribe**. You'll see a permission request appear with the text you provided. Select **OK** to provide Gangstribe the proper permission:

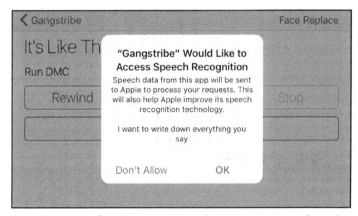

Of course nothing happens after you provide authorization — you haven't yet set up speech recognition! It's now time to test the limits of the framework with DJ Sammy D's renditions of popular rap music.

Transcribing the file

Back in **RecordingViewController.swift**, find the `RecordingViewController` extension at the bottom of the file. Add the following method to transcribe a file found at the passed `url`:

```
fileprivate func transcribeFile(url: URL) {

  // 1
  guard let recognizer = SFSpeechRecognizer() else {
    print("Speech recognition not available for specified
locale")
    return
  }

  if !recognizer.isAvailable {
    print("Speech recognition not currently available")
    return
  }

  // 2
  updateUIForTranscriptionInProgress()
  let request = SFSpeechURLRecognitionRequest(url: url)

  // 3
  recognizer.recognitionTask(with: request) {
    [unowned self] (result, error) in
    guard let result = result else {
      print("There was an error transcribing that file")
      return
    }

    // 4
    if result.isFinal {
      self.updateUIWithCompletedTranscription(
        result.bestTranscription.formattedString)
    }
  }
}
```

Here are the details on how this transcribes the passed file:

1. The default `SFSpeechRecognizer` initializer provides a recognizer for the device's locale, returning `nil` if there is no such recognizer. `isAvailable` checks if the `recognizer` is ready, failing in such cases as missing network connectivity.

2. `updateUIForTranscriptionInProgress()` is provided with the starter to disable the Transcribe button and start an activity indicator animation while the transcription is in process. A `SFSpeechURLRecognitionRequest` is created for the file found at `url`, creating an interface to the transcription engine for that recording.

3. `recognitionTask(with:resultHandler:)` processes the transcription `request`, repeatedly triggering a completion closure. The passed `result` is unwrapped in a guard, which prints an error on failure.

4. The `isFinal` property will be true when the entire transcription is complete. `updateUIWithCompletedTranscription(_:)` stops the activity indicator, re-enables the button and displays the passed string in a text view. `bestTranscription` contains the transcription Speech Recognizer is most confident is accurate, and `formattedString` provides it in String format for display in the text view.

> **Note**: Where there is a `bestTranscription`, there can of course be lesser ones. `SFSpeechRecognitionResult` has a `transcriptions` property that contains an array of transcriptions sorted in order of confidence. As you see with Siri and Keyboard Dictation, a transcription can change as more context arrives, and this array illustrates that type of progression.

Now you need to call this new code when the user taps the Transcribe button. In `handleTranscribeButtonTapped(_:)` replace `//TODO: Kick off the transcription` with the following:

```
self.transcribeFile(url: recording.audio)
```

After successful authorization, the button handler now calls `transcribeFile(url:)` with the URL of the currently selected recording.

Build and run, select **Gangsta's Paradise**, and then tap the **Transcribe** button. You'll see the activity indicator for a while, and then the text view will eventually populate with the transcription:

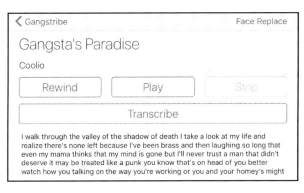

Transcription and locales

The results aren't bad, considering Coolio doesn't seem to own a copy of Webster's Dictionary. Depending on the locale of your device, there could be another reason things are a bit off. The above screenshot was a transcription completed on a device configured for US English, while DJ Sammy D has a slightly different dialect.

But you don't need to book a flight overseas to fix this. When creating a recognizer, you have the option of specifying a locale — that's what you'll do next.

> **Note:** Even if your device is set to en_GB (English - United Kingdom) as Sam's is, the locale settings are important to Gangstribe. In just a bit, you'll transcribe text in an entirely different language!

Still in **RecordingViewController.swift**, find `transcribeFile(url:)` and replace the following two lines:

```
fileprivate func transcribeFile(url: URL) {
  guard let recognizer = SFSpeechRecognizer() else {
```

with the code below:

```
fileprivate func transcribeFile(url: URL, locale: Locale?) {
  let locale = locale ?? Locale.current

  guard let recognizer = SFSpeechRecognizer(locale: locale) else
  {
```

You've added an optional `Locale` parameter which will specify the locale of the file being transcribed. If `locale` is `nil` when unwrapped, you fall back to the device's locale. You then initialize the `SFSpeechRecognizer` with this locale.

Now to modify where this is called. Find `handleTranscribeButtonTapped(_:)` and replace the `transcribeFile(url:)` call with the following:

```
self.transcribeFile(url: recording.audio, locale:
recording.locale)
```

You use the new method signature, passing the locale stored with the `recording` object.

> **Note:** If you want to see the locale associated with a Gangstribe recording, open **Recording.swift** and look at the `recordingNames` array up top. Each element

> contains the song name, artist, audio file name and locale. You can find information on how locale identifiers are derived in Apple's Internationalization and Localization Guide here — apple.co/1HVWDQa

Build and run, and complete another transcription on **Gangsta's Paradise**. Assuming your first run was with a locale other than en_GB, you should see some differences.

```
❮ Gangstribe                              Face Replace

Gangsta's Paradise

Coolio

  ┌──────────────┐ ┌──────────────┐ ┌──────────────┐
  │    Rewind    │ │     Play     │ │     Stop     │
  └──────────────┘ └──────────────┘ └──────────────┘
  ┌────────────────────────────────────────────────┐
  │                   Transcribe                    │
  └────────────────────────────────────────────────┘

  As I walk through the valley of the shadow of death I take a look at my life and
  realise there's nothing left because I've been Brassington laughing so long that
  even my mamma thinks that my mind is gone but I ain't never trust a man that
  didn't deserve it may be treated like a punk you know that's unheard-of you
  better watch how you're talking and way of working or you and your Homies
```

In both transcription screenshots, look for the words following *treated like a punk you know that's*. With the correct locale set, the next words read *unheard-of* whereas the American English transcription heard *on head of*. This is a great example of the power of this framework with its understanding of a wide range of languages and dialects.

> **Note:** Keep in mind that your transcriptions may differ from the screenshots. The engine evolves over time and it does customize itself based on its knowledge of you.

You can probably understand different dialects of languages you speak pretty well. But you're probably significantly weaker when it comes to understanding languages you don't speak. The Speech Recognition engine understands over 50 different languages and dialects, so it likely has you beat here.

Now that you are passing the locale of files you're transcribing, you'll be able to successfully transcribe a recording in any supported language. Build and run, and select the song **Raise Your Hands**, which is in Thai. Play it, and then tap **Transcribe** to see the transcribed content.

❮ Gangstribe   Face Replace

Raise Your Hands
โจอี้ บอย

| Rewind | Play | Stop |

Transcribe

อยากสวยอยากอยากใสอยากเด่นแต่ต้นเรียนไม่เก่งขอให้ยกมือขึ้น

Flawless transcription! Presumably.

Live speech recognition

Live transcription is very similar to file transcription. The primary difference in the process is a different request type — **SFSpeechAudioBufferRecognitionRequest** — which is used for live transcriptions.

As the name implies, this type of request reads from an audio buffer. Your task will be to append live audio buffers to this request as they arrive from the source. Once connected, the actual transcription process will be identical to the one for recorded audio.

Another consideration for live audio is that you'll need a way to stop a transcription when the user is done speaking. This requires maintaining a reference to the **SFSpeechRecognitionTask** so that it can later be canceled.

Gangstribe has some pretty cool tricks up its sleeve. For this feature, you'll not only transcribe live audio, but you'll use the transcriptions to trigger some visual effects. With the use of the FaceReplace library, speaking the name of a supported emoji will plaster it right over your face!

Connect to the audio buffer

To do this, you'll have to configure the audio engine and hook it up to a recognition request. But before you start recording and transcribing, you need to request authorization to use speech recognition in this controller.

Open **LiveTranscribeViewController.swift** and add the following to the top of the file by the other imports:

```
import Speech
```

Now the live transcription controller has access to Speech Recognition.

Next find `viewDidLoad()` and replace the line `startRecording()` with the following:

```
SFSpeechRecognizer.requestAuthorization {
  [unowned self] (authStatus) in
  switch authStatus {
  case .authorized:
    self.startRecording()
  case .denied:
    print("Speech recognition authorization denied")
  case .restricted:
    print("Not available on this device")
  case .notDetermined:
    print("Not determined")
  }
}
```

Just as you did with pre-recorded audio, you're calling `requestAuthorization(_:)` to obtain or confirm access to Speech Recognition.

For the `authorized` status, you call `startRecording()` which currently just does some preparation — you'll implement the rest shortly. For failures, you print relevant error messages.

Next, add the following properties at the top of `LiveTranscribeViewController`:

```
let audioEngine = AVAudioEngine()
let speechRecognizer = SFSpeechRecognizer()
let request = SFSpeechAudioBufferRecognitionRequest()
var recognitionTask: SFSpeechRecognitionTask?
```

- **audioEngine** is an `AVAudioEngine` object you'll use to process input audio signals from the microphone.

- **speechRecognizer** is the `SFSpeechRecognizer` you'll use for live transcriptions.

- **request** is the `SFSpeechAudioBufferRecognitionRequest` the speech recognizer will use to tap into the audio engine.

- **recognitionTask** will hold a reference to the `SFSpeechRecognitionTask` kicked off when transcription begins.

Now find `startRecording()` in a `LiveTranscribeViewController` extension in this same file. This is called when the Face Replace view loads, but it doesn't yet do any recording. Add the following code to the bottom of the method:

```
// 1
guard let node = audioEngine.inputNode else {
  print("Couldn't get an input node!")
  return
}
```

```
let recordingFormat = node.outputFormat(forBus: 0)

// 2
node.installTap(onBus: 0, bufferSize: 1024,
                format: recordingFormat) { [unowned self]
  (buffer, _) in
  self.request.append(buffer)
}

// 3
audioEngine.prepare()
try audioEngine.start()
```

This code does the following:

1. Obtains the input audio `node` associated with the device's microphone, as well as its corresponding `outputFormat`.

2. Installs a tap on the output bus of `node`, using the same recording format. When the buffer is filled, the closure returns the data in `buffer` which is appended to the `SFSpeechAudioBufferRecognitionRequest`. The `request` is now tapped into the live input node.

3. Prepares and starts the `audioEngine` to start recording, and thus gets data going to the tap.

Because starting the audio engine throws, you need to signify this on the method. Change the method definition to match the following:

```
fileprivate func startRecording() throws {
```

With this change, you likewise need to modify where the method gets called. Find `viewDidLoad()` and replace `self.startRecording()` with the following:

```
do {
  try self.startRecording()
} catch let error {
  print("There was a problem starting recording: \
(error.localizedDescription)")
}
```

`startRecording()` is now wrapped in a `do-catch`, printing the error if it fails.

There is one last thing to do before you can kick off a recording — ask for user permission. The framework does this for you, but you need to provide another key in the plist with an explanation. Open **Info.plist** and add the key `Privacy - Microphone Usage Description` providing the String value `I want to record you live`.

Key		Type	Value
▼ Information Property List		Dictionary	(19 items)
Localization native development region	⬍	String	en
Executable file	⬍	String	$(EXECUTABLE_NAME)
Bundle identifier	⬍	String	$(PRODUCT_BUNDLE_IDENTIFIER)
InfoDictionary version	⬍	String	6.0
Bundle name	⬍	String	$(PRODUCT_NAME)
Bundle OS Type code	⬍	String	APPL
Bundle versions string, short	⬍	String	1.0
Bundle version	⬍	String	1
Application requires iPhone environment	⬍	Boolean	YES
Privacy - Camera Usage Description	⬍	String	Let me look at your face
Privacy - Speech Recognition Usage Description	⬍	String	I want to write down everything you say
Privacy - Microphone Usage Description	⬍ ⊕ ⊖	String	⬍ I want to record you live

Build and run, choose a recording, then select **Face Replace** from the navigation bar. You'll immediately be greeted with a prompt requesting permission to use the microphone. Hit **OK** so that Gangstribe can eventually transcribe what you say:

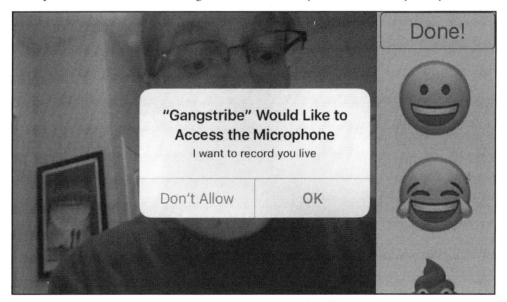

With the tap in place, and recording started, you can finally kick off the speech recognition task.

In **LiveTranscribeViewController.swift**, go back to startRecording() and add the following at the bottom of the method:

```
recognitionTask = speechRecognizer?.recognitionTask(with:
request) {
  [unowned self]
  (result, _) in
  if let transcription = result?.bestTranscription {
```

```
    self.transcriptionOutputLabel.text =
  transcription.formattedString
    }
  }
```

`recognitionTask(with:resultHandler:)` is called with the `request` connected to the tap, kicking off transcription of live audio. The task is saved in `recognitionTask` for later use.

In the closure, you get `bestTranscription` from the result. You then update the label that displays the transcription with the formatted string of the `transcription`.

Build and run, and tap the **Face Replace** button in the navigation bar. Start talking, and you'll now see a real time transcription from speech recognition!

> **Note:** Apple has hinted at some throttling limits, including an utterance duration limit of "about one minute". If you stay in live transcription long enough, you'll probably see it stop responding. Now you know why!

But there's a problem. If you try opening Face Replace enough times, it will crash spectacularly. You're currently leaking the `SFSpeechAudioBufferRecognitionRequest` because you've never stopping transcription or recording!

Add the following method to the `LiveTranscribeViewController` extension that also contains `startRecording()`:

```
fileprivate func stopRecording() {
  audioEngine.stop()
  request.endAudio()
  recognitionTask?.cancel()
}
```

Calling `stop()` on the audio engine releases all resources associated with it. `endAudio()` tells the request that it shouldn't expect any more incoming audio, and causes it to stop listening. `cancel()` is called on the recognition task to let it know its work is done so that it can free up resources.

You'll want to call this when the user taps the **Done!** button before you dismiss the controller. Add the following to `handleDoneTapped(_:)`, just before the `dismiss`:

```
stopRecording()
```

The audio engine and speech recognizer will now get cleaned up each time the user finishes with a live recording. Good job cleaning up your toys! :]

Transcription segments

The live transcription below your video is pretty cool, but it's not what you set out to do. It's time to dig into these transcriptions and use them to trigger the emoji face replacement!

First, you need to understand a bit more about the data contained in the `SFTranscription` objects returned in `SFSpeechRecognitionResult` objects. You've been accessing these with the `bestTranscription` property of results returned to the `recognitionTask(with:resultHandler:)` closure.

`SFTranscription` has a `segments` property containing an array of all `SFTranscriptionSegment` objects returned from the request. Among other things, a `SFTranscriptionSegment` has a `substring` containing the transcribed String for that segment, as well as its `duration` from the start of the transcription. Generally, each segment will consist of a single word.

Each time the live transcription returns a new result, you want to look at the most recent segment to see if it matches an emoji keyword.

First add the following property to at the top of the class:

```
var mostRecentlyProcessedSegmentDuration: TimeInterval = 0
```

`mostRecentlyProcessedSegmentDuration` tracks the timestamp of the last processed segment. Because the segment duration is from the start of transcription, the highest duration indicates the latest segment.

Now add the following to the top of `startRecording()`:

```
mostRecentlyProcessedSegmentDuration = 0
```

This will reset the tracked duration each time recording starts.

Now add the following new method to the bottom of the last
`LiveTranscribeViewController` extension:

```
// 1
fileprivate func updateUIWithTranscription(_ transcription:
SFTranscription) {
  self.transcriptionOutputLabel.text =
transcription.formattedString

  // 2
  if let lastSegment = transcription.segments.last,
    lastSegment.duration > mostRecentlyProcessedSegmentDuration
  {
    mostRecentlyProcessedSegmentDuration = lastSegment.duration
    // 3
    faceSource.selectFace(lastSegment.substring)
  }
}
```

Here's what this code does:

1. This defines a new method that accepts an `SFTranscription` and uses it to update
    the UI with results. First, it updates the transcription label at the bottom of the
    screen with the results; this will soon replace similar code found in
    `startRecording()`.

2. This unwraps the `last` segment from the passed `transcription`. It then checks
    that the segment's duration is higher than the
    `mostRecentlyProcessedSegmentDuration` to avoid an older segment being
    processed if it returns out of order. The new duration is then saved in
    `mostRecentlyProcessedSegmentDuration`.

3. `selectFace()`, part of the Face Replace code, accepts the `substring` of this new
    transcription, and completes a face replace if it matches one of the emoji names.

In `startRecording()`, replace the following line:

```
self.transcriptionOutputLabel.text =
transcription.formattedString
```

with:

```
self.updateUIWithTranscription(transcription)
```

`updateUIWithTranscription()` is now called each time the `resultHandler` is
executed. It will update the transcription label as well as triggering a face replace if
appropriate. Because this new method updates the transcription label, you removed the
code that previously did it here.

Build and run and select **Face Replace**. This time, say the name of one of the emojis. Try "cry" as your first attempt.

The speech recognizer will transcribe the word "cry" and feed it to the `FaceSource` object, which will attach the cry emoji to your face. What a time to be alive!

> **Note**: For a full list of available keywords, open **FaceSource.swift** and look for the `names` array. Each of these map to one of the emojis in the `faces` array above it.

Usage guidelines

While they aren't yet clearly defined, Apple has provided some usage guidelines for Speech Recognition. Apple will be enforcing the following types of limitations:

* Per device per day

* Per app per day (global limitations for all users of your app)

* One minute limitation for a single utterance (from start to end of a recognition task)

Apple hasn't provided any numbers for device and app daily limits. These rules are likely to mature and become more concrete as Apple sees how third party developers use the framework.

Apple also emphasizes that you must make it very clear to users when they are being recorded. While it isn't currently in the review guidelines, it's in your best interest to follow this closely to avoid rejections. You also wouldn't want to invade your user's privacy!

Finally, Apple suggests presenting transcription results before acting on them. Sending a text message via Siri is a great example of this: she'll present editable transcription results and delay before sending the message. Transcription is certainly not perfect, and you want to protect users from the frustration and possible embarrassment of mistakes.

Where to go from here?

In this chapter, you learned everything you need to know to get basic speech recognition working in your apps. It's an extremely powerful feature where the framework does the heavy lifting. With just a few lines of code, you can bring a lot of magic to your apps.

There isn't currently much documentation on Speech Recognition, so your best bet is to explore the headers in the source for more detail. Here are a couple of other places to go for more info:

- WWDC Speech Recognition API Session - apple.co/2aSMrlw
- Apple Speech Recognition sample project (SpeakToMe) - apple.co/2aSO6HS

Chapter 8: User Notifications

By Jeff Rames

Consider your favorite apps. It's likely that a good portion of them leverage some type of User Notification.

Remote push notifications date all the way back to iOS 3, while local notifications were introduced iOS 4. Notifications engage users with your app, keep you up to date, and provide near real-time communication with others.

For all their importance, User Notifications haven't changed much over the years. However, iOS 10 has introduced sweeping changes to the way User Notifications work for developers:

- **Media attachments** can now be added to notifications, including audio, video and images.

- New **Notification Content extensions** let you create custom interfaces for notifications.

- **Managing notifications** is now possible with interfaces in the new user notification center.

- New **Notification Service app extensions** let you process remote notification payloads before they're delivered.

In this chapter, you'll explore all of these new features. Let's get started!

> **Note:** For most of this chapter, you'll be fine with the iOS simulator, and don't need any prior experience with user notifications. However, to work with Notification Service app extensions in the final section of this chapter, you'll need a device running iOS 10 and a basic understanding of configuring remote

notifications. For more background information on notifications, check out *Push Notifications Tutorial: Getting Started* at raywenderlich.com/123862.

Getting started

The sample app for this chapter is **cuddlePix**, which aims to spread cheer with visually rich notifications containing pictures of cuddly cacti.

Note: While cuddlePix employs only the most cuddly digital cacti, remember to use caution when cuddling a real cactus. Real world prototyping of cuddlePix indicated that some cacti can be quite painful. :]

When complete, the app will act as a management dashboard for notification statuses and configuration data, as well as a scheduler for local notifications. It will also define custom notifications complete with custom actions.

Open the starter project for this chapter, and set your team in the CuddlePix Target General Signing settings. Then build and run to see what you have to work with. You'll be greeted by an empty table view that will eventually house the notification status and configuration information.

Tap the + bar button, and you'll see an interface for scheduling multiple local notifications over the next hour, or scheduling a single one in five seconds' time. These don't do anything at present - that's where you come in.

Take a few minutes and explore the below items in the starter project:

- **NotificationTableViewController.swift** contains the table view controller and displays a sectioned table using a datasource built from a struct and protocol found in **TableSection.swift**.

- **ConfigurationViewController.swift** manages the view that schedules notifications, centered around a mostly stubbed-out method `scheduleRandomNotification(in:completion:)` that will ultimately create and schedule notifications.

- **Main.storyboard** defines the simple UI you've already seen in full while testing the app.

- **Utilities** contains some helpers you'll use during this tutorial.

- **Supporting Files** contains artwork attributions, the plist, and images you'll display in your notifications.

The User Notifications framework

Gone are the days of handling notifications via your application delegate. Enter **UserNotifications.framework**, which does everything its predecessor did, along with enabling all of the new user notification functionality such as attachments, Notification Service extensions, foreground notifications, and more.

The core of the new framework is `UNUserNotificationCenter`, which is accessed via a singleton. It manages user authorization, defines notifications and associated actions, schedules local notifications, and provides a management interface for existing notifications.

The first step in using `UNUserNotificationCenter` is to ask the user to authorize your app to use notifications. Open **NotificationTableViewController.swift** and add the following to `viewDidLoad()`, just below the call to `super`:

```
UNUserNotificationCenter.current()
  .requestAuthorization(options: [.alert, .sound]) {
    (granted, error) in
    if granted {
      self.loadNotificationData()
    } else {
      print(error?.localizedDescription)
    }
  }
```

`UNUserNotificationCenter.current()` returns the singleton user notification center.

You then call `requestAuthorization(options:completionHandler:)` to request authorization to present notifications. You pass in an array of `UNAuthorizationOptions` to indicate what options you're requesting — in this case, `alert` and `sound` notifications. If access is granted, you call the currently stubbed out `loadNotificationData()`; otherwise you print the passed error.

Build and run, and you'll see an authorization prompt as soon as `NotificationTableViewController` loads. Be sure to tap **Allow**.

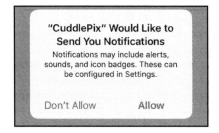

Scheduling notifications

Now that you have permission from the user, it's time to take this new framework for a spin and schedule some notifications!

Open **ConfigurationViewController.swift** and review the following code:

- Pressing the **Cuddle me now!** button triggers `handleCuddleMeNow(_:)`, which passes a delay of 5 seconds to `scheduleRandomNotification(in:completion:)`.

- The **Schedule** button triggers `scheduleRandomNotifications(_:completion:)`, which calls `scheduleRandomNotification(in:completion:)` with various delays to space out repeat notifications over an hour.

- Right now `scheduleRandomNotification(in:completion:)` obtains the URL of a random image in the bundle and prints it to the console, but it doesn't yet schedule a notification. That's your first task.

To create a local notification, you need to provide some content and a trigger condition.

In `scheduleRandomNotification(in:completion:)`, delete `print("Schedule notification with \(imageURL)")` and add the following in its place:

```
// 1
let content = UNMutableNotificationContent()
content.title = "New cuddlePix!"
content.subtitle = "What a treat"
content.body = "Cheer yourself up with a hug 🐱"
```

```
//TODO: Add attachment

// 2
let trigger = UNTimeIntervalNotificationTrigger(
  timeInterval: seconds, repeats: false)
```

Note: You can select an emoji from the Xcode editor with **Command + Control + Spacebar**. Don't stress if you can't find this exact emoji, as it doesn't matter for this tutorial.

Here's what you're doing in the code above:

1. You create a `UNMutableNotificationContent`, which defines what is displayed on the notification — in this case, you're setting a `title`, `subtitle` and `body`. This is also where you'd set things like badges, sounds and attachments. As the comment teases, you'll add an attachment here a bit later in the tutorial.

2. A `UNTimeIntervalNotificationTrigger` needs to know when to fire and if it should repeat. You're passing through the `seconds` parameter for the delay, and creating a one-time notification. You can also trigger user notifications via location or calendar triggers.

Next up, you need to create the notification request and schedule it.

Replace the `completion()` call with the following:

```
// 1
let request = UNNotificationRequest(
  identifier: randomImageName, content: content, trigger:
trigger)

// 2
UNUserNotificationCenter.current().add(request,
withCompletionHandler: { (error) in
  if let error = error {
    print(error)
    completion(false)
  } else {
    completion(true)
  }
})
```

Here's the breakdown:

1. You create a `UNNotificationRequest` from the `content` and `trigger` you created above. You also provide the required unique identifier (the name of the randomly selected image) to use later when managing the request.

2. You then call `add(_:withCompletionHandler)` on the shared user notification center to add your `request` to the notification queue. Take a look at the completion handler: if an error exists, you print it to the console and inform the caller. If the call was successful, you call the `completion(success:)` closure indicating success, which ultimately notifies its delegate `NotificationTableViewController` that a refresh of pending notifications is necessary. You'll learn more about `NotificationTableViewController` later in the chapter.

Build and run, tap the **+** bar item, tap **Cuddle me now!** then quickly background the application (you can use **Command + Shift + H** to background the application if you are using the Simulator). Five seconds after you created the notification, you'll see the notification banner complete with your custom content:

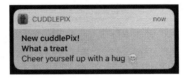

Adding attachments

When you have such a beautiful cactus image, it seems a bit wasteful to only use it for the unique notification identifier. It would be nice to display this image in the notification itself as well.

To do this, back in `scheduleRandomNotification(in:completion:)`, add the following just below the `imageURL` declaration at the beginning of the method:

```
let attachment = try! UNNotificationAttachment(identifier:
    randomImageName, url: imageURL, options: .none)
```

A `UNNotificationAttachment` is an image, video, or audio attachment that is included with a notification. It requires an identifier — you've used `randomImageName` — as well as a URL that points to a local resource of a supported type.

Note this method throws an error if the media isn't readable or otherwise isn't supported. But since you've included these images in your bundle, it's fairly safe to disable error propagation with a `try!`.

Next, replace `//TODO: Add attachment` with the following:

```
content.attachments = [attachment]
```

Here you're setting `attachments` to the single image attachment wrapped in an array. This makes it available for display when the notification fires using default notification handling for image attachments.

> **Note:** When the notification is scheduled, a security-scoped bookmark is created for the attachment so Notification Content extensions have access to the file.

Build and run, initiate a notification with **Cuddle me now!** then return to the home screen as you did before. You'll be greeted with a notification containing a random cactus picture on the right side of the banner. Force tap, or select and drag down on the banner, and you'll be treated to an expanded view of the huggable cactus.

Foreground notifications

The **UNUserNotificationCenterDelegate** protocol defines methods for handling incoming notifications and their actions, including an enhancement to iOS 10 notifications: the ability to display system notification banners in the foreground.

Open **AppDelegate.swift** and add the following at the end of the file:

```
extension AppDelegate: UNUserNotificationCenterDelegate {
  func userNotificationCenter(_ center:
UNUserNotificationCenter,
      willPresent notification: UNNotification,
      withCompletionHandler completionHandler:
      @escaping (UNNotificationPresentationOptions) -> Void) {
        completionHandler(.alert)
  }
}
```

This extends `AppDelegate` to adopt the `UNUserNotificationCenterDelegate` protocol. The optional `userNotificationCenter(_:willPresent:withCompletionHandler:)` is called when a notification is received in the foreground, and gives you an opportunity to act upon that notification. Inside, you call the `completionHandler()`, which determines if and how the alert should be presented.

The `.alert` notification option indicates you want to present the alert, but with no badge updates or sounds. You could also choose to suppress the alert here by passing an empty array.

In `application(_:didFinishLaunchingWithOptions:)`, add the following just before the `return`:

```
UNUserNotificationCenter.current().delegate = self
```

This sets your app's delegate as the `UNUserNotificationCenterDelegate` so the user notification center will pass along this message when a foreground notification is received.

Build and run, and schedule a notification as you've done before. This time, leave cuddlePix in the foreground and you'll see a system banner appear in the foreground:

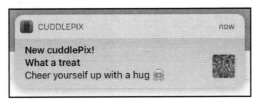

Think back to all the times you had to build your own banner for these situations. Take a deep breath — that's all in the past now! :]

UNUserNotificationCenter

You're my hero!

Managing notifications

You've probably experienced the frustration of clearing out countless missed and outdated notifications in Notification Center. Think of an app that posts sports scores in real-time; you likely care only about the most recent score. iOS 10 gives developers the ability to realize this improved user experience.

The accessor methods of **UNUserNotificationCenter** let you read an app's user notification settings (the user permissions) so you can stay up-to-date on changes. But more excitingly, the *delete* accessors let you programmatically remove pending and delivered notifications to free your users from a wall of unnecessary notifications.

Finally, the accessor methods let you read and and set notification categories – you'll learn about those a little later in this chapter.

Querying Notification Center

You'll start by reading the notification settings and displaying them in cuddlePix's initial table view.

Open **NotificationTableViewController.swift** and find `loadNotificationData(callback:)`. Your code calls this when the table is refreshed, an authorization is returned, a notification is scheduled or a notification is received. Right now, it simply reloads the table.

Add the following just below the `group` declaration near the top:

```
// 1
let notificationCenter = UNUserNotificationCenter.current()
let dataSaveQueue = DispatchQueue(label:
  "com.raywenderlich.CuddlePix.dataSave")

// 2
group.enter()
// 3
notificationCenter.getNotificationSettings { (settings) in
  let settingsProvider = SettingTableSectionProvider(settings:
    settings, name: "Notification Settings")
  // 4
  dataSaveQueue.async(execute: {
    self.tableSectionProviders[.settings] = settingsProvider
    group.leave()
  })
}
```

This code queries for notification settings and updates the table datasource object that displays them.

1. You create `notificationCenter` to reference the shared notification center more concisely. Then you create a `DispatchQueue` to prevent concurrency issues when updating the table view data source.

2. You then enter a dispatch group to ensure all data fetch calls have completed before you refresh the table. Note the project already refreshes in a `group.notify(callback:)` closure for this reason.

3. You call `getNotificationSettings(callback:)` to fetch current notification settings from Notification Center. You pass the results of the query to the callback closure via `settings`, which in turn you use to initialize a `SettingTableSectionProvider`.

   `SettingTableSectionProvider` is from the starter project; it extracts interesting information from the provided `UNNotificationSettings` for presentation in a table view cell.

4. Using the `dataSaveQueue`, you asynchronously update the settings section of `tableSectionProviders` with the newly created `settingsProvider`. The table management is all provided by the starter project; all you need to do is set the provider so as to provide the data to the table view. Finally, you leave `group` to release your hold on the dispatch group.

Build and run, and you'll see a **Notification Settings** section in the table view that represents the current status of notification settings for cuddlePix.

To test it out, go to iOS Settings, find **CuddlePix** and toggle some of the switches. Return to cuddlePix, pull to refresh, and you'll see the updated status:

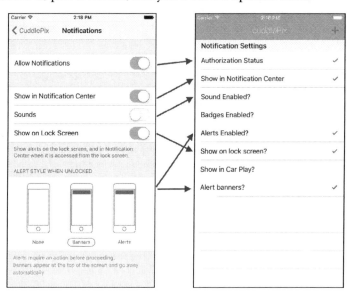

Knowing your user's settings can help you tailor your notifications to suit.

It's just as easy to fetch information about pending and delivered notifications.

Add the following code just below the closing bracket of the `getNotificationSettings(completionHandler:)` closure:

```
group.enter()
notificationCenter.getPendingNotificationRequests { (requests)
in
  let pendingRequestsProvider =
    PendingNotificationsTableSectionProvider(requests:
      requests, name: "Pending Notifications")
  dataSaveQueue.async(execute: {
    self.tableSectionProviders[.pending] =
pendingRequestsProvider
    group.leave()
  })
}

group.enter()
notificationCenter.getDeliveredNotifications { (notifications)
in
  let deliveredNotificationsProvider =
    DeliveredNotificationsTableSectionProvider(notifications:
      notifications, name: "Delivered Notifications")
  dataSaveQueue.async(execute: {
    self.tableSectionProviders[.delivered]
      = deliveredNotificationsProvider
    group.leave()
  })
}
```

This implements two additional fetches that are similar to the settings fetch you coded earlier and update each `tableSectionProviders` respectively. `getPendingNotificationRequests(completionHandler:)` fetches notifications that are pending; that is, scheduled, but not yet delivered. `getDeliveredNotifications(completionHandler:)` fetches those notifications that have been delivered, but not yet deleted.

Build and run, schedule a notification, and you'll see it appear under **Pending Notifications**. Once it's been delivered, pull to refresh and you'll see it under **Delivered Notifications**.

Delivered notifications persist until they're deleted. To test this, expand a notification when the banner appears then select the **X** in the upper right. Refresh the table, then check to see if the notification still exists. You can also delete a notification by pulling down Notification Center and clearing it from the **Missed** list.

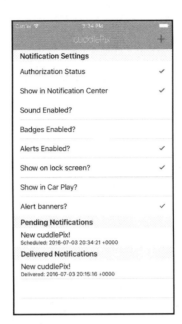

> **Note:** Remember that your notifications use the randomly selected image name as their unique identifier. Because there are only a handful of images in cuddlePix, you're bound to get some notifications with duplicate content and identifiers. If you dismiss a notification with a delivered duplicate, you will notice both it and its duplicate get deleted.

It would be even nicer if you didn't have to pull to refresh when a new notification arrives.

Add the following to **AppDelegate.swift** at the top of `userNotificationCenter(_:willPresent:withCompletionHandler)`:

```
NotificationCenter.default.post(name:
  userNotificationReceivedNotificationName, object: .none)
```

`userNotificationReceivedNotificationName` is a system notification cuddlePix uses to reload the status table. You've placed it here, because `userNotificationCenter(_:willPresent:withCompletionHandler)` triggers whenever a notification arrives.

A very compelling application of this "status awareness" is to prevent repeat notifications if an identical notification is still in "delivered" status.

Modifying notifications

Consider again the app that reports sport scores. Rather than littering Notification Center with outdated score alerts, you could update the same notification and bump it to the top of the notification list each time an update comes through.

Updating notifications is straightforward. You simply create a new `UNNotificationRequest` with the same identifier as the existing notification, pass it your updated content, and add it to `UNUserNotificationCenter`. Once the trigger conditions are met, it will overwrite the existing notification that has a matching identifier.

For cuddlePix, notifications are serious business. Consider the scenario where you scheduled 10 notifications, when you meant to only schedule five. Too much of a good thing can get pretty prickly, so you're going to make your notification strategy a little more *succulent* and delete pending notifications.

Open **NotificationTableViewController.swift**; you'll see `tableView` editing methods near the end of the data source methods extension. Deletion is enabled for rows in the **pending** section, but committing the delete doesn't do anything. Time to fix that.

Add the following to `tableView(_:commit:forRowAt:)`:

```
// 1
guard let section =
  NotificationTableSection(rawValue: indexPath.section),
  editingStyle == .delete && section == .pending else { return }

// 2
guard let provider = tableSectionProviders[.pending]
  as? PendingNotificationsTableSectionProvider else { return }

let request = provider.requests[indexPath.row]

// 3
UNUserNotificationCenter.current()
  .removePendingNotificationRequests(withIdentifiers:
    [request.identifier])
loadNotificationData(callback: {
  self.tableView.deleteRows(at: [indexPath], with: .automatic)
})
```

This method executes when you attempt an insertion or deletion on the `tableView`. Taking it step-by-step:

1. You check that the selected cell came from the `pending` section of the table and that the attempted operation was a `delete`. If not, return.

2. You unwrap and typecast the `tableSectionProviders` datasource object associated with pending notifications, and return if the operation fails. You then set `request` to the `UNNotificationRequest` represented by the selected cell.

3. You call `removePendingNotificationRequests(withIdentifiers:)` on the user notification center to delete the notification matching your request's identifier. Then you call `loadNotificationData(callback:)` to refresh the datasource, deleting the row in the callback closure.

Build and run, create a new notification, and swipe the cell in the **Pending Notifications** section to reveal the delete button. Tap **Delete** quickly before the notification is delivered. Because you've deleted it from the user notification center before it was delivered, the notification will never be shown, and the cell will be deleted.

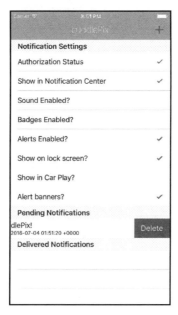

Notification content extensions

Another major change to notifications in iOS 10 is the introduction of Notification Content extensions, which let you provide custom interfaces for the expanded version of your notifications. Interaction is limited, though — the notification view won't pass along gestures, but the extension can update the view in response to **actions**, which you'll learn about a little later.

To make a Notification Content extension, you must adopt the **UNNotificationContentExtension** protocol in your extension view controller. This protocol defines optional methods that notify the extension when it's being presented, help it respond to actions, and assist in media playback.

The interface can contain anything you might normally place in a view, including playable media such as video and audio. However, the extension runs as a separate binary from your app, and you don't have direct access to the app's resources. For this reason, any required resources that aren't included in the extension bundle are passed via attachments of type **UNNotificationAttachment**.

Creating an extension with an attachment

Let's try this out. Select **File\New\Target** in Xcode; choose the **iOS\Application Extension\Notification Content** template then select **Next**.

Enter **ContentExtension** for the Product Name, select the **Team** associated with your developer account, choose **Swift** as the Language, then hit **Finish**. If prompted, choose to **Activate** the scheme.

You've created a new target and project group, both named **ContentExtension**. In the group, you have a view controller, storyboard, and plist necessary for configuring the extension. You'll visit each of these in turn while implementing the extension.

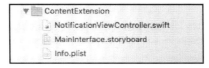

Open **MainInterface.storyboard** and take a look; you'll see a single view controller of type `NotificationViewController` — this is the controller created when you generated the extension. Inside is a single view with a "Hello World" label connected to an outlet in the controller.

For cuddlePix, your goal is to create something similar to the default expanded view, but just a tad more cuddly. A cactus picture with a hug emoji in the corner should do quite nicely! :]

To start, delete the existing label and change the view's background color to white. Set the view height to **320** to give yourself more room to work. Add an Image View and pin it to the edges of the superview:

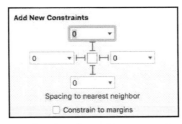

Select the Image View and go to the Attributes Inspector. In the View section, set the Content Mode to **Aspect Fill** to ensure as many pixels as possible are filled with beautiful, poky, cactusy goodness:

To clean things up, select the **Resolve Auto Layout Issues** button in the lower right and then select **Update Frames** in the **All Views in Notification View Controller** section. This will cause your Image View to resize to match the constraints, and the Auto Layout warnings should resolve as well.

Next, drag a label just under the image view in the document outline pane on the left-hand side of Interface Builder:

Pin it to the bottom left of the view with the following constraints:

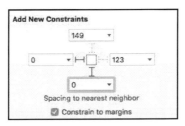

Now to add a big spiny cactus hug! With the label selected, change the Text in the attribute inspector to a hug emoji. To do this, use **Control + Command + Spacebar** to bring up the picker, and select the 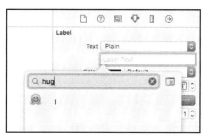 .

Set the font size of the label to **100** so your hug emoji is more visible. Click **Update Frames** again to resize the label to match the new content.

Now, open **NotificationViewController.swift** in the Assistant Editor so that you can wire up some outlets.

First, delete the following line:

```
@IBOutlet var label: UILabel?
```

That outlet was associated with the label you deleted from the storyboard template. You'll see an error now as you're still referencing it.

Delete the following in `didReceive(_:)` to resolve that:

```
self.label?.text = notification.request.content.body
```

Next, Control-drag from the image view in the storyboard to the spot where you just deleted the old outlet. Name it **imageView** and select **Connect**.

With the interface done, close the storyboard and open
NotificationViewController.swift in the Standard editor.

Remember that didReceive(_:) is called when a notification arrives; this is where you
should perform any required view configuration. For this extension, that means
populating the image view with the cactus picture from the notification.

Add the following to didReceive(_:):

```
// 1
guard let attachment =
notification.request.content.attachments.first
  else { return }
// 2
if attachment.url.startAccessingSecurityScopedResource() {
  let imageData = try? Data.init(contentsOf: attachment.url)
  if let imageData = imageData {
    imageView.image = UIImage(data: imageData)
  }
  attachment.url.stopAccessingSecurityScopedResource()
}
```

Here's what the above does:

1. The passed-in UNNotification (notification) contains a reference to the original
   UNNotificationRequest (request) that generated it. A request has
   UNNotificationContent (content) which, among other things, contains an array
   of UNNotificationAttachments (attachments). In a guard, you grab the first of
   those attachments — you know you've only included one — and you place it in
   attachment.

2. Attachments in the user notification center live inside your app's sandbox – not the
   extension's – therefore you must access them via security-scoped URLs.
   startAccessingSecurityScopedResource() makes the file available to the
   extension when it successfully returns, and
   stopAccessingSecurityScopedResource() indicates you're finished with the
   resource. In between, you load imageView using Data obtained from the file pointed
   to by this URL.

The extension is all set. But when a notification triggers for cuddlePix, how is the the
system supposed to know what, if any, extension to send it to?

..notification gnomes?

Gnomes are a good guess, but they're notoriously unreliable. :] Instead, the user notification center relies on a key defined in the extension's plist to identify the types of notifications it should handle.

Open **Info.plist** in the **ContentExtension** group and expand NSExtension, then NSExtensionAttributes, to reveal **UNNotificationExtensionCategory**. This key takes a string (or array of strings) identifying the notifications it should handle. Enter **newCuddlePix** here, which you'll later use in the content of your notification requests.

> **Note**: In the same plist dictionary, you'll see another required key: UNNotificationExtensionInitialContentSizeRatio. Because the system starts to present a notification before it loads your extension, it needs something on which to base the initial content size. You provide a ratio of the notification's height to its width, and the system will animate any expansion or contraction once the extension view loads.
>
> cuddlePix's extension view frame is set to fill the full width of a notification, so in this case you leave it at the default ratio of 1.

The operating system knows that notifications using the *newCuddlePix* category should go to your extension, but you haven't yet set this category on your outgoing notifications. Open **ConfigurationViewController.swift** and find scheduleRandomNotification(in:completion:) where you generate instances of UNNotificationRequest.

Add the following after the spot where you declare content:

```
content.categoryIdentifier = newCuddlePixCategoryName
```

The UNNotificationRequest created in this method will now use newCuddlePixCategoryName as a categoryIdentifier for its content. newCuddlePixCategoryName is a string constant defined in the starter that matches the one you placed in the extension plist: "newCuddlePix".

When the system prepares to deliver a notification, it will check the notification's category identifier and try to find an extension registered to handle it. In this case, that is the extension you just created.

> **Note:** For a remote notification to invoke your Notification Content extension, you'd need to add this same category identifier as the value for the `category` key in the payload dictionary.

Make sure you have the **CuddlePix** scheme selected, then build and run. Next, switch to the **ContentExtension** scheme then build and run again. When you're prompted what to run the extension with, select **CuddlePix** and **Run**:

In cuddlePix, generate a new notification with **Cuddle me now!**. When the banner appears, expand it either by force touching on a compatible device, or selecting the notification and dragging down in the simulator. You'll now see the new custom view from your extension:

> **Note:** You'll notice that the custom UI you designed is presented *above* the default
> banner content. In this case, that's what you want, as your custom view didn't
> implement any of this text.
>
> However, if you shifted the titles and messages to the extension, you might want
> to remove the system-generated banner at the bottom. You could do this by
> adding the `UNNotificationExtensionDefaultContentHidden` key to your
> extension plist with a value of `true`.

Handling notification actions

So far, the custom notification for cuddlePix isn't all that different from the default one.
However, a custom view *does* provide quite a lot of opportunity depending on your
needs. For example, a ride-sharing app could provide a map of your ride's location, while
a sports app could provide a large scoreboard.

The feature that makes extensions shine in cuddlePix is *interactivity*. While Notification
Content extensions don't allow touch handling, where the touches aren't passed to the
controller, they *do* provide interaction through custom action handlers.

Before iOS 10, custom actions were forwarded on to the application and handled in an
application delegate method. This worked great for things like responding to a message
where there wasn't any need to see the results of the action.

Because Notification Content extensions can handle actions directly, that means the
notification view can be updated with results. For instance, when you accept an
invitation, you could display an updated calendar view right there in the notification
showing the new event.

The driver behind this is the new **UNNotificationCategory**, which uniquely defines a
notification type and references actions the type can act upon. The actions are defined
with **UNNotificationAction** objects that, in turn, uniquely define actions. When
configured and added to the `UNUserNotificationCenter`, these objects help direct
actionable notifications to the right handlers in your app or extensions.

Defining the action

The goal of cuddlePix is to spread cheer, and what better way to do that than shower
your cuddly cactus with stars? You're going to wire up an action for "starring" a cactus,
which will kick off an animation in your custom notification view.

To start, you need to register a notification category and action in the app.

Open **AppDelegate.swift** and add the following method to `AppDelegate`:

```
func configureUserNotifications() {
  // 1
  let starAction = UNNotificationAction(identifier:
    "star", title: "🌟 star my cuddle 🌟 ", options: [])
  // 2
  let category =
    UNNotificationCategory(identifier: newCuddlePixCategoryName,
      actions: [starAction],
      intentIdentifiers: [],
      options: [])
  // 3
  UNUserNotificationCenter.current()
    .setNotificationCategories([category])
}
```

Taking each numbered comment in turn:

1. A `UNNotificationAction` has two jobs: it provides the data used to display an action to the user, and it uniquely identifies actions so controllers can act upon them. It requires a title for the first job and a unique identifier string for the second. Here you've created a `starAction` with a recognizable identifier and title.

2. You defined a `UNNotificationCategory` with the string constant set up for this notification: `newCuddlePixCategoryName`. You've wrapped `starAction` in an array and passed it to `actions`, which requires all custom actions in the order you want them displayed.

3. You pass the new `category` to the `UNUserNotificationCenter` with `setNotificationCategories()`, which accepts an array of categories and registers cuddlePix as supporting them.

Add the following code just before the `return` statement in `application(_:didFinishLaunchingWithOptions:)`:

```
configureUserNotifications()
```

This ensures category registration occurs as soon as the app starts.

Build and run the **CuddlePix** scheme, followed by the **ContentExtension** scheme, which you should choose to run with CuddlePix. Create a notification and expand it via force touch or a drag down when it arrives.

You'll now see your custom action at the bottom of the notification.

Select **star my cuddle**; the notification will simply dismiss, because you haven't yet implemented the action to be performed.

Handling and forwarding extension responses

Notification extensions get first crack at handling an action response. In fact, they determine whether or not to forward the request along to the app when they finish.

Inside ContentExtension, open **NotificationViewController.swift** and you'll see your controller already adheres to `UNNotificationContentExtension`. This provides an optional method for handling responses.

Add the following to `NotificationViewController`:

```
internal func didReceive(_ response: UNNotificationResponse,
                completionHandler completion:
    @escaping (UNNotificationContentExtensionResponseOption) ->
Void) {
  // 1
  if response.actionIdentifier == "star" {
    // TODO Show Stars
    let time = DispatchTime.now() +
      DispatchTimeInterval.milliseconds(2000)
    DispatchQueue.main.asyncAfter(deadline: time) {
      // 2
      completion(.dismissAndForwardAction)
    }
  }
}
```

didReceive(_:completionHandler:) is called with the action response and a completion closure. The closure must be called when you're done with the action, and it requires a parameter indicating what should happen next. Here's what's going on in more detail:

1. When you set up UNNotificationAction, you gave the star action an identifier of star, which you check here to catch responses of this type. Inside, you have a TODO for implementing the star animation that you'll soon revisit. You let the animation continue for two seconds via DispatchQueue.main.asyncAfter before calling the completion closure.

2. completion takes an enum value defined by UNNotificationContentExtensionResponseOption. In this case, you've used dismissAndForwardAction, which dismisses the notification and gives the app an opportunity to act on the response. Alternative values include doNotDismiss, which keeps the notification on screen, and dismiss, which doesn't pass the action along to the app after dismissal.

Your current implementation of the star action leaves something to be desired — specifically, the stars! The starter project already contains everything you need for this animation, but it's not yet available to the Notification Content extension's target.

In the project navigator, expand the **Utiltiies** and the **Star Animator** group and select both files inside:

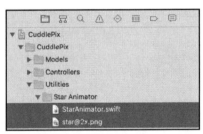

Open the File Inspector in the utilities pane of Xcode and select **ContentExtension** under **Target Membership**:

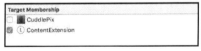

Back in **NotificationViewController.swift**, replace // TODO Show Stars with:

```
imageView.showStars()
```

This uses a UIImageView extension defined in the **StarAnimator.swift** file you just added to the target. showStars() uses Core Animation to create a shower of stars over the image view.

Build and run the extension and the app as you've done before. Create and expand a notification, then select **star my cuddle** and you'll see an awesome star shower over your cactus before the notification dismisses:

Your extension has done its job, and the cuddle has been starred. But recall that you called `dismissAndForwardAction` in the completion closure. Where is it being forwarded *to*?

The answer is that it's forwarded to the app, but right now the `UNUserNotificationCenterDelegate` in cuddlePix isn't expecting anything.

Open **AppDelegate.swift** and add the following method to the `UNUserNotificationCenterDelegate` extension:

```
func userNotificationCenter(_ center: UNUserNotificationCenter,
                            didReceive response:
  UNNotificationResponse,
                            withCompletionHandler
  completionHandler: @escaping () -> Void) {
    print("Response received for \(response.actionIdentifier)")
    completionHandler()
}
```

`userNotificationCenter(_:didReceive:withCompletionHandler)` will let you know a notification action was selected. Inside, you print out the `actionIdentifier` of the response, simply to confirm things are working as they should. You then call `completionHandler()` which accepts no arguments and is required to notify the user notification center that you're done handling the action.

Build and run the **CuddlePix** scheme, then trigger a notification. Expand the notification and select **star my cuddle**. Watch the console and you should see the below text print:

```
Response received for star
```

To recap, here's the flow of messages that takes place when you receive a notification in the foreground and respond to an action in a Notification Content extension:

1. **userNotificationCenter(_:willPresent:withCompletionHandler:)** is called in the `UNUserNotificationCenterDelegate` (only in the foreground), and determines if the notification should present itself.

2. **didReceive(_:)** is called in the `UNNotificationContentExtension` and provides an opportunity to configure the custom notification's interface.

3. **didReceive(_:completionHandler:)** is called in the `UNNotificationContentExtension` after the user selects a response action.

4. **userNotificationCenter(_:didReceive:withCompletionHandler:)** is called in the `UNUserNotificationCenterDelegate` if the `UNNotificationContentExtension` passes it along via the `dismissAndForwardAction` response option.

Notification Service app extensions

Believe it or not, another major feature awaits in the form of Notification Service extensions. These let you intercept remote notifications and modify the payload. Common use cases would include adding a media attachment to the notification, or decrypting content.

cuddlePix doesn't really demand end-to-end encryption, so instead you'll add an image attachment to incoming remote notifications. But first, you need to set up a development environment. Because the simulator cannot register for remote notifications, you'll need a device with iOS 10 to test.

Start by configuring cuddlePix for push with your Apple Developer account. First select the **CuddlePix** target and **General** tab. In the **Signing** section, select your **Team** and then in **Bundle Identifier** enter a unique **Identifier**.

Now switch to the **Capabilities** tab and switch **Push Notifications** on for the CuddlePix target. cuddlePix is now set up to receive tokens from the Apple Push Notification Service (APNS).

Select the **ContentExtension** target and change the *com.razeware.CuddlePix* prefix in its bundle identifier to match the unique identifier you used for the **CuddlePix** target (leaving .ContentExtension at the end of the identifier). Also set your **Team** as you did in the other target. Apple requires that your extensions have a prefix that matches the main app.

You'll also need a way to send test pushes. For this, you'll use a popular open source tool called **Pusher**, which sends push notifications directly to APNS. To start, follow the instructions in the **Installation** section of their GitHub readme to get the app running: github.com/noodlewerk/NWPusher.

Pusher's readme also has a **Getting Started** section that guides you through creating the required SSL certificate; follow this to create a Development certificate. You may also find the section titled *Creating an SSL Certificate and PEM file* in *Push Notifications Tutorial: Getting Started* useful. You can find it here - raywenderlich.com/123862.

With your p12 file in hand, go back to Pusher and select it in the **Select Push Certificate** dropdown. You may need to choose **Import PCKS #12 file (.p12)** and manually select it if it doesn't appear here.

Pusher requires a push token so it can tell APNS where to send the notification.

Head back to Xcode and open **AppDelegate.swift**. Add the following just before the
`return` statement in `application(_:didFinishLaunchingWithOptions)`:

```
application.registerForRemoteNotifications()
```

When cuddlePix starts up, it will now register for notifications. Remember – this will
only work when run on a device.

Add the following at the bottom of the app delegate, just below the final bracket:

```
extension AppDelegate {
  // 1
  func application(_ application: UIApplication,
didFailToRegisterForRemoteNotificationsWithError error: Error) {
      print("Registration for remote notifications failed")
      print(error.localizedDescription)
  }

  // 2
  func application(_ application: UIApplication,
    didRegisterForRemoteNotificationsWithDeviceToken
deviceToken: Data) {
      print("Registered with device token: \
(deviceToken.hexString)")
  }
}
```

This extension contains `UIApplicationDelegate` methods for handling responses from
APNS:

1. `application(_:didFailToRegisterForRemoteNotificationsWithError:)` is
   called when registration fails. Here, you print the error message.

2. `application(_:didRegisterForRemoteNotificationsWithDeviceToken:)` is
   called when registration is successful, and returns the `deviceToken`. You use
   `hexString`, a helper method included with the starter project, to convert it to hex
   format and print it to the console.

Build and run on a device, and check the debug console for your device token, prefixed
with the string `Registered with device token`. Copy the hex string and paste it into
the **Device Push Token** field in Pusher. Then paste the following in the payload field,
using **Paste and Match Style** to avoid formatting issues:

```
{
  "aps":{
    "alert":{
      "title":"New cuddlePix!",
      "subtitle":"From your friend",
      "body":"Cheer yourself up with this remote hug 🤗"
```

```
        },
        "category":"newCuddlePix"
    }
}
```

Your setup should now look like this:

Select **Push** in the lower right of Pusher and, if everything is configured properly, you should see a push that looks like this:

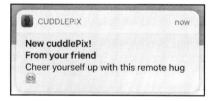

The default notification banner is here, but if you expand it, the image view will be blank. You passed in the category of `newCuddlePix`, identifying your Notification Content extension – but you didn't provide an attachment to load. That's just not possible from a remote payload...but that's where Notification Service extensions come in.

Creating and configuring a Notification Service extension

The plan is to modify your payload to include the URL of an attachment you'll download in the Notification Service extension and use to create an attachment. Update the JSON in the payload section in Pusher to match the following:

```
{
    "aps":{
        "alert":{
            "title":"New cuddlePix!",
            "subtitle":"From your friend",
            "body":"Cheer yourself up with this remote hug 😺"
```

```
    },
      "category":"newCuddlePix",
    "mutable-content": 1
  },
    "attachment-url": "https://wolverine.raywenderlich.com/books/
  i10t/notifications/i10t-feature.png"
  }
```

This contains two new keys:

1. `mutable-content` takes a boolean and indicates whether or not the notification should be modifiable by a Notification Service extension. You set it to **1** to override the default of 0, which prevents a Notification Service app extension from running.

2. `attachment-url` resides outside of the main payload, and is of your own design; the key name and content are not dictated by the user notification services. You'll write code in the extension to grab this and use it to load an image in the notification.

With the content in mind, it's time to start creating the Notification Service extension to load the `content-url` and build an attachment with it.

Select **File\New\Target** in Xcode, and choose the **iOS\Application Extension\Notification Service Extension** template. Name it **ServiceExtension**, make sure your correct **Team** is selected, select **Swift** as the Language, and hit **Finish**. If prompted, choose to **Activate** the scheme.

This will create a target called **ServiceExtension**. It will also add the following files to your project:

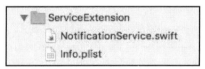

Take a look at **NotificationService.swift**, which contains a class `NotificationService` that inherits from `UNNotificationServiceExtension`. `UNNotificationServiceExtension` is the central class for Notification Service extensions, and it contains two important methods overridden in the template code:

1. **didReceive(_:withContentHandler)** is called when a notification is received and routed to the extension, and is given a limited amount of time to modify the notification contents. It accepts a `UNNotificationRequest`, from which it creates `bestAttemptContent`, a mutable copy of the notification content. The template unwraps this, appends `[modified]` to the end of the title, then calls the content handler, passing the updated content.

2. **serviceExtensionTimeWillExpire()** is called to provide a best attempt at updating notification content in cases where

didReceive(_:UNNotificationServiceExtension) doesn't return quickly enough. The template contains a property bestAttemptContent that didReceive(_:UNNotificationServiceExtension) uses while updating content. Here, serviceExtensionTimeWillExpire() unwraps bestAttemptContent and sends it along to the content handler.

You'll modify this code to handle downloading the attachment-url. First, add the following import to the top of the file:

```
import MobileCoreServices
```

You'll need this for referencing a file type constant in just a moment.

In didReceive(_:withContentHandler), delete the template code inside the if let bestAttemptContent = bestAttemptContent block. Add the following in its place:

```
// 1
guard let attachmentString = bestAttemptContent
  .userInfo["attachment-url"] as? String,
  let attachmentUrl = URL(string: attachmentString) else
{ return }

// 2
let session = URLSession(configuration:
  URLSessionConfiguration.default)
let attachmentDownloadTask = session.downloadTask(with:
  attachmentUrl, completionHandler: { (url, response, error) in
    if let error = error {
      print("Error downloading: \(error.localizedDescription)")
    } else if let url = url {
      // 3
      let attachment = try! UNNotificationAttachment(identifier:
        attachmentString, url: url, options:
        [UNNotificationAttachmentOptionsTypeHintKey:
kUTTypePNG])
      bestAttemptContent.attachments = [attachment]
    }
    // 5
    contentHandler(bestAttemptContent)
})
// 4
attachmentDownloadTask.resume()
```

Here's what this does:

1. This gets the string value for attachment-url found in userInfo of the request content copy. It then creates a URL from this string and saves it in attachmentUrl. If this guard isn't successful, it bails out early with a return.

2. `session` is an instance of `URLSession` used when creating a `downloadTask` to get the image at `attachmentUrl`. In the completion handler, an error is printed on failure.

3. On success, a `UNNotificationAttachment` is created using the `attachmentString` as a unique identifier and the local `url` as the content. `UNNotificationAttachmentOptionsTypeHintKey` provides a hint as to the file type; in this case, `kUTTypePNG` is used as the file is known to be a PNG. The resulting attachment is set on `bestAttemptContent`.

4. The `completionHandler` is called, passing over the modified notification content. This signifies the extension's work is done, and sends back the updated notification. This must be done whether or not the attempt was successful. If unsuccessful, the original request is sent back.

5. Once the `downloadTask` is defined, it kicks off with `resume()`. This leads to the `attachmentDownloadTask` `completionHandler` executing on completion, which in turn calls the `contentHandler` to complete processing.

`serviceExtensionTimeWillExpire()` is already in good shape with the template code. It will return whatever you currently have in `bestAttemptContent`.

Build and run the **ServiceExtension** scheme on your device, making sure to run with **cuddlePix**. Now return to **Pusher** where you should have already copied the new payload containing `attachment-url`. Hit **Push** and you should see a remotely-sourced cuddle, complete with an image of something truly beautiful:

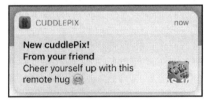

The Notification Service extension intercepted the remote push, downloaded the image in the URL provided in the payload and attached it to the notification. Pretty cool!

Where to go from here?

In this chapter, you got up close and personal with some cuddly cacti while checking out all the new features in notifications.

You learned how to create custom notification interfaces, respond to actions in Notification Content extensions and the app, query and modify existing notifications, and enhance remote notifications with Notification Service extensions. I imagine you've already come up with some ideas on your own to enhance your apps with these basic concepts.

For more detail on any of these topics, be sure to check out **Apple's UserNotifications API Reference** at apple.co/29F1nzE

Also check out the great WWDC 2016 videos that cover all of these new features:

- Advanced Notifications (Session 708)—apple.co/29t7c6v
- Introduction to Notifications (Session 707)—apple.co/29Wv6D6

Chapter 9: Property Animators
By Rich Turton

If you've done any animations in UIKit, you've probably used the `UIView` animation methods `UIView.animate(withDuration:animations:)` and friends.

iOS 10 has introduced a new way to write animation code: using `UIViewPropertyAnimator`. This isn't a replacement for the existing API, nor is it objectively "better", but it does give you a level of control that wasn't possible before.

In this chapter, you'll learn about the following new features that Property Animators give you access to:

• Detailed control over animation timing curves

• A superior spring animation

• Monitoring and altering of animation state

• Pausing, reversing and scrubbing through animations or even abandoning them part-way through

The fine control over animation timing alone would make a Property Animator an improvement for your existing `UIView` animations. But where they really shine is when you create animations that aren't just fire-and-forget.

For example, if you're animating something in response to user gestures, or if you want the user to be able to grab an animating object and do something else with it, then Property Animators are your new best friend.

Getting started

Open the **Animalation** project in the starter materials for this chapter. This is a demonstration app which you'll modify to add extra animation capabilities. There are two view controllers, some animated transition support files, and some utility files. Build and run the project:

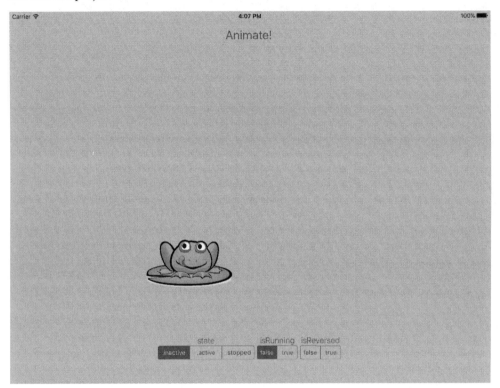

Tap the **Animate** button at the top, and the frog will move to a random position. This happens with a traditional call to `UIView.animate(withDuration:)` in **ViewController.swift**:

```
func animateAnimalTo(location: CGPoint) {
  // TODO
  UIView.animate(withDuration: 3) {
    self.imageContainer.center = location
  }
}
```

Watch carefully as the frog moves. It starts slowly, then gets faster, then slows down again before it stops.

That's due to the animation's **timing curve**. UIView.animate(withDuration:) uses a built-in timing curve called curveEaseInOut, which represents this slow/fast/slow behavior. There are a few other timing curve options provided by Apple, but your choices are quite limited.

Often, you want precise control over an animation's timing curve, and this is one of the features that Property Animators give you. Before we get into the code, here's a quick explanation of timing curves.

Timing is everything

Consider a very simple animation, ten seconds in length, where a view moves along a line, from x = 0 to x = 10.

At any given second, how far along the line is the view? The answer to this question is given by the animation's **timing curve**. The simplest timing curve isn't curved at all — it's called the **linear** curve. Animations using the linear curve move along at a constant speed: after 1 second, the view is at position 1. After 2 seconds, position 2, and so on. You could plot this on a graph like so:

This doesn't lead to very fluid or natural-looking animations; in real life, things don't go from not moving at all to moving at a constant rate, and then suddenly stopping when they get to the end.

For that reason, the UIView animation API uses an **ease-in, ease-out** timing curve. On a graph, that looks more like this:

You can see that for the first quarter or so of the time, your animation doesn't make much progress. It then speeds up and slows again near the end. To the eye, the animated object accelerates, moves then decelerates and stops. This looks a lot more natural and is what you saw with the frog animation.

`UIView` animations offer you four choices of timing curve: **linear** and **ease-in-ease-out**, which you've seen above; **ease-in**, which accelerates at the start but ends suddenly; and **ease-out**, which starts suddenly and decelerates at the end.

`UIViewPropertyAnimator`, however, offers you nearly limitless control over the timing curve of your animations. In addition to the four pre-baked options above, you can supply your own **cubic Bézier timing curve**.

Cubic Bézier timing curves

Your own cubic *what* now?

Don't panic. You've been looking at these types of curves already. A cubic Bézier curve goes from point A to point D, while also doing its very best to get near points B and C on the way, like a dog running across the park, being distracted by interesting trees.

Let's review the examples from earlier. In both examples above, point A is in the bottom left and point D is in the top right.

With the linear curve, points B and C happen to be in an exact straight line:

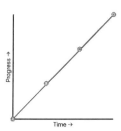

With ease-in-ease-out, point B is directly to the right of point A, and point C is directly to the left of point D. You can imagine the line being pulled from A towards B, then C takes over, then D:

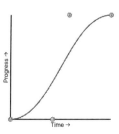

Finally, here's what the ease-in and ease-out curves look like. With the ease-in curve, point C is directly under point D, and with the ease-out curve, B is under A:

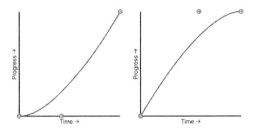

But what if you want something custom? You could set up the four points like this and make a custom animation curve:

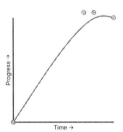

Here, points B and C are above the top of the graph, so the animation would actually overshoot and then come back to its final position.

Points B and C in these diagrams are the **control points** of the animation curve. They define the shape of the line as it travels from A to D.

Controlling your frog

With that covered, it's now time to write some code. :] Open **ViewController.swift** and find `animateAnimalTo(location:)`. Replace the body of the method with this code:

```
imageMoveAnimator = UIViewPropertyAnimator(
    duration: 3,
    curve: .easeInOut) {
      self.imageContainer.center = location
}
imageMoveAnimator?.startAnimation()
```

There's already a property in the starter project to hold the animator, so you create a new Property Animator and assign it. After the Animator is created, you need to call `startAnimation()` to set it running.

> **Note:** Why do you need to assign the Animator to a property? Well, you don't *need* to, but one of the major features of Property Animators is that you can take control of the animation at any point, and without holding a reference to it, that's not possible.

Build and run the project, hit the animate button, and... well, it looks exactly the same. You've used the `.easeInOut` timing curve, which is the same as the default curve used for `UIView` animations.

Let's take a look at a custom timing curve. When frogs jump, they have an explosive burst of acceleration, then they land gently. In terms of timing curves, that looks something like this:

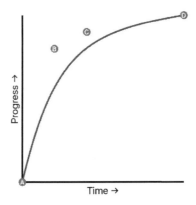

You can see the two control points on the diagram. Let's try it out!

Replace the contents of `animateAnimalTo(location:)` with the following:

```
let controlPoint1 = CGPoint(x: 0.2, y: 0.8) // B on the diagram
let controlPoint2 = CGPoint(x: 0.4, y: 0.9) // C on the diagram
imageMoveAnimator = UIViewPropertyAnimator(
    duration: 3,
    controlPoint1: controlPoint1,
    controlPoint2: controlPoint2) {
        self.imageContainer.center = location
}
imageMoveAnimator?.startAnimation()
```

The two control points correspond to the labelled points on the diagram as indicated by the comments. The timing curve always runs from (`0`, `0`) at **A** to (`1`, `1`) at **D**. Build and run and you'll see that the frog starts to move very quickly and then slows down — exactly as you wanted!

Challenge: Play around with the control points to see what effects you can get. What happens if any control point coordinate is greater than 1.0, or less than 0.0?

Spring animations

The level of control over the timing curve goes even further than this. The two initializers you've used so far, passing in a curve or control points, are actually convenience initializers. All they do is create and pass on a `UITimingCurveProvider` object.

`UITimingCurveProvider` is a protocol that provides the relationship between elapsed time and animation progress. Unfortunately, the protocol doesn't go as far as to let you have *total* control, but it does give you access to another cool feature: springs!

Note: "Wait!" you cry. "We already had spring animations!" Yes, you did, but they weren't very customizable. `UIView` spring require a duration, as well as the various parameters describing the spring. To get natural-looking spring animations, you had to keep tweaking the duration value.

Why? Well, imagine an actual spring. If you stretch it between your hands and let go, the duration of the spring's motion is really a function of the properties of the spring (What is it made of? How thick is it?) and how far you stretched it. Similarly, the duration of the animation should be driven from the properties of the spring, not tacked on and the animation forced to fit.

Apple has provided an implementation of `UITimingCurveProvider` to create timing curves for springs, called `UISpringTimingParameters`. To use `UISpringTimingParameters` you need to provide three values to describe the spring system:

- The **mass** of the object attached to the spring.

- The **stiffness** of the spring.

- The **damping**; these are any factors that would act to slow down the movement of the system, like friction or air resistance.

The amount of damping applied will give you one of three outcomes: the system can be **under-damped**, meaning it will bounce around for a while before it settles; **critically damped**, meaning it will settle as quickly as possible without bouncing at all; or **over-damped**, meaning it will settle without bouncing, but not quite as quickly.

In most cases, you'll want a slightly under-damped system — without that, your spring animations won't look particularly *springy*. But you don't have to guess at what values to use. The critical damping ratio is 2 times the square root of the product of the mass and stiffness values. You'll put this into action now.

Replace the contents of animateAnimalTo(location:) with the following:

```
//1
let mass: CGFloat = 1.0
let stiffness: CGFloat = 10.0
//2
let criticalDamping = 2 * sqrt(mass * stiffness)
//3
let damping = criticalDamping * 0.5
//4
let parameters = UISpringTimingParameters(
  mass: mass,
  stiffness: stiffness,
  damping: damping,
  initialVelocity: .zero)
//5
imageMoveAnimator = UIViewPropertyAnimator(
  duration: 3,
  timingParameters: parameters)
imageMoveAnimator?.addAnimations {
  self.imageContainer.center = location
}
imageMoveAnimator?.startAnimation()
```

Here's the breakdown:

1. Create constants for the mass and stiffness values.

2. Derive the critical damping ratio using the formula stated above.

3. Reduce this ratio to give an under-damped spring.

4. Create a spring timing parameters object.

5. Use the designated initializer, passing in the new timing parameters.

Note that since you're using spring timing parameters, *duration is ignored*. You also have to add the animations separately when using this initializer.

Build and run, and you'll see the frog move in a more spring-like fashion.

Challenge: Experiment with the mass and stiffness used in section 1 and the multiplier used in section 3, and see what effect this has on the animation.

Note: If for some reason you don't find specifying your own spring parameters exciting, there is also a convenience initializer `init(dampingRatio:, initialVelocity:)` for `UISpringTimingParameters` where 1.0 is a critically damped spring and values less than 1.0 will be under-damped.

Initial velocity

There's one additional value when you create the spring timing parameters — the initial velocity. This means you can tell the spring system that the object has momentum at the start of the animation — in which case it can make the animation look more natural.

Build and run the app, and drag the frog around. Notice that when you release the frog, he moves back to where he started. Then try moving the frog quickly, and release your mouse while you're still moving the frog. You'll see that when you let go, the frog suddenly starts moving in the opposite direction. It doesn't look quite right: you'd expect the frog to continue moving in the direction you were dragging for a bit before he moves back to the initial point.

The initial velocity is a `CGVector`, measured in units that correspond to the total animation distance — that is, if you are animating something by 100 points, and the object is already moving at 100 points per second, the vector would have a magnitude of 1.0.

You're going to amend the app so that the velocity of the pan gesture used to move the frog is taken into account in the spring animation. First, change the `animateAnimalTo(location:)` method signature to include a velocity parameter:

```
func animateAnimalTo(location: CGPoint,
                     initialVelocity: CGVector = .zero)
{
```

Use this value instead of `.zero` when making the timing parameters:

```
initialVelocity: initialVelocity)
```

Now find `handleDragImage(_:)`. Replace the body of the `.ended:` case with the following code:

```
case .ended:
  if let imageDragStartPosition = imageDragStartPosition {
    //1
    let animationVelocity = sender.velocity(in: view)
    //2
    let animationDistance =
```

```
    imageContainer.center.distance(toPoint: imageDragStartPosition)
      //3
      let normalisedVelocity = animationVelocity.normalise(weight:
   animationDistance)
      //4
      let initialVelocity = normalisedVelocity.toVector
      animateAnimalTo(
        location: imageDragStartPosition,
        initialVelocity: initialVelocity)
    }
    imageDragStartPosition = .none
```

Taking each numbered comment in turn:

1. The pan gesture has a `velocity(in:)` method describing how fast it's moving measured in points per second. This is returned as a `CGPoint` rather than a `CGVector`, but both structures are very similar.

2. A convenience method included in the starter project calculates the distance in points from the current position to the animation's end position. This is one "unit" when talking about the animation.

3. Another convenience method uses that distance to convert the gesture velocity into animation units.

4. Finally, the `CGPoint` is converted to a `CGVector` so it can be passed to the animation method.

Build and run and fling the frog about — you will see that the animation takes your initial gesture into account.

Inspecting in-progress animations

What else can you get out of a Property Animator, besides fancy timing curves? Well, you can query what's happening at any point in the animation. The Property Animator has the following properties that tell you what's happening:

*   `state`: This is `.inactive`, `.active` or `.stopped`.

*   `isRunning`: This is a `Bool` telling you if the animation is running or not.

*   `isReversed`: This is a `Bool` telling you if the animation is reversed or not.

The `state` property is also observable via key-value-observing (KVO). KVO is quite tedious to set up, so that work has been done for you in
ViewController+Observers.swift.

Let's try it out. Add this line to the start of
`animateAnimalTo(location:initialVelocity:)`:

```
removeAnimatorObservers(animator: imageMoveAnimator)
```

And this line just above where you call `startAnimation()`:

```
addAnimatorObservers(animator: imageMoveAnimator)
```

These lines link up the segmented control at the bottom of the app to the current state of the animator. Build and run, start an animation and keep an eye on the segmented control. You can see `state` change before your eyes:

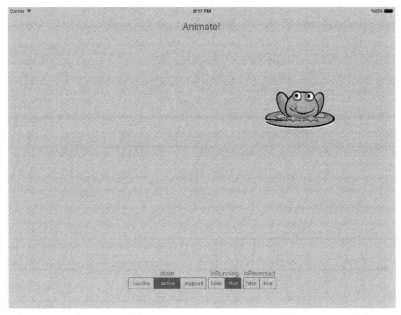

As you explore more features of the Property Animator you'll see more of these segments light up. This is where Property Animators start to get *really* interesting!

Pausing and scrubbing

With `UIView` animations, you set them going and then usually forget about them unless you also added a completion block. With Property Animators, you can reach in at any point during the animation and stop it. You can, for example, use this for animations the user can interrupt by touching the screen. Interactions like this make your users feel incredibly connected to what's happening in the app.

The Animalation project already has a handler for tapping the image view, but at the moment it doesn't do anything. In **ViewController.swift**, find handleTapOnImage(_:) and add the following code:

```
//1
guard let imageMoveAnimator = imageMoveAnimator else {
  return
}
//2
progressSlider.isHidden = true
//3
switch imageMoveAnimator.state {
case .active:
  if imageMoveAnimator.isRunning {
    //4
    imageMoveAnimator.pauseAnimation()
    progressSlider.isHidden = false
    progressSlider.value =
Float(imageMoveAnimator.fractionComplete)
  } else {
    //5
    imageMoveAnimator.startAnimation()
  }
default:
  break
}
```

Here's the step-by-step breakdown:

1. If there's no imageMoveAnimator, there's no point in doing anything, so you simply break out of the method.

2. On the provided screen you have a slider, which has currently been hidden. The slider should also be hidden in most cases when the image is tapped, so you set that here.

3. If you're testing values of an enum, it's almost always better to use a switch, even if in this case you're only interested in one outcome. Remember the possible values are .active, .inactive and .stopped.

4. If the Animator is running, then you pause it, show the slider and set the slider's value to the .fractionComplete value of the animator. UIKit currently uses CGFloat rather than Float in almost all cases, but we're starting to see a switch in the Apple APIs that favors a simpler syntax such as Float. The UISlider's value is one such example, so here you have to convert between Float and CGFloat.

5. If the Animator *isn't* running, you set it off again.

Next, add in the implementation for handleProgressSliderChanged(_:):

```
imageMoveAnimator?.fractionComplete = CGFloat(sender.value)
```

This is the reverse of what you did when pausing the animation — the value of the slider is used to set the .fractionComplete property of the animator.

Build and run the app and try to tap the frog while it's moving:

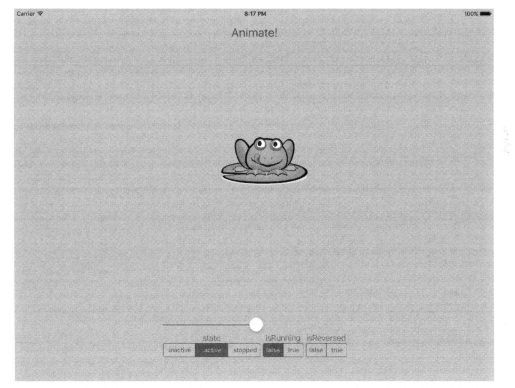

You can see the slider appear and the animation stop. Moving the slider back and forth moves the frog along its path — but note that it follows the straight point-to-point path, rather than the overshooting and oscillation coming from the spring. That's because the slider moves the animation along the **progress** axis of those charts from earlier, not the **time** axis.

It's important to note here that *pausing* an animation isn't the same as *stopping* one. Notice that the **state** indicator stays on .active when you've paused the animation.

Stopping

When a Property Animator stops, it ends all animation at the current point and, more importantly, updates the properties of the animated views to match those at the current point.

If you've ever tried to get in-flight values out of an interrupted `UIView` animation so that you can seamlessly stop it, you'll be quite excited to read this.

Inside `handleTapOnImage(_:)`, add the following line at the end of the method:

```
stopButton.isHidden = progressSlider.isHidden
```

This will show or hide the stop button in sync with the progress slider.

Find `handleStopButtonTapped(_:)` and replace the comment with the following implementation:

```
guard let imageMoveAnimator = imageMoveAnimator else {
  return
}
switch imageMoveAnimator.state {
//1
case .active:
  imageMoveAnimator.stopAnimation(false)
//2
case .inactive:
  break
//3
case .stopped:
  imageMoveAnimator.finishAnimation(at: .current)
}
```

Stopping an Animator is, or can be, a two-stage process. Above, you have the standard `guard` checking that the Animator object exists, then a switch on the state:

1. For an active Animator, you tell it to stop. The parameter indicates if the Animator should immediately end and become inactive (`true`), or if it should move to the stopped state and await further instructions (`false`)

2. There's nothing to do for the inactive state.

3. A stopped Animator should be finished at the current position.

Build and run the project, then do the following:

- Tap the animate button to start the animation.

- Tap the frog to pause the animation.

- Tap the stop button to stop the animation.

- Tap the stop button *again* to finish the animation.

If you're feeling a little confused at this point, don't worry. A Property Animator can be paused, stopped or finished, and those all mean different things:

Paused

State: `.active`

Running: `true`

This is a running Animator on which you've called `pauseAnimation()`. All of the animations are still in play. The animations can be modified, and the Animator can be started again by calling `startAnimation()`.

Stopped

State: `.stopped`

Running: `false`

This is a running or paused Animator on which you've called `stopAnimation(_:)`, passing `false`. All of the animations are removed, and the views that were being animated have their properties updated to the current state as determined by the animation. The completion block has not been called. You can manually finish the animation by calling `finishAnimation(at:)`, passing `.end`, `.start` or `.current`.

Finished

State: `.inactive`

Running: `false`

This is either an Animator that's reached the end of its animations naturally; a running Animator on which you've called `stopAnimation(_:)`, passing `true`; or a stopped Animator on which you've called `finishAnimation(at:)`. Note that you cannot call `finishAnimation(at:)` on anything other than a stopped animator.

The animated views will have their properties set to match the end point of the animation, and the completion block for the Animator will be called.

We haven't yet discussed completion blocks for Property Animators. They're a little different to those from `UIView` animations, where you get a `Bool` indicating if the animation was completed or not. One of the main reasons they're different is because a Property Animator can be run in reverse.

Reversing

You might be thinking "Why would I ever want to run an animation in reverse?" A good use case is when you're working with gesture-driven interfaces. Imagine using something like a swipe gesture to dismiss a presented view, where, during the dismiss animation, the user decides not to dismiss it, and swipes back slightly in the other direction.

A Property Animator can take all of this into account and run the animation back to the start point, without having to store or recalculate anything.

To demonstrate this in the sample app, you're going to change the function of the **Animate** button. If you tap it while an animation is running, it's going to reverse the animation.

In **ViewController.swift** find `handleAnimateButtonTapped(_:)` and replace the implementation with the following:

```
if let imageMoveAnimator = imageMoveAnimator,
imageMoveAnimator.isRunning {
  imageMoveAnimator.isReversed = !imageMoveAnimator.isReversed
} else {
  animateAnimalToRandomLocation()
}
```

For a running animation, this will toggle the reversed property; otherwise, it will start the animation as before.

Build and run, then tap the animate button — then tap it again. You'll see the frog return to its original position, but using the spring timing to settle naturally back into place! You can see that the **isReversed** indicator on the screen updates appropriately.

Note: At the time of writing this chapter, there appears to be a bug in Xcode 8 beta 4 where isReversed does not update properly.

You now have three different ways that the animation can end: it can finish normally, you can stop it half way, or you can reverse it to finish where it started. This is useful information to know when you have a completion block on the animation, so you're now going to add one now.

In `animateAnimalTo(location: initialVelocity:)`, add the following code after you call `addAnimations(_:)`:

```
imageMoveAnimator?.addCompletion { position in
  switch position {
```

```
    case .end: print("End")
    case .start: print("Start")
    case .current: print("Current")
    }
  }
```

The completion block takes a `UIViewAnimatingPosition` enum as its argument, which tells you what state the Animator was in when it finished.

Build and run the project and try to obtain all three completion block printouts by ending the animation at the end, start or somewhere in the middle.

For a more practical demonstration of the various states of a completion block, you're going to add a second animation and run the two of them together.

Multiple animators

You can add as many changes as you like to a single Property Animator, but it's also possible to have several Animators working on the same view. You're going to add a second Animator to run alongside the first, which will change the animal image displayed.

In **ViewController.swift** add the following array of images, before the class declaration of ViewController:

```
let animalImages = [
  #imageLiteral(resourceName: "bear"),
  #imageLiteral(resourceName: "frog"),
  #imageLiteral(resourceName: "wolf"),
  #imageLiteral(resourceName: "cat")
]
```

You'll see the pasted code transform into image literals... how cool is that?

Next, underneath the declaration for `imageMoveAnimator`, add a declaration for the second animator:

```
var imageChangeAnimator: UIViewPropertyAnimator?
```

In the extension where `animateAnimalToRandomLocation()` lives, add the following new method:

```
func animateRandomAnimalChange() {
  //1
  let randomIndex =
```

```
      Int(arc4random_uniform(UInt32(animalImages.count)))
        let randomImage = animalImages[randomIndex]
        //2
        let duration = imageMoveAnimator?.duration ?? 3.0

        //3
        let snapshot =
    animalImageView.snapshotView(afterScreenUpdates: false)!
        imageContainer.addSubview(snapshot)
        animalImageView.alpha = 0
        animalImageView.image = randomImage

        //4
        imageChangeAnimator = UIViewPropertyAnimator(
            duration: duration,
            curve: .linear) {
              self.animalImageView.alpha = 1
              snapshot.alpha = 0
        }

        //5
        imageChangeAnimator?.addCompletion({ (position) in
            snapshot.removeFromSuperview()
        })

        //6
        imageChangeAnimator?.startAnimation()
    }
```

Here's the play-by-play:

1. Select a random destination image from the array you just created.

2. You want the duration of this animation to match that from the move animation. Remember that a spring animation ignores the duration you pass in. Instead, the duration is calculated based on the spring parameters and is available for you to use via the `duration` property.

3. Here you set up the animation: you take a snapshot of the current animal, add that to the image container, make the actual image view invisible and set the new image.

4. Create a new Animator with a linear timing curve (you don't really want a spring for a fade animation) and within that, fade in the image view and fade out the snapshot for a cross-dissolve effect.

5. When the animation is complete, remove the snapshot.

6. Finally, start the animation.

Add a call to this method in `handleAnimateButtonTapped(_:)`, right after the call to `animateAnimalToRandomLocation()`:

```
animateRandomAnimalChange()
```

Build and run and hit the animate button, and you'll see the image cross-fade while it moves:

> **Note:** The animal won't always change. Sometimes the randomly selected animal is the same as the one that's already there!

If you pause the animation, you'll see that the cross-fade merrily continues. This might be what you want — it can be handy to have independent animations on the same object. However, for this app, you're going to sync up the state of the two animators.

Find `handleTapOnImage(_:)` and where you pause or start `imageMoveAnimator`, do the same to `imageChangeAnimator`:

```
case .active:
  if imageMoveAnimator.isRunning {
    imageMoveAnimator.pauseAnimation()
    imageChangeAnimator?.pauseAnimation()
```

```
    progressSlider.isHidden = false
    progressSlider.value =
  Float(imageMoveAnimator.fractionComplete)
  } else {
    imageMoveAnimator.startAnimation()
    imageChangeAnimator?.startAnimation()
  }
```

Change `handleProgressSliderChanged(_:)` to adjust the second Animator by adding this line:

```
imageChangeAnimator?.fractionComplete = CGFloat(sender.value)
```

In `handleAnimateButtonTapped(_:)`, after you set the reversed state of the move animator, mirror it for the image change animator:

```
imageChangeAnimator?.isReversed = imageMoveAnimator.isReversed
```

Finally, you need to handle the stopping. You're not going to do quite the same thing here — abandoning the fade animation half way through would look rather odd. In `handleStopButtonTapped(_:)`, after you stop the move animator, simply pause the image change animator:

```
imageChangeAnimator?.pauseAnimation()
```

After you finish the move animator in the `.stopped` case, add the following code:

```
if let imageChangeAnimator = imageChangeAnimator,
   let timing = imageChangeAnimator.timingParameters {
  imageChangeAnimator.continueAnimation(
    withTimingParameters: timing,
    durationFactor: 0.2)
}
```

`continueAnimation` lets you swap in a brand new timing curve (or spring) and a duration factor, which is used as a multiplier of the original animation duration. You can only do this to a paused animator. This means your fade animation will quickly finish, while the move animation has stopped. This is an example of the great flexibility and control that Property Animators can give you.

Build and run the app, and try pausing, scrubbing, stopping, finishing (remember to tap "stop" *twice* to finish) and reversing the animation. You'll notice a problem when you reverse — the animal disappears! Where's your doggone frog gone?

Remember what's happening in the fade animation — a snapshot of the old image is added, the image view is updated and made transparent, then a cross fade happens. In the completion block, the snapshot is removed.

If the animation is reversed, when it "finishes" (i.e. returns to the start), the image view is transparent and the snapshot view is removed, which means you can't see anything. You need to do different things in the completion block depending on which position the animation ended in.

Go to `animateRandomAnimalChange()` and add the following line before you take the snapshot:

```
let originalImage = animalImageView.image
```

This keeps a reference to the original animal, which you'll need if the animation is reversed. Add the following code to the completion block of the `imageChangeAnimator`:

```
if position == .start {
  self.animalImageView.image = originalImage
  self.animalImageView.alpha = 1
}
```

This code restores the alpha and the image as they were before the animation started.

Build and run again, reverse the animation and behold! No more disappearing animals!

View controller transitions

Property Animators, or to be specific, objects that conform to `UIViewImplicitlyAnimating`, can also be plugged in to your interactive view controller transitions. Previously, you could start an interactive transition, track a gesture, and then hand it off to finish or be canceled by the system — but after that point, the user had no control. When you add Property Animators to the mix, you can switch multiple times between interactive and non-interactive modes, making your users feel really connected to what's happening on the screen.

Setting up and building interactive transitions is a complex topic outside the scope of this chapter. See https://www.raywenderlich.com/110536/custom-uiviewcontroller-transitions or our book *iOS Animations By Tutorials* for an overview. The starter project already contains an interactive transition; you're going to amend this to make it use Property Animators and become interruptible.

First, take a look at the existing transition. Open **Main.storyboard**, find the **Animals** button on the bottom right of the main view controller and make it visible by unchecking the **Hidden** box. Build and run the project and tap the button.

To dismiss the controller interactively, pull down:

Once you've let go, the animation will either return to the top or complete.

If you try and grab the screen as it's disappearing (the transition is super slow to help you with this!), nothing will happen.

To make an interactive transition super-duper interruptibly interactive, there's a new method to implement on your `UIViewControllerAnimatedTransitioning` object. Open **DropDownDismissAnimator.swift**. This is a standard transition Animator object. Add the following new method:

```
func interruptibleAnimator(using transitionContext:
UIViewControllerContextTransitioning) ->
UIViewImplicitlyAnimating {
  let animator = UIViewPropertyAnimator(
    duration: transitionDuration(using: transitionContext),
    curve: .easeInOut) {
      self.performAnimations(using: transitionContext)
  }
  return animator
}
```

This creates a new Property Animator that simply calls the same animation method, `UIView` animations and all, that is currently used by the transition.

The project uses a subclass of `UIPercentDrivenInteractiveTransition` for the interaction controller for this transition. Percent driven transitions have a new method, `pause()`, to switch the transition context from non-interactive to interactive mode.

You want this to happen when the user starts another pan gesture. Open **DropDownInteractionController.swift** , which is the interaction controller. This class uses a pan gesture to update the progress of the transition, and when the gesture ends, sets it back to non-interactive mode with either `finish()` or `cancel()` depending on the position of the view.

Add two new properties, underneath `isInteractive`:

```
var hasStarted = false
var interruptedPercent: CGFloat = 0
```

You will use `hasStarted` to decide if a new pan gesture is the start of a new dismissal, or an attempt to interrupt an ongoing dismissal. If you do interrupt an ongoing dismissal, `interruptedPercent` will be used to make sure the pan gesture's translation takes the current position of the view into account.

Inside `handle(pan:)`, amend the calculation of `percent`:

```
let percent = (translation / pan.view!.bounds.height) +
  interruptedPercent
```

You're adding the interrupted percent on here, because if the dismissal was already 50% through when the user touches the screen, that needs to be reflected in the position of the view.

Inside the same method, replace the `.began` case in the switch statement with the following code:

```
case .began:
  if !hasStarted {
    hasStarted = true
    isInteractive = true
    interruptedPercent = 0
    viewController?.dismiss(animated: true, completion: nil)
  } else {
    pause()
    interruptedPercent = percentComplete
  }
```

If this isn't the first gesture in the dismissal, the transition is paused and the current percentage is taken from it. The transition must be paused **before** you read the percentage, otherwise you'll get an inaccurate figure.

Finally, switch over to **AppDelegate.swift** and add the following line to the `animationCleanup` closure created in `animationController(forDismissed:)`:

```
interactionController?.hasStarted = false
```

This ensures that the interaction controller is properly reset when the animations are complete.

Build and run the project, show the animals view, then have fun interrupting yourself and wobbling the view up and down!

Where to go from here?

Congratulations! You've had a good exploration of the new powers available to you now that you can use Property Animators! Go forth and fill your apps with interruptible, interactive animations, including an extra level of awesomeness in your view controller transitions.

The WWDC video, 2016 session 216, available at https://developer.apple.com/videos/play/wwdc2016/216/ is full of useful information.

Chapter 10: Measurements and Units

By Rich Turton

You've probably written code like this:

```
let distance: CGFloat // Distance is in miles
```

When dealing with real-world units in code, it's easy just to use one of the built-in numeric types and try to remember all the places you're supposed to use units along with the number, like the following:

```
distanceLabel.text = "\(distance) miles"
```

But that's not quite correct if there's only one mile, or if the mile has a lot of decimal places, so you'd have to add even more code to counter this. Then it doesn't localize properly, so you add some *more* code. Then people want to see their distances in kilometers, so you add a preference and some conversion logic.

If this is a familiar story, you're in luck. The Foundation framework has some exciting new additions this year for solving exactly these problems. You're going to learn about Measurement and Unit, and how they allow you to do the following:

- Get rid of fiddly conversions

- Use strongly typed values that prevent you from making unit mistakes; for example, using yards when you meant Kelvin

- Show values to the user in terms they understand

- Get all this power for your *own* measurements and units.

Date intervals

Another exciting addition to Foundation this year is the date interval — a period from one `Date` to another.

Again, this represents a problem that is commonly solved by having to write a lot of code that you probably don't test (admit it), and you almost certainly don't test for international users. Date intervals and the associated date interval formatter will make your life easier when you need to work with dates.

As I'm sure you can agree, dates are hard, so all help is welcome!

Measurement and Unit

To get started, you're going to learn about two new types that will make a *measurable* improvement to your code. :]

The `Measurement` struct doesn't sound like much. It has just two properties:

- `value`, which is a `Double`

- `unit`, which is a `Unit`

`Unit` is even more minimal — it has just one propert:

- `symbol`, which is a `String`

This minimal implementation gives you some benefits. Given a `Measurement`, you'd know right away what its units were, and be able to format it for display using the symbol that comes with the unit. But the real power of the system comes from two things:

- The `Unit` subclasses that are included with Foundation

- The use of generics to associate a particular `Measurement` with a given `Unit`

Unit subclasses

`Dimension` is a subclass of `Unit` in Foundation. This represents units that have a dimension, such as length or temperature. Dimensions have a base unit and a converter that can interpret the value to and from the base unit.

`Dimension` is an abstract class, which means you're expected to subclass it to make your own dimensions. A wide variety are already included in Foundation.

As an example, there is a `UnitLength` class. This is a subclass of `Dimension` used to represent lengths or distances. The base unit is the meter, which is the SI unit for length.

> **Note:** SI stands for Système International, the internationally agreed system of measurements. Readers from the US, brace yourselves for learning that you are measuring almost everything "incorrectly". :]

`UnitLength` has over 20 class variables which are instances of `UnitLength`. Each one has a different converter so that it can be translated to and from meters.

`UnitLength.meters`, for example, has a converter that does nothing, because the unit is already in the base unit. `UnitLength.miles` will have a converter that knows that there are around 0.000621371 miles per meter.

Units and generics

When you create a `Measurement`, you give it a value and a unit. That unit becomes a generic constraint on the measurement. Knowing that a measurement is associated with a particular `Unit` means that Swift won't let you do things with two measurements that don't use the same unit, and it means that you *can* do useful things with measurements that do — like math.

I want to ride my bicycle

A triathlon is a fun event if your idea of fun is spending all day hurting. That means the annual raywenderlich.com team triathlon event is particularly fun!

The annual raywenderlich.com team triathalon includes:

- a 25km bike ride

- a 3 nautical mile swim

- a half marathon run

Let's see how we can create some measurements representing these lengths using the new classes in Foundation. Open a new playground and enter the following code:

```
let cycleRide = Measurement(value: 25,
  unit: UnitLength.kilometers)
let swim = Measurement(value: 3,
  unit: UnitLength.nauticalMiles)
```

Here you define the length of the cycle and swim using the new `Measurement` class. You simply set the `value` and choose the appropriate `unit`: simple!

But what about the half marathon?

A marathon is 26 miles, 385 yards. This awkward number comes from the 1908 London Olympics, where the organizers planned a course of 26 miles, then had to add an extra bit so that the race would finish neatly in front of the Royal Box. Do you know what 26 miles, 385 yards is in "Decimal miles"? I don't, and now, I don't have to.

To create a measurement of a marathon, add the following to the playground:

```
let marathon = Measurement(value: 26, unit: UnitLength.miles)
    + Measurement(value: 385, unit: UnitLength.yards)
```

Notice that you've been able to add these measurements together, even though one is in miles and the other is in yards. That's because the units are all `UnitLength`. The final value of `marathon` is in the base unit, because that's the only result that makes sense when adding two different instances together. Add the following code to the playground to take a look at the units in use:

```
marathon.unit.symbol
swim.unit.symbol
cycleRide.unit.symbol
```

The results sidebar shows the units in use for each measurement:

```
"m"
"NM"
"km"
```

These stand for meters, nautical miles, and kilometer respectively.

Remember that the raywenderlich.com team triathalon is a half-marathon, not a full marathon. You don't really think computer geeks like us could run a full marathon, do you? :]

So next, add the following code to find the length of a half-marathon:

```
let run = marathon / 2
```

Then you can get the total distance covered in the triathlon like this:

```
let triathlon = cycleRide + swim + run
```

As you might expect, `triathlon` shows up in the results sidebar in meters:

```
51653.442 m
```

This isn't particularly useful, but generics can help you here. `Measurement` instances with a `Unit` subclassing `Dimension` have a useful extra feature: they can convert to other units, or be converted to other units. To see the triathlon total in miles, add this line:

```
triathlon.converted(to: .miles)
```

The results sidebar will now show you 32.096 miles and change.

In addition to mathematical operations, you can also compare measurements of the same `Unit`. To find out if the cycle ride is longer than the run, you can do this:

```
cycleRide > run
```

It's true: A 25km cycle ride is longer than running a half marathon. Which would you rather do?

If all of this exercise has left you feeling short of energy, the next section should help.

Uranium Fever

You've almost certainly heard of Einstein's equation $E = mc^2$. It states that the energy (E) contained in a mass (m) is equal to the mass multiplied by the square of the speed of light (c). In this equation, energy is measured in joules, mass in kilograms, and the speed of light in meters per second.

Light is really rather fast — 299,792,458 meters per second. This suggests that everything contains huge amounts of energy. Perhaps luckily, that energy is quite hard to release.

One way to convert mass into energy is nuclear fission. The type commonly used in nuclear power stations works a little like this (it's a bit more complicated in reality, but you're not here to get a nuclear physics degree):

• Uranium-235 gets hit by a neutron

• Uranium-235 absorbs the neutron and briefly becomes Uranium-236

• Then it breaks apart into Krypton-92, Barium-141 and three more neutrons

• Those neutrons carry on to hit more Uranium-235...

> **Note:** If you *do* have a nuclear physics degree, congratulations on your change of career, but please don't get upset about errors or simplifications in this chapter.

You're going to do some calculations in the playground to work out what is happening in this reaction.

First of all, you're going to define a unit to deal with atomic masses. Atoms aren't very heavy things on their own, and physicists use *Atomic Mass Units* to talk about them. One atomic mass unit is approximately the mass of a proton or neutron, and is approximately 1.661 x 10 to the -27th power kilograms. That's quite a small number.

Add the following code to the playground to create this instance of `UnitMass`:

```
let amus = UnitMass(symbol: "amu",
  converter: UnitConverterLinear(coefficient: 1.661e-27))
```

This is your first custom unit. You'll look at converters in more detail later on, but for now, understand that you're saying you've got a new way of representing mass, and you've specified how your new way relates to the base unit for `UnitMass`, which is the kilogram.

Add measurements to describe the elements that go in to the nuclear reaction:

```
let u235 = Measurement(value: 235.043924, unit: amus)
let neutron = Measurement(value: 1.008665, unit: amus)
let massBefore = u235 + neutron
```

Now add measurements to describe the products of the fission reaction:

```
let kr92 = Measurement(value: 91.926156, unit: amus)
let ba141 = Measurement(value: 140.914411, unit: amus)
let massAfter = kr92 + ba141 + (3 * neutron)
```

`massAfter` is less than `massBefore`. What's happened? It's been converted to energy! You can use $E = mc^2$ to find out how much energy.

This function uses Einstein's equation to convert mass into energy:

```
func emc2(mass: Measurement<UnitMass>) ->
Measurement<UnitEnergy> {
  let speedOfLight = Measurement(value: 299792458,
    unit: UnitSpeed.metersPerSecond)
  let energy = mass.converted(to: .kilograms).value *
    pow(speedOfLight.value, 2)
  return Measurement(value: energy, unit: UnitEnergy.joules)
}
```

> **Note:** In the calculation you have to use the `value` of the measurement. That's because relationships between different dimensions (like mass and speed) aren't yet defined in Foundation. For example, you can't divide a `UnitLength` by a `UnitDuration` and get a `UnitSpeed`.

Find out how much energy is released in the fission of a single Uranium-235 atom like this:

```
let massDifference = massBefore - massAfter
let energy = emc2(mass: massDifference)
```

That gives you a very small number of joules. You don't run a nuclear reactor with a single atom of uranium, though; you use a rod or some pellets of the stuff. So how much energy is contained in a given weight of uranium?

The first step is to do a little chemical calculation. You want to find out how many atoms of uranium are in a given mass. That's done by this function:

```
func atoms(atomicMass: Double, substanceMass:
Measurement<UnitMass>) -> Double {
    let grams = substanceMass.converted(to: .grams)
    let moles = grams.value / atomicMass
    let avogadro = 6.0221409e+23
    return moles * avogadro
}
```

This formula uses a special number called Avogadro's number which defines the number of atoms in a *mole*, which is in turn approximately the number of amus that weigh one gram. Don't worry too much about understanding the formula, but note that you can pass in any `UnitMass` you like and get a value out of the other end.

Use this function to get the number of atoms in 1 lb of uranium, then multiply that by the value you obtained earlier for the energy released by a single atom:

```
let numberOfAtoms = atoms(atomicMass: u235.value, substanceMass:
Measurement(value: 1, unit: .pounds))
let energyPerPound = energy * numberOfAtoms
```

The number has now gone from a meaninglessly small number to a meaninglessly large one. Let's do a final calculation to give it some context. The average American home uses 11,700 kWh (kilowatt hours) of electricity per year. `UnitEnergy` has you covered:

```
let kwh = energyPerPound.converted(to: .kilowattHours)
kwh.value / 11700
```

You should come up with a number close to 766. A pound of uranium can power 766 American homes for a year!

In the results sidebar in the playground, the numbers are often displayed with lots of decimal places or exponentials. In the next section, you're going to take control of presenting your measurements with `MeasurementFormatter`.

Measure for MeasurementFormatter

`MeasurementFormatter` is a `Formatter` subclass just like `DateFormatter` and `NumberFormatter`. It can take a lot of the work out of presenting your measurements to the user, as it will automatically use the preferred units for the user's locale.

> **Note:** Unlike date and number formatters, measurement formatters are one-way. You can't use them to take a string like "1 kWh" and turn it into a `Measurement`.

It's getting hot in here

Open a new playground to start exploring measurement formatters.

Create a measurement representing a pleasantly warm Northern European summer's day:

```
let temperature = Measurement(value: 24, unit:
UnitTemperature.celsius)
```

Now, create a measurement formatter and use it to get a string from the measurement:

```
let formatter = MeasurementFormatter()
formatter.string(from: temperature)
```

Because the locale in playgrounds is the US by default, your sensible measurement has been changed into "nonsense units" that only one country in the world understands. Fix that by setting a more sensible locale:

```
formatter.locale = Locale(identifier: "en_GB")
formatter.string(from: temperature)
```

Measurement formatter has a property, `UnitOptions`, which acts as a sort of grab bag of random options which didn't really fit elsewhere. There are only three options in there, one of which specifically relates to temperature.

Add these lines:

```
formatter.unitOptions = .temperatureWithoutUnit
formatter.string(from: temperature)
```

This tells the formatter to skip the letter indicating the temperature scale. This option also stops the formatter changing the scale to match the locale, as that would be hopelessly confusing. Check by changing the locale back:

```
formatter.locale = Locale(identifier: "en_US")
formatter.string(from: temperature)
```

The second unit option you can specify tells the formatter not to change the units you've passed in. Add the following lines to see this in action:

```
formatter.unitOptions = .providedUnit
formatter.string(from: temperature)
```

You'll see that the formatter is using Celsius again, even though it is still in the US locale.

The third option doesn't relate to temperatures. You'll look at that in the next section.

I would walk 500 miles

Remember earlier, when you added miles to yards to nautical miles to kilometers, and the answer was given in meters?

The number of meters was quite high, and to present a meaningful value to the user you would have to have a conversion step to a more sensible unit, and you may need to write code to determine what that more sensible unit should be. Measurement formatters can do this for you, for some kinds of units.

Add the following code to the playground:

```
let run = Measurement(value: 20000, unit: UnitLength.meters)
formatter.string(from: run)
```

The formatter gives you `20,000 m` as the result; the formatter you're using has a locale of the US, but is set to use the provided unit. Now add these lines:

```
formatter.unitOptions = [.naturalScale, .providedUnit]
formatter.string(from: run)
```

Now you get a more sensible `20 km`. `.naturalScale` works together with `.providedUnit` to stay within the measurement system given by the measurement, but to move up and down through related units.

```
let speck = Measurement(value: 0.0002, unit: UnitLength.meters)
formatter.string(from: speck)
```

This gives you the result `0.2 mm`.

The `unitStyle` option on the formatter will tell it to present the full names or abbreviations of units where possible:

```
formatter.unitStyle = .long
formatter.string(from: run)
```

This gives you the result `20 kilometers`.

The default value is `.medium`, which prints the symbol of the unit in use. There is currently no public API to provide extended or shorter names or symbols for your own units.

The final aspect of a measurement formatter you can customize is the way the numbers themselves are presented. What do we know that's good at formatting numbers? A number formatter!

You can create a number formatter and give it to the measurement formatter:

```
let numberFormatter = NumberFormatter()
numberFormatter.numberStyle = .spellOut
formatter.numberFormatter = numberFormatter
formatter.string(from: run)
```

This gives you the result `twenty kilometers`.

Up next, you're going to learn how to go beyond the units provided to you by Foundation.

(Custom) Dimension

The base class for units is `Unit`. This is an abstract class, designed for subclassing. Foundation comes with a single subclass, `Dimension`, which is *also* an abstract class. There are lots of subclasses of `Dimension`, each one of which represents a specific quantifiable *thing*, like length or area or time. The base unit for the dimension is defined at the class level — there is a class function, `baseUnit()`, which returns the instance used as the base unit.

Instances feature a symbol and a converter for translating to and from the base unit. Again, Foundation loads each `Dimension` subclass with class variables giving you pre-made common units.

This is a little complicated to understand. Here's a diagram to clarify things:

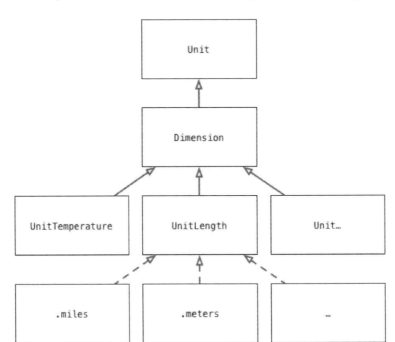

To instantiate a `Dimension` or one of its subclasses, you pass in a symbol and a converter. The converter, as its name suggests, is responsible for converting the value of the unit back and forth from the base unit specified at class level.

The converter has to be a subclass of `UnitConverter`, which, in a pattern that should be familiar by now, is an abstract superclass. There is one subclass provided — `UnitConverterLinear` — which allows linear conversion between units.

Most things you measure start at zero; zero miles is zero meters is zero furlongs. This means that a simple coefficient (multiplication factor) is good enough for most conversions.

Some things, like temperature, are a little more complicated. When people were inventing temperature scales, they had no concept of absolute zero, so they placed zero somewhere sensible (when water freezes) or somewhere silly (the temperature of equal parts ice and salt). To cope with these situations you need a constant as well as the coefficient.

`UnitConverterLinear` is created with a coefficient and a constant; the constant has a default value of zero. When you made the `amus UnitMass` instance, you used a linear converter. You're going to look at an example in more detail now.

Chain of fools

It seems like in Olde England when people would have a thing that needed measuring, they would look around them, pick the first thing they saw and use that as a unit. Hence we have poppyseed, finger, hand, foot, rod, chain, and many more.

It turns out that a chain is 20.1168 meters. So, you could create a unit to use in measurements like this:

```
let chains = UnitLength(symbol: "ch",
  converter: UnitConverterLinear(coefficient: 20.1168))
```

This is similar to the code you used earlier when creating amus. However, imagine that you believe the chain is such a useful unit of measure, you want it to be available everywhere, just like the meter or the mile. To do this, you create an extension on UnitLength and add a new class variable. Add the following code to a new playground:

```
extension UnitLength {
  class var chains: UnitLength {
    return UnitLength(symbol: "ch",
      converter: UnitConverterLinear(coefficient: 20.1168))
  }
}
```

You can then use this unit just like any other. A cricket pitch is one chain from wicket to wicket:

```
let cricketPitch = Measurement(value: 1, unit:
UnitLength.chains)
```

This works just like any of the built-in units. You can do a few conversions:

```
cricketPitch.converted(to: .baseUnit())
cricketPitch.converted(to: .furlongs)
(80 * cricketPitch).converted(to: .miles)
```

This gives the values you'd expect; a chain is 20.1168 meters, as you've defined, and in a rare occurrence of the number 10 in Imperial measurements, a chain is 0.1 furlongs. There are 8 furlongs in a mile, so 80 chains, give or take a bit of rounding, is a mile.

So to get a fully-qualified extra unit added to any dimension, all you need to do is provide a class variable, and all that needs to have is a symbol and a converter. Go and sing a few verses of Unchained Melody to celebrate, but don't get too carried away — the next part is a little more complicated.

Turning it up to 11

You'll probably have heard of **decibels** (dB), associated with how loud things are. The decibel is actually a measure of the *ratio* of two values, and not only that, it's done on a logarithmic scale.

Decibels are used to measure changes in amplitude or power. Because of the logarithmic scale, they allow you to talk about quite large changes and still use sensible numbers. For example, a doubling of power is approximately 3dB, but increasing power by a factor of 1 million is only 60dB.

Converting between power ratios and decibels is therefore not possible with the linear unit converter, because the relationship between the two is not linear. You're going to make a new subclass of `UnitConverter` to express this relationship, and a new `Dimension` subclass to hold your units.

> **Note:** Don't worry too much about following or understanding the math in this example. The idea is to learn about creating a new dimension and a new converter.

First, the converter. Make a new subclass of `UnitConverter` in your playground:

```
// 1
class UnitConverterLogarithmic: UnitConverter, NSCopying {
  // 2
  let coefficient: Double
  let logBase: Double
  // 3
  init(coefficient: Double, logBase: Double) {
    self.coefficient = coefficient
    self.logBase = logBase
  }
  // 4
  func copy(with zone: NSZone? = nil) -> Any {
    return self
  }
}
```

Here's the breakdown:

1. You're subclassing `UnitConverter`. Subclasses must also implement `NSCopying`, though that isn't mentioned in the documentation at the time of writing this chapter.

2. These are the two properties needed to perform logarithmic conversions. A coefficient and a log base.

3. This is the initializer which allows you to set the two properties.

4. This is the implementation required for `NSCopying`. Your class is immutable, so you can just return `self`.

There are two methods you must override to make a working converter to convert to and from the base unit. These calculations are the standard methods for dealing with logarithms; it isn't important for the chapter that you follow the math. Add the following methods to your converter class:

```
override func baseUnitValue(fromValue value: Double) -> Double {
  return coefficient * log(value) / log(logBase)
}

override func value(fromBaseUnitValue baseUnitValue: Double) ->
Double {
  return exp(baseUnitValue * log(logBase) / coefficient)
}
```

These two methods allow your converter to convert measurements to and from the base unit. That's your unit converter done. Now for the `Dimension` subclass. The thing you're measuring is a ratio, so you're going to call the subclass `UnitRatio`. Add the following code to the playground:

```
class UnitRatio: Dimension {

  class var decibels: UnitRatio {
    return UnitRatio(symbol: "dB",
      converter: UnitConverterLinear(coefficient: 1))
  }

  override class func baseUnit() -> UnitRatio {
    return UnitRatio.decibels
  }
}
```

This has created a new `Dimension` subclass. There's a single instance, `decibels`. This is set up just like the `chains` that you added to `UnitLength`. Decibels is going to be the base unit, so to "convert" it doesn't need to do any work, since the linear converter with a coefficient of 1 will do the job.

The class method `baseUnit()` has to be implemented for all `Dimension` subclasses. This just returns the `decibels` class variable.

Now you can add the two ratios that can be converted to decibels — amplitude and power. Add the following class variables to `UnitRatio`:

```
class var amplitudeRatio: UnitRatio {
  return UnitRatio(symbol: "", converter:
    UnitConverterLogarithmic(coefficient: 20, logBase: 10))
```

```
}

class var powerRatio: UnitRatio {
  return UnitRatio(symbol: "", converter:
    UnitConverterLogarithmic(coefficient: 10, logBase: 10))
}
```

Now you're ready to use your new dimension. To double the volume of something, that's a power ratio of 2. Add this code to create that measurement, and convert it to decibels:

```
let doubleVolume = Measurement(value: 2, unit:
UnitRatio.powerRatio)
doubleVolume.converted(to: .decibels)
```

That's approximately three decibels, which is what you expected from the introduction to this section.

To take your amp "up to 11" from 10 is a power ratio of 1.1:

```
let upTo11 = Measurement(value: 1.1, unit: UnitRatio.powerRatio)
upTo11.converted(to: .decibels)
```

That's only 0.4dB. Doesn't sound quite as impressive, does it?

You've covered a lot of theory here — congratulations! From tiring sports to rocking out, via a spot of nuclear physics. But you're not done. If you need a holiday after all that, the next section will help you out.

24 Hours From Tulsa

Any app that deals with dates probably has to deal with date intervals as well. You might be dealing with events that have start and end times. How do you display that event? How do you do calculations and comparisons between events?

All of this was possible to write yourself, but it was easy to get wrong. `DateInterval` and `DateIntervalFormatter` are here to help.

A `DateInterval` has a start `Date` and a duration, so it represents a specific *period* of time, in the same way a `Date` represents a specific *point* in time.

You can create a date interval in two ways: either with a start date and a duration, or with a start date and end date. You can't make an interval with an end date before the start date.

In a new playground page, add this code:

```
let today = Date()
let twentyFourHours: TimeInterval = 60 * 60 * 24
let tomorrow = today + twentyFourHours
let overmorrow = tomorrow + twentyFourHours

let next24Hours = DateInterval(start: today, duration:
twentyFourHours)
let nowTillThen = DateInterval(start: today, end: tomorrow)
```

This sets up some useful dates and then creates two date intervals using each method. They both represent the same period of time, and you can test this equality:

```
next24Hours == nowTillThen
```

This code evaluates to true. You can perform other comparisons between intervals:

```
let next48Hours = DateInterval(start: today, end: overmorrow)
next48Hours > next24Hours //true
```

If date intervals start at the same time, the longest interval counts as the larger of the two.

```
let allTomorrow = DateInterval(start: tomorrow, end: overmorrow)
allTomorrow > next24Hours //true
allTomorrow > next48Hours //true
```

If two date intervals start at different times, the one with the latest start date is larger, and the lengths of the intervals are not compared.

There are more useful methods on DateInterval. Add this code to the playground to create an interval covering a normal working week:

```
// 1
let calendar = Calendar.current
var components = calendar.dateComponents([.year, .weekOfYear],
  from: Date())
// 2
components.weekday = 2
components.hour = 8
let startOfWeek = calendar.date(from: components)!
// 3
components.weekday = 6
components.hour = 17
let endOfWeek = calendar.date(from: components)!
// 4
let workingWeek = DateInterval(start: startOfWeek,
  end: endOfWeek)
```

Here's the breakdown:

1. Get a reference to the current calendar and then get the year and week components of the current date.

2. Set the weekday to `Monday` and the hour to 8 and use this to create 8am on Monday. Note that this is the correct way to work with dates. Adding time intervals will let you down when you happen to fall across a daylight savings change!

3. Set the weekday to `Friday` and the hour to 17 to make 5pm on Friday. Cocktail time!

4. Create a date interval with those two dates.

It turns out you've won a surprise holiday! It's two weeks long, and it starts right now! ("Now" being 1pm on Friday. You have to allow a little poetic license here because you could be following this chapter at any point in the week, but the code has to work the same way!).

Add this code to represent your holiday:

```
components.hour = 13
let startOfHoliday = calendar.date(from: components)!
let endOfHoliday = calendar.date(byAdding: .day,
   value: 14, to: startOfHoliday)!
let holiday = DateInterval(start: startOfHoliday,
   end: endOfHoliday)
```

This creates the 1pm on Friday date, adds 14 days to get the end date, and makes a new interval.

You can find out if the holiday start date falls within the working week like this:

```
workingWeek.contains(startOfHoliday) //true
```

You can find out if the holiday and the working week intersect each other like this:

```
workingWeek.intersects(holiday) //true
```

And, most excitingly, you can see exactly how much of the working week you're missing out on by going on your holiday:

```
let freedom = workingWeek.intersection(with: holiday)
```

This gives you a date interval beginning at 1pm on Friday and ending at 5pm. The method returns an optional; if the two intervals don't intersect, you get `.none` back.

You may have noticed that these date intervals are tricky to read in the results bar of the playground. You can change that with `DateIntervalFormatter`.

`DateIntervalFormatter` isn't too exciting; you configure it just like a `DateFormatter`, and it then applies the format to the start and end dates of the interval and puts a hyphen in between them. But it does save you having to do that step yourself.

Add the following code to the playground:

```
let formatter = DateIntervalFormatter()
formatter.dateStyle = .none
formatter.string(from: freedom!)
```

You knew the freedom interval only covered part of a day, so it made sense to hide the dates from the formatter. The options available for date interval formatters are the same as those for date formatters, so if you can use date formatters, you're all set.

Where to go from here?

The classes covered in this chapter aren't going to give your users mind-blowing new features, nor do they deal with particularly exciting or shiny things. But what they *do* give you is rock-solid, useful functionality, and give you more time to spend working on what makes your app unique. That's what Foundation is there for, after all: for you to build on top of!

Chapter 11: What's New with Core Data

By Rich Turton

You know what nobody likes? Typing boilerplate code. But there's another type of typing nobody likes as well — explicit typing, especially when Swift's implicit typing will do.

The new Core Data updates in iOS 10 involve less of both kinds of typing:

- **Less typing of boilerplate code** because there are new convenience methods, classes and code generations.

- **Less explicit typing** because Generic Fairy Dust™ has been sprinkled over fetch requests and fetched results controllers. The compiler now knows what class of managed object you're dealing with.

There are also some useful new features at the managed object context and persistent store coordinator level, which may change the way you're structuring your code.

If the previous two paragraphs made no sense to you, then check out our book *Core Data By Tutorials* to learn the basics of Core Data first.

If you're already familiar with Core Data, then read on to find out what's new!

In this chapter, you're going to take an app and convert it to use Core Data, using some of the handy new Core Data features in iOS 10.

The app is TaterRater, which is incredibly handy for creating ratings notes about your favorite varieties of potato. Later, you'll make a greater TaterRater using Core Dater — er, *Data*.

Getting spudded

Open the starter project, build and run, then take a look around.

The app has a split view controller holding a master list and a detail view. The detail view lets you set your own score for a particular variety of potato, view the average score given by the millions of other potato fans worldwide and view your personal potato notes.

You can edit your notes by bringing up a modal view controller which holds a text view.

The **Model** group has a text file that holds a list of potato varieties and a single model class in **Potato.swift** which represents the app's model.

You're going to start by replacing that model class with a Core Data model.

An eye to new data models

With the **Model** group selected, choose **File\New\File…**. Select **Data Model** from the **Core Data** group:

Name the file **TaterRater.xcdatamodeld**. When the model editor opens, add a new entity called **Potato** and the following attributes:

- `crowdRating` of type **Float**

- `notes` of type **String**

- `userRating` of type **Integer 16**

- `variety` of type **String**

The model editor should look like this:

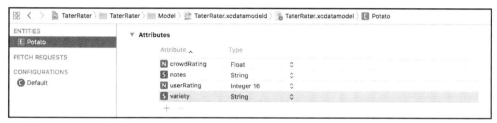

The `Potato` entity will replace the `Potato` class that currently exists in the app. You've created and typed the properties to match the existing class, so the existing code will still compile. Delete the **Potato.swift** file from the **Model** group.

Still in the model editor open the Data Model Inspector with the **Potato** entity selected. Fill in the **Name** field to say **Potato**, if it's not already.

There are some new options in the **Class** section. Take a look at the **Codegen** field. There are three options here which control how the code for that particular entity will be created:

- **Manual / None**: no files will be created.

- **Class Definition**: a full class definition will be created.

- **Category / Extension**: An extension with the core data attributes declared within will be created.

Choose **Class Definition**:

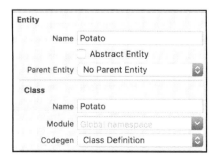

Build and run your project. It will crash, but at runtime. Does that surprise you? You removed the **Potato.swift** file and you haven't generated an `NSManagedObject` subclass file yet, but your app built just fine. What's happening?

Xcode now automatically generates the code to implement your subclasses. It puts the generated files into the Derived Data folder for the project, to further underline the idea that you're not supposed to be editing them yourself. It does this every time you change the model file.

See for yourself what has been created by finding some code that uses your entity. For example, open **AppDelegate.swift**, then Command-click on the `Potato` type to see the class definition:

```
import Foundation
import CoreData

@objc(Potato)
public class Potato: NSManagedObject {

}
```

Back in **AppDelegate.swift**, Command-click on one of the properties, such as `variety`, to see how the properties are implemented:

```
import Foundation
import CoreData

extension Potato {

    @nonobjc public class func fetchRequest() ->
NSFetchRequest<Potato> {
        return NSFetchRequest<Potato>(entityName: "Potato");
    }

    @NSManaged public var crowdRating: Float
    @NSManaged public var notes: String?
    @NSManaged public var userRating: Int16
    @NSManaged public var variety: String?

}
```

Note: If you select **Manual / None** in the model editor, then these files will not be created. If you select **Category / Extension**, only the second file will be created, and you'll have to define the class yourself. If you want the files to be included in your project directly, then choosing **Manual / None** then **Editor\Create NSManagedObject subclass…** will give you the original behavior.

Automatic code generation can make it easier to make changes in your model. However, it does not free you of the responsibility for versioning your model when you make changes to it. Lightweight migration still requires versions.

You've created your model and Xcode has made the implementations for you. But why did the app crash at runtime? The problem lies in the App Delegate, where you are creating a list of model objects based on the list of potato varieties in the text file.

The error given is **Failed to call designated initializer on NSManagedObject class 'Potato'**. At the moment the code tries to create a new potato with a blank initializer: Potato(). This doesn't work for managed objects. It's time to set up Core Data for this app and give yourself some context.

A stack with a peel

Setting up the Core Data stack used to be quite a bit of work. You'd need to create the model, then a persistent store coordinator, then a managed object context. The code to do that was rather long, and almost exactly the same for each project.

The new NSPersistentContainer class now wraps up all of that tedious work for you, as well as offering some handy new features.

Open **AppDelegate.swift** and add the following line to the top of the file:

```
import CoreData
```

Inside the class definition, add a new property:

```
var coreDataStack: NSPersistentContainer!
```

Add this to the start of application(_:didFinishLaunchingWithOptions:):

```
coreDataStack = NSPersistentContainer(name: "TaterRater")
```

This single line of code retrieves your model using the name you pass in and creates a persistent store coordinator configured with a sensible set of default options. You can change these by setting the persistentStoreDescriptions property of the persistent container. These are the properties and settings you'd normally pass to the persistent store coordinator: the URL, migration options and so forth.

One interesting new option is that you can instruct the persistent container to set up its stores asynchronously. If you have a large data set or a complex migration, then you previously had to do extra work to make sure that migrations didn't block during launching, resulting in the watchdog killing the app off. Now it's a simple setting.

You can set up asynchronous loading like this, after you've created the persistent container (but don't add this code to the project):

```
coreDataStack.persistentStoreDescriptions.first?
  .shouldAddStoreAsynchronously = true
```

For this project you'll leave the setting to its default, which lets the stores be set up synchronously. In most cases this is fine.

Add the following code right after you make the persistent container:

```
coreDataStack.loadPersistentStores {
  description, error in
  if let error = error {
    print("Error creating persistent stores: \
(error.localizedDescription)")
    fatalError()
  }
}
```

This code creates the SQL files if they aren't there already. It performs any lightweight migrations that may be required. These are the things that normally happen using `addPersistentStore...` on the persistent store coordinator.

Because you haven't told the persistent container to set its stores up asynchronously, this method blocks until the work is complete. With asynchronous setup, execution continues, so you'd have to load some sort of waiting UI at launch, then in the completion block above perform a segue to show your actual UI. The completion block is called on the calling thread.

Find the line later on in the same method where each `Potato` is created. Replace the empty initializer `let potato = Potato()` with this:

```
let potato = Potato(context: coreDataStack.viewContext)
```

This line contains two new Core Data features:

- *Finally* you can create a managed object subclass just with a context. No more entity descriptions, entity names or casting!

- The persistent container has a property, `viewContext`, which is a managed object context running on the main queue, directly connected to the persistent store coordinator. You'll learn more about the context hierarchy later.

Build and run the app now and everything will work exactly as it did before — except now you're using managed objects under the hood.

Next, you'll change the table view around so that it works with a fetched results controller instead of an array of objects.

Frenched russet controllers

Open **PotatoTableViewController.swift**. Import the core data module:

```
import CoreData
```

Then add new properties to hold the fetched results controller and the context:

```
var resultsController: NSFetchedResultsController<Potato>!
var context: NSManagedObjectContext!
```

Here's another new feature: fetched results controllers are now typed. This means that all of the arrays and objects that you get out of them are of known types. You'll see the benefits of this shortly.

Add the following code to the end of `viewDidLoad()`:

```
// 1
let request: NSFetchRequest<Potato> = Potato.fetchRequest()
// 2
let descriptor = NSSortDescriptor(key: #keyPath(Potato.variety),
ascending: true)
// 3
request.sortDescriptors = [descriptor]
// 4
resultsController = NSFetchedResultsController(fetchRequest:
request, managedObjectContext: context, sectionNameKeyPath: nil,
cacheName: nil)
do {
  try resultsController.performFetch()
} catch {
  print("Error performing fetch \(error.localizedDescription)")
}
```

Here's the breakdown:

1. Here you use the `fetchRequest()` method that is part of the generated managed object subclass code you saw earlier.

   Unfortunately this seems to clash with the new, magically typed `fetchRequest()` that has been added to `NSManagedObject`. If you don't use the type annotation, then the compiler doesn't know which method you want to use and will give you an error.

Hopefully the file generation will be fixed in a future version so that the new method can be used directly.

2. The new #keyPath syntax prevents you from mistyping keys when creating sort descriptors. You should definitely use it.

3. The sort descriptor is added to the fetch request.

4. Creating the fetched results controller and performing the fetch hasn't changed.

Now replace the implementations of the datasource methods. Change numberOfSections(in:) to this:

```
return resultsController.sections?.count ?? 0
```

This is unchanged from last year. sections is an optional so you need the nil coalescing operator to make sure you always return a valid number.

Change tableView(_: numberOfRowsInSection:) to this:

```
return resultsController.sections?[section].numberOfObjects ?? 0
```

Again, this is nothing new. You're getting the section info object from the results controller and returning the row count.

Inside configureCell(_: atIndexPath:), replace the first line with this:

```
let potato = resultsController.object(at: indexPath)
```

Notice that you don't need to tell Swift what type of object this is. Because the fetched results controller now has type information, when you say potato, the compiler says Potato. No need to call the whole thing off.

Make a similar change in prepare(for: sender:). The final line of the method gets the selected object to pass to the detail view controller. Replace that line with this one:

```
detail.potato = resultsController.object(at: path)
```

Finally, you can delete the potatoes property from the view controller. This will give you an error because you're passing in that property from the app delegate when the app launches. Switch back to **AppDelegate.swift** and change the error line to this:

```
potatoList.context = coreDataStack.viewContext
```

Now the table is using the same main thread managed object context that you used to load in the objects.

Build and run just to confirm that you now have a results-controller driven table view.

You'll see a warning about the `potatoes` constant not being used any more — you're going to fix that soon.

A fetched results controller isn't particularly useful unless it has a delegate. The standard fetched results controller delegate code hasn't changed except for getting slightly shorter due to Swift 3 renaming, so I won't go through the details.

Open **PotatoTableViewController.swift** and add the following extension:

```swift
extension PotatoTableViewController:
NSFetchedResultsControllerDelegate {

  func controllerWillChangeContent(_ controller:
NSFetchedResultsController<NSFetchRequestResult>) {
    tableView.beginUpdates()
  }

  func controller(_ controller:
NSFetchedResultsController<NSFetchRequestResult>,
    didChange anObject: Any, at indexPath: IndexPath?,
    for type: NSFetchedResultsChangeType,
    newIndexPath: IndexPath?) {
    switch type {
    case .delete:
      guard let indexPath = indexPath else { return }
      tableView.deleteRows(at: [indexPath], with: .automatic)
    case .insert:
      guard let newIndexPath = newIndexPath else { return }
      tableView.insertRows(at: [newIndexPath], with: .automatic)
    case .update:
      guard let indexPath = indexPath else { return }
      if let cell = tableView.cellForRow(at: indexPath) {
        configureCell(cell, atIndexPath: indexPath)
      }
    case .move:
      guard let indexPath = indexPath,
      let newIndexPath = newIndexPath else { return }
      tableView.deleteRows(at: [indexPath], with: .automatic)
      tableView.insertRows(at: [newIndexPath], with: .automatic)
    }
  }

  func controllerDidChangeContent(_ controller:
NSFetchedResultsController<NSFetchRequestResult>) {
    tableView.endUpdates()
  }

}
```

Back up in `viewDidLoad()` assign the result controller's delegate just before you perform the fetch:

```
resultsController.delegate = self
```

Build and run again, and change the ratings on some of your favorite potatoes. You'll see the ratings update instantly on the cells if you're running on an iPad, otherwise you'll have to navigate back. That's the power of a fetched results controller.

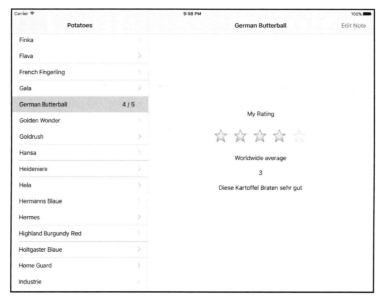

Currently the app creates the list of potatoes from scratch every time it launches. One of the main features of Core Data is that it can be used for persistence, so you're going to actually save things now. To demonstrate another new feature, you'll going to offload that initial list creation to a background task.

Digging in to the background

Add a new Swift file to the **Model** group, and call it **PotatoTasks.swift**. Add the following code:

```
import CoreData

extension NSPersistentContainer {

  func importPotatoes() {
    // 1
```

```
    performBackgroundTask { context in
      // 2
      let request: NSFetchRequest<Potato> =
Potato.fetchRequest()
      do {
        // 3
        if try context.count(for: request) == 0 {
          // TODO: Import some spuds
        }
      } catch {
        print("Error importing potatoes: \
(error.localizedDescription)")
      }
    }
  }
}
```

Here's the breakdown:

1. performBackgroundTask(_:) is a built-in method on NSPersistentContainer
    that takes a block with a managed object context as a parameter, does some work
    with it and then disposes of the context. The context is confined to a private queue.
    There's also a method to get a background context directly if you want to manage the
    object yourself.

2. This is the same code to generate a typed fetch request that you've already seen.

3. This is another new method, this time on the context itself. count(for:) is a
    throwing version of countForFetchRequest(_: error:).

Replace the TODO: comment with this code, which is very similar to the code that was
used in the app delegate:

```
sleep(3)
guard let spudsURL = Bundle.main.url(forResource: "Potatoes",
withExtension: "txt") else { return }
let spuds = try String(contentsOf: spudsURL)
let spudList = spuds.components(separatedBy: .newlines)
for spud in spudList {
  let potato = Potato(context: context)
  potato.variety = spud
  potato.crowdRating = Float(arc4random_uniform(50)) / Float(10)
}

try context.save()
```

The sleep line is there so that you can pretend you're loading data from a server. At the
end of the object creation, the private context is saved. if you didn't do this, everything
would be lost as the context is discarded at the end of the block.

Switch back to **AppDelegate.swift** and in `application(_:
didFinishLaunchingWithOptions)` replace all of the code from after the
`loadPersistentStores(_:)` call to just before the `return true` statement with this:

```
coreDataStack.importPotatoes()

if let split = window?.rootViewController as?
UISplitViewController {

  if
    let primaryNav = split.viewControllers.first as?
UINavigationController,
    let potatoList = primaryNav.topViewController as?
PotatoTableViewController {
      potatoList.context = coreDataStack.viewContext
  }

  split.delegate = self
  split.preferredDisplayMode = .allVisible
}
```

This code removes all of the potato creation code and calls the new extension method
which loads the data in a background queue. Build and run the app and...

Where are your potatoes? You may have expected them to make their way to the main
thread managed object context after the background context saved. Usually, you'd make
a background context as a child of the main thread context. But that isn't what
`NSPersistentContainer` gives you.

If you build and run the app again, then you'll see your list. This gives you a clue as to what is happening. The previous way to deal with multiple managed object contexts looked a little something like this:

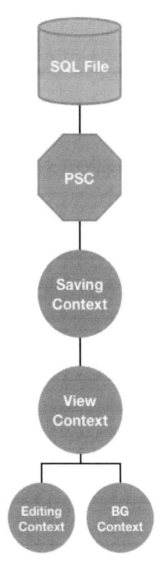

You only had one context that would talk to the persistent store coordinator. Typically that was a background queue context whose only job was to perform saves. Under that was the main thread context, which represented the "truth" of your app. Subsequent background operations or foreground editing contexts would be children of that main thread context.

This was necessary because the persistent store coordinator and SQL store could not handle multiple readers or writers without having to use locks. In iOS 10, the SQL store has been improved to allow multiple readers and a single writer, and the persistent store coordinator no longer uses locks. This means that a context hierarchy now looks more like this:

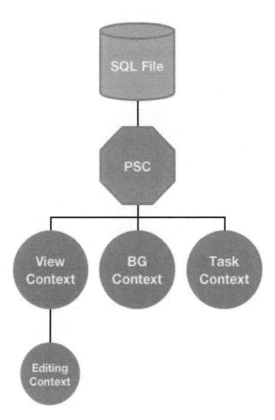

The background contexts that the persistent container gives you talk directly to the persistent store coordinator — they aren't children of the main thread context. The background context adds all of the potatoes, then saves. This is written to the SQL store by the persistent store coordinator. The main thread context has no idea this is happening, unless it is forced to re-run the fetch requests.

This would have presented a problem in older versions of iOS. You'd have to listen for save change notifications and do the merges yourself, like a savage. Luckily, this is the future. In **AppDelegate.swift**, before the `importPotatoes()` line, add the following code:

```
coreDataStack.viewContext.automaticallyMergesChangesFromParent =
  true
```

This is a new property on `NSManagedObjectContext`, and very useful it is too. Essentially it does all of that merging process for you. If the context is directly beneath the persistent store coordinator, then it will receive updates whenever a sibling context linked to the coordinator saves. If the context is a child context of another context, then it will receive updates whenever the parent context saves.

> **Note:** Because the changes are merged when the parent *saves*, this means that changes don't automatically cascade down. For example, if you had a background task which saved straight to the persistent store, and the view context was merging changes, then those background changes would appear in the view context. However, if the view context itself had a child context, the changes would not cascade down even if the child context was set to automatically merge.

Delete the app from your simulator or device (because the data is already there) and build and run again. You'll see the empty list of potatoes for a while, then once the background context has done its work, the new data will automatically appear!

iCloud Core Data gets mashed

Not announced at WWDC was one slightly nasty surprise: all of the symbols and methods associated with iCloud Core Data sync have been removed.

iCloud has always had something of a troubled relationship with Core Data and it seems Apple has finally decided to end it. According to the documentation, the existing methods will still work (for whatever definition of "work" you had before), but it's difficult to recommend starting a new project and relying on iCloud.

Perhaps with this year's changes, the simplification of setup and more convenient code, Apple is positioning Core Data as a more accessible, default choice model layer in your app, and you're supposed to use CloudKit or some other method to sync. There is no "official" guidance on the matter.

Where to go from here?

Our *Core Data By Tutorials* book is completely updated for iOS 10 and contains much more information about all of the goodies and new features listed here, as well as a solid grounding in what Core Data is, and how it works.

Chapter 12: What's New with Photography

By Rich Turton

iOS 10 introduced two major improvements to taking and editing photos and videos:

• For the first time, your apps can now take and edit live photos.

• Also, there is a new photo capture pipeline which allows you to give rich UI responses for various stages of image capture and processing.

In this chapter you'll learn about the new photo capturing methods by creating a selfie-taking app. You'll then level up by adding live photo capabilities, and finish off by editing live photos.

You'll be building the app from scratch, so you'll also find out about lots of pre-existing AVFoundation goodies involved in photography along the way.

Smile, you're on camera!

For this project, you'll need to run on a device with a front-facing camera — there's no camera on the simulator. raywenderlich.com readers are a good-looking bunch of people, so this app will only allow you to use the front camera — when you look this good, why would you want to take pictures in the other direction? :]

For the later sections, you'll also need a device that supports Live Photos.

Create a new Xcode project using the **Single View Application** template, named **PhotoMe**. Make it for **iPhone** only. Leave the Core Data, Unit Tests and UI Tests boxes unchecked, and save the projet somewhere.

Choose your team in the **Signing** section in the target's **General** settings tab to allow you to run on a device, and untick all of the **Device Orientation** options except **Portrait**. Using a single orientation keeps things simple for the demo.

Right-click on **Info.plist** and choose **Open As > Source Code**. Add the following values just above the final `</dict>` tag:

```
<key>NSCameraUsageDescription</key>
<string>PhotoMe needs the camera to take photos. Duh!</string>
<key>NSMicrophoneUsageDescription</key>
<string>PhotoMe needs the microphone to record audio with Live
Photos.</string>
<key>NSPhotoLibraryUsageDescription</key>
<string>PhotoMe will save photos in the Photo Library.</string>
```

This is required to access to the camera, microphone and photo library.

`AVFoundation` contains a specialist `CALayer` subclass, `AVCaptureVideoPreviewLayer`, which you can can use to show the user what the camera is currently seeing. There's no support for this in Interface Builder, so you need to make a `UIView` subclass to deal with it.

Create a new file, using the **Cocoa Touch Class** template. Name the new class **CameraPreviewView**, and make it a subclass of **UIView**. Replace the contents of the file with the following:

```swift
import UIKit
import AVFoundation
import Photos

class CameraPreviewView: UIView {
    //1
    override static var layerClass: AnyClass {
        return AVCaptureVideoPreviewLayer.self
    }
    //2
    var cameraPreviewLayer: AVCaptureVideoPreviewLayer {
        return layer as! AVCaptureVideoPreviewLayer
    }
    //3
    var session: AVCaptureSession? {
        get {
            return cameraPreviewLayer.session
        }
        set {
            cameraPreviewLayer.session = newValue
        }
    }
}
```

Here's the breakdown:

1. Views have a `layerClass` class property which can specify a specific `CALayer` subclass to use for the main layer. Here, you specify `AVCaptureVideoPreviewLayer`.

2. This is a convenience method to give you a typed property for the view's layer.

3. The capture preview layer needs have an `AVCaptureSession` to show input from the camera, so this property passes through a session to the underlying layer.

Open **Main.storyboard** and drag in a view. Drag the resizing handles to make the view touch the top, left and right sides of the scene. Use the pinning menu to pin it to those edges, then Control-drag from the view to itself to create an aspect ratio constraint. Edit this new constraint to give a 3:4 aspect ratio.

With the new view selected, open the **Identity** Inspector and set the **Class** to **CameraPreviewView**. At this point your storyboard should look like this:

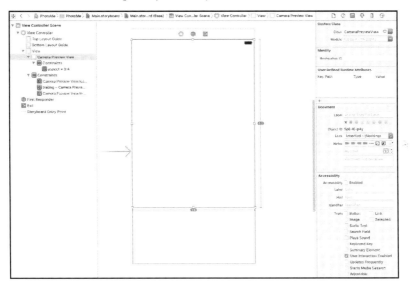

Open the assistant editor and Control-drag into **ViewController.swift** to make a new outlet from the camera preview view. Name it **cameraPreviewView**.

Still in **ViewController.swift**, add the following `import` statement:

```
import AVFoundation
```

Then add these properties:

```
fileprivate let session = AVCaptureSession()
fileprivate let sessionQueue = DispatchQueue(
```

```
    label: "com.razeware.PhotoMe.session-queue")
    var videoDeviceInput: AVCaptureDeviceInput!
```

An `AVCaptureSession` is the object that handles the input from the cameras and microphones. Most of the methods relating to capture and processing are asynchronous and can be handled on background queues, so you create a new queue to deal with everything session-related. The capture device input represents the actual camera / microphone that is capturing the audio and video.

Now add the following code to `viewDidLoad()`:

```
//1
cameraPreviewView.session = session
//2
sessionQueue.suspend()
//3
AVCaptureDevice.requestAccess(forMediaType: AVMediaTypeVideo) {
    success in
    if !success {
        print("Come on, it's a camera app!")
        return
    }
    //4
    self.sessionQueue.resume()
}
```

Here's the breakdown:

1. Pass through the capture session to the view so it can display the output.

2. Suspend the session queue, so nothing can happen with the session.

3. Ask for permission to access the camera and microphone. Both of these are required for live photos, which you'll add later.

4. Once permission is granted, resume the queue.

You're almost ready to get your face on the screen. First, you need to configure the capture session. Add the following method to do this:

```
private func prepareCaptureSession() {
    // 1
    session.beginConfiguration()
    session.sessionPreset = AVCaptureSessionPresetPhoto

    do {
        // 2
        let videoDevice = AVCaptureDevice.defaultDevice(
            withDeviceType: .builtInWideAngleCamera,
            mediaType: AVMediaTypeVideo,
```

```
            position: .front)
        // 3
        let videoDeviceInput = try
            AVCaptureDeviceInput(device: videoDevice)

        // 4
        if session.canAddInput(videoDeviceInput) {
            session.addInput(videoDeviceInput)
            self.videoDeviceInput = videoDeviceInput

            // 5
            DispatchQueue.main.async {
                self.cameraPreviewView.cameraPreviewLayer
                    .connection.videoOrientation = .portrait
            }
        } else {
            print("Couldn't add device to the session")
            return
        }
    } catch {
        print("Couldn't create video device input: \(error)")
        return
    }

    // 6
    session.commitConfiguration()
}
```

Here's what's happening above:

1. `beginConfiguration()` tells the session that you're about to add a series of configuration changes, which are committed at the end. Next you configure the session to use some preset values that are good for high quality photo output. There are other presets available for video output, at varying quality and resolutions.

2. Create a device representing the front facing camera.

3. Create a device input representing the data the device can capture.

4. Add the input to the session, and store it in the property you declared earlier.

5. Back on the main queue, tell the preview layer that you'll be dealing with portrait only.

6. If everything went OK, commit all of the changes to the session.

At the end of `viewDidLoad()`, add this code to call the new method on the session queue:

```
sessionQueue.async {
    [unowned self] in
```

```
        self.prepareCaptureSession()
    }
```

This means it won't get called until permission has been granted, and the main queue won't be blocked while the configuration happens.

Finally, you need to start the session running. Add this `viewWillAppear(_:)` implementation:

```
override func viewWillAppear(_ animated: Bool) {
    super.viewWillAppear(animated)
    sessionQueue.async {
        self.session.startRunning()
    }
}
```

`startRunning()` is a blocking call that can take some time to complete, so you call it on the dedicated queue created earlier.

Build and run on your device with a front-facing camera, grant permission for the camera, and you should see your lovely face on the device!

In this section you've created an **input**, which represents the front camera of your device, and a **session**, which handles the data coming from the input. Next up, you're going to add a way of getting output from the session.

Taking a photo

New to iOS 10 is the `AVCapturePhotoOutput` class. This replaces `AVCaptureStillImageOutput`, which is deprecated in iOS 10. Learning about the cool new features of this class takes up the next few sections of this chapter.

Start by adding a new property to **ViewController.swift** to hold an output object:

```
fileprivate let photoOutput = AVCapturePhotoOutput()
```

The output has to be configured and added to the capture session. In `prepareCaptureSession()`, just before the `commitConfiguration()` call, add this code:

```
if session.canAddOutput(photoOutput) {
    session.addOutput(photoOutput)
    photoOutput.isHighResolutionCaptureEnabled = true
} else {
    print("Unable to add photo output")
    return
}
```

The `isHighResolutionCaptureEnabled` property sets up the output to generate full-size photos, as opposed to the smaller images that are used to feed the on-screen preview. You must set this to `true` *before* the session has started running, otherwise the session has to reconfigure itself mid-flight, which will make the preview stutter and discard any photos that are in progress.

Now that an output object is created and configured, there are three more steps necessary to actually take a photo:

1. Add a "take photo" button to the UI so that the user can get their duck-face ready.

2. Create an `AVCapturePhotoSettings` object which contains the information about how the photo should be taken, such as the flash mode to use or other details.

3. Tell the output object to capture a photo, passing in the settings and a delegate object.

First, you'll take care of the UI. Open **Main.storyboard** and make things look a little more camera-like by setting the main view's background color to black, and the **Global Tint** color to a tasteful orange using the File Inspector. Set the camera preview view's background color to black as well.

Drag in a **Visual Effect View With Blur** and pin it to the left, bottom and right edges of the main view (but **not** the top). Set the **Blur Style** to **Dark**.

Drag a **button** into the visual effect view, and change the label to **Take Photo!**, with a font size of **20.0**. With the button selected, click the **Stack** button or choose **Editor > Embed In > Stack View** to create a vertical stack view. You'll be adding more controls here as your camera gets more sophisticated, so a stack view is a good idea.

Add constraints to center the stack view horizontally in the superview, then pin it to the **top** of the superview with a spacing of **5** and to the **bottom** with a spacing of **20**. Update any frames that Xcode complains about, and you should end up with something like this:

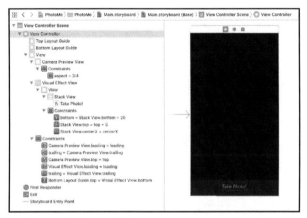

Open the assistant editor and Control-drag to create an outlet and action for the button in **ViewController.swift**:

```swift
@IBOutlet weak var shutterButton: UIButton!
@IBAction func handleShutterButtonTap(_ sender: UIButton) {
}
```

The action is going to call a separate method, capturePhoto(). Add this in a new extension:

```swift
extension ViewController {
    fileprivate func capturePhoto() {
        // 1
        let cameraPreviewLayerOrientation = cameraPreviewView
            .cameraPreviewLayer.connection.videoOrientation

        // 2
        sessionQueue.async {
            if let connection = self.photoOutput
                .connection(withMediaType: AVMediaTypeVideo) {
                connection.videoOrientation =
                cameraPreviewLayerOrientation
            }
```

```
        // 3
        let photoSettings = AVCapturePhotoSettings()
        photoSettings.flashMode = .off
        photoSettings.isHighResolutionPhotoEnabled = true

    }
  }
}
```

This method creates the settings object mentioned earlier. Here's the breakdown:

1. The output connection needs to know what orientation the camera is in. You could cheat here since the camera is fixed to portrait, but this is useful stuff to know.

2. Again, all work relating to the actual capture is pushed off onto the session queue. First, an AVCaptureConnection is obtained from the AVCapturePhotoOutput object. A connection represents a stream of media coming from one of the inputs, through the session, to the output. You pass the orientation to the connection.

3. The photo settings is created and configured. For basic JPEG capture, there aren't many things to configure.

Add a call to capturePhoto() from handleShutterButtonTap(_:):

```
capturePhoto()
```

The app isn't ready to take a photo yet. First, a little bit of theory.

Processing a captured photo takes a certain amount of time. You may have noticed when taking photos in the standard Camera app that you can hit the shutter button lots of times and it can take a while before the photos show up in the thumbnail preview. There's a lot of work to be done on the raw data captured by the camera's sensor before you get a JPEG (or RAW) file saved to disk with embedded EXIF data, thumbnails and so on.

Because it's possible (and indeed, desirable — your user doesn't want to miss her perfect shot!) to take another photo without waiting for the first one to finish processing, it would get hopelessly confusing if the view controller was the photo output's delegate. In each delegate method you'd have to work out which particular photo capture you were dealing with.

To make things easier to understand, you will create a separate object whose only job is to act as the delegate for the photo output. The view controller will hold a dictionary of these delegate objects. It just so happens that each AVCapturePhotoSettings object is single-use only and comes with a unique identifier to enforce that, which you'll use as a key for the dictionary.

Create a new Swift file called **PhotoCaptureDelegate.swift**. Add the following implementation:

```swift
import AVFoundation
import Photos

class PhotoCaptureDelegate: NSObject {
    // 1
    var photoCaptureBegins: (() -> ())? = .none
    var photoCaptured: (() -> ())? = .none
    fileprivate let completionHandler: (PhotoCaptureDelegate,
PHAsset?) -> ()

    // 2
    fileprivate var photoData: Data? = .none

    // 3
    init(completionHandler: @escaping (PhotoCaptureDelegate,
PHAsset?) -> ()) {
        self.completionHandler = completionHandler
    }

    // 4
    fileprivate func cleanup(asset: PHAsset? = .none) {
        completionHandler(self, asset)
    }
}
```

Here's the explanation:

1. You'll supply closures to execute at key points in the photo capture process. These are when the capture begins and ends, then when the captured image has been processed and everything is complete.

2. A property to hold the data captured from the output

3. `init` ensures that a completion closure is passed in; the other event closures are optional.

4. This method calls the completion closure once everything is completed.

This diagram shows the various stages of the photo capture process:

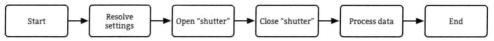

Each stage is associated with delegate method calls. Some of these delegate calls are relevant to the view controller (hence the various closures), and some can be handled within the delegate object itself. The delegate methods aren't mentioned specifically in the diagram because *they are the longest method signatures in the universe,* so there are comments indicating when each one is called.

Add the following extension:

```
extension PhotoCaptureDelegate: AVCapturePhotoCaptureDelegate {
    // Process data completed
    func capture(_ captureOutput: AVCapturePhotoOutput,
                didFinishProcessingPhotoSampleBuffer
        photoSampleBuffer: CMSampleBuffer?,
                previewPhotoSampleBuffer: CMSampleBuffer?,
                resolvedSettings:
AVCaptureResolvedPhotoSettings,
                bracketSettings:
AVCaptureBracketedStillImageSettings?,
                error: Error?) {

        guard let photoSampleBuffer = photoSampleBuffer else {
            print("Error capturing photo \(error)")
            return
        }
        photoData = AVCapturePhotoOutput
            .jpegPhotoDataRepresentation(
                forJPEGSampleBuffer: photoSampleBuffer,
                previewPhotoSampleBuffer:
previewPhotoSampleBuffer)
    }
}
```

See? That's quite the method name. This one is called when the sensor data from the capture has been processed. All you do here is use a class method on AVCapturePhotoOutput to create the JPEG data and save it to the property. Now add this method to the same extension:

```
// Entire process completed
func capture(_ captureOutput: AVCapturePhotoOutput,
            didFinishCaptureForResolvedSettings
    resolvedSettings: AVCaptureResolvedPhotoSettings,
            error: Error?) {

    // 1
    guard error == nil, let photoData = photoData else {
        print("Error \(error) or no data")
        cleanup()
        return
    }

    // 2
    PHPhotoLibrary.requestAuthorization {
        [unowned self]
        (status) in
        // 3
        guard status == .authorized  else {
            print("Need authorisation to write to the photo
```

```
library")
            self.cleanup()
            return
        }
        // 4
        var assetIdentifier: String?
        PHPhotoLibrary.shared().performChanges({
            let creationRequest =
PHAssetCreationRequest.forAsset()
            let placeholder = creationRequest
                .placeholderForCreatedAsset

            creationRequest.addResource(with: .photo,
                                        data: photoData,
options: .none)

            assetIdentifier = placeholder?.localIdentifier

        }, completionHandler: { (success, error) in
            if let error = error {
                print("Error saving to the photo library: \
(error)")
            }
            var asset: PHAsset? = .none
            if let assetIdentifier = assetIdentifier {
                asset = PHAsset.fetchAssets(
                    withLocalIdentifiers: [assetIdentifier],
                    options: .none).firstObject
            }
            self.cleanup(asset: asset)
        })
    }
}
```

This method is called when the entire capture and processing is finished with. It's the last delegate method to be called. Here's the breakdown:

1. Check to make sure everything is as expected.

2. Request access to the photo library. The first time this runs, the user will be prompted to allow permission.

3. If access is not granted, your camera app is of limited utility.

4. Save the captured data to the photo library and obtain a PHAsset, which is an object representing a photo or movie from the photos library. The Photos framework isn't the topic for this chapter, so you only get a summary explanation: You ask to create an asset, then attempt to create one, and if all is well, you end up with a full PHAsset.

Note that the `cleanup(asset:)` method is called in all cases. Switch back to
ViewController.swift and add a property to hold the list of delegates discussed earlier:

```
fileprivate var photoCaptureDelegates =
    [Int64 : PhotoCaptureDelegate]()
```

Now add the following code to the end of the closure that is performed on the session
queue in `capturePhoto()`:

```
// 1
let uniqueID = photoSettings.uniqueID
let photoCaptureDelegate = PhotoCaptureDelegate() {
    [unowned self] (photoCaptureDelegate, asset) in
    self.sessionQueue.async { [unowned self] in
        self.photoCaptureDelegates[uniqueID] = .none
    }
}

// 2
self.photoCaptureDelegates[uniqueID] = photoCaptureDelegate

// 3
self.photoOutput.capturePhoto(
    with: photoSettings, delegate: photoCaptureDelegate)
```

This code kicks off the capture process:

1. Create the delegate and, in a cruel twist of fate, tell it to remove itself from memory
    when it's finished.

2. Store the delegate in the dictionary

3. Start the capture process, passing in the delegate and the settings object.

Build and run, and you'll see your new photo UI:

Tap the Take Photo button and you'll be prompted for access to the photo library. Allow this and then switch to the Photos app – there's your selfie! That's nice, but it could use a little UI polish. You'll add that next.

Making it fabulous

You get a shutter noise for free, but it would be nice to see something on the screen as well. You can use the capture begins and capture ends delegate methods for this. In capturePhoto(), after you create the delegate object, add the following code:

```
photoCaptureDelegate.photoCaptureBegins = { [unowned self] in
    DispatchQueue.main.async {
        self.shutterButton.isEnabled = false
        self.cameraPreviewView.cameraPreviewLayer.opacity = 0
        UIView.animate(withDuration: 0.2) {
            self.cameraPreviewView.cameraPreviewLayer.opacity =
1
        }
    }
}

photoCaptureDelegate.photoCaptured = { [unowned self] in
    DispatchQueue.main.async {
        self.shutterButton.isEnabled = true
    }
}
```

You pass in two closures, one to be executed when the capture starts, and one when it ends. When the capture begins, you blank out and fade back in to give a shutter effect and disable the shutter button. When the capture is complete, the shutter button is enabled again.

Open **PhotoCaptureDelegate.swift** and add the following to the AVCapturePhotoCaptureDelegate extension:

```
func capture(_ captureOutput: AVCapturePhotoOutput,
            willCapturePhotoForResolvedSettings
    resolvedSettings: AVCaptureResolvedPhotoSettings) {
    photoCaptureBegins?()
}

func capture(_ captureOutput: AVCapturePhotoOutput,
            didCapturePhotoForResolvedSettings
    resolvedSettings: AVCaptureResolvedPhotoSettings) {
    photoCaptured?()
}
```

Some more very wordy methods, that just execute the closures that have been passed in for these event points.

Build and run and take some more photos, and you'll see a camera-like animation each time you hit the button.

The built-in camera app has a nice feature where it shows a thumbnail of the last photo you took in the corner. You're going to add that to PhotoMe. You may have noticed the `previewPhotoSampleBuffer` parameter in the extraordinarily long delegate method called when the photo sample buffer is processed. This gets used to make an embedded preview in the JPEG file that is created, but you can also use it to make in-app thumbnails.

Add a new property to `PhotoCaptureDelegate` to hold a closure to be executed when a thumbnail is captured:

```
var thumbnailCaptured: ((UIImage?) -> ())? = .none
```

Then add this code to the end of the `...didFinishProcessingPhotoSampleBuffer...` method:

```
if let thumbnailCaptured = thumbnailCaptured,
    let previewPhotoSampleBuffer = previewPhotoSampleBuffer,
    let cvImageBuffer =
CMSampleBufferGetImageBuffer(previewPhotoSampleBuffer) {

    let ciThumbnail = CIImage(cvImageBuffer: cvImageBuffer)
    let context = CIContext(options:
[kCIContextUseSoftwareRenderer: false])
    let thumbnail = UIImage(cgImage:
context.createCGImage(ciThumbnail, from: ciThumbnail.extent)!,
scale: 2.0, orientation: .right)

    thumbnailCaptured(thumbnail)
}
```

This is a faintly ludicrous game of pass-the-parcel where you make the `CMSampleBuffer` into a `CVImageBuffer`, then a `CIImage`, then a `CGImage`, then a `UIImage`. It's a good job this is all happening on a background thread! :]

The next part sounds more complicated than it is. You're going to add a whole stack of stack views. There's a diagram afterwards to help you. Open **Main.storyboard** and drag a **Horizontal Stack View** in to the existing stack view, at the same level as the shutter button. Add two **Vertical Stack Views** to the new stack view. Add a **Horizontal Stack View** to the first vertical stack view, and to *that* stack view add a switch and a label.

Set the **Value** of the switch to **Off**, and the text of the label to **Capture Thumbnail**, with the text color set to white.

Add an image view to the second vertical stack view. Add a width constraint to the image view to make it 80 points wide, then add an aspect ratio constraint to make it 1:1 (square). Check **Clip to Bounds** and set the **Content Mode** to **Aspect Fill**.

Take a deep breath, then check what you have against this diagram. Rename each stack view to match, because you'll be adding more views later on and this will stop you getting confused:

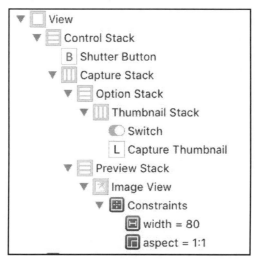

Select the **Capture Stack** and set the **Alignment** to **Center** and the **Spacing** to **20**.

Select the **Option Stack** and set the **Alignment** to **Leading** and the **Spacing** to **5**.

Select the **Thumbnail Stack** and set the **Spacing** to **5**.

Use the **Resolve Autolayout Issues** menu to update all of the frames if necessary.

At this point, you should see something that looks like this:

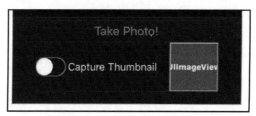

Open the assistant editor and make two new outlets from **ViewController.swift** to the switch and image view:

```
@IBOutlet weak var previewImageView: UIImageView!
@IBOutlet weak var thumbnailSwitch: UISwitch!
```

If the user has turned the thumbnail switch on, you need to add a preview format to the photo settings object. In **ViewController.swift**, add the following to capturePhoto() before the delegate object is created:

```
if self.thumbnailSwitch.isOn
    && photoSettings.availablePreviewPhotoPixelFormatTypes
    .count > 0 {
    photoSettings.previewPhotoFormat = [
        kCVPixelBufferPixelFormatTypeKey as String :
            photoSettings
                .availablePreviewPhotoPixelFormatTypes.first!,
        kCVPixelBufferWidthKey as String : 160,
        kCVPixelBufferHeightKey as String : 160
    ]
}
```

This tells the photo settings that you want to create a 160x160 preview image, in the same format as the main photo. Still in capturePhoto(), add the following code after you've created the delegate object:

```
photoCaptureDelegate.thumbnailCaptured = { [unowned self] image
in
    DispatchQueue.main.async {
        self.previewImageView.image = image
    }
}
```

This will set the preview image once the thumbnail is captured and processed. Build and run, turn the thumbnail switch on and take a photo. Check out that preview!

Live photos

What you've done so far is really a slightly nicer version of what you could already do with `AVCaptureStillImageOutput`. In the next two sections you'll get on to totally new stuff: taking live photos, and editing them!

Open **Main.storyboard** and drag a new **Horizontal Stack View** into the **Option Stack**, above the **Thumbnail Stack**. Name the new stack view **Live Photo Stack** and set the **Spacing** to 5. Drag in a switch and a label, set the label text to **Live Photo Mode** and the text color to white, and set the switch to **Off**. This will control your capture of live photos.

Drag a label to the top of the **Control Stack**, set the text color to the same orange you're using for the overall tint, the text to "capturing...", and the font size to **35**. Set the new label to **Hidden**. This will tell the user if a live photo capture is still rolling.

Open the assistant editor and create outlets to the new switch and the "capturing..." label:

```
@IBOutlet weak var livePhotoSwitch: UISwitch!
@IBOutlet weak var capturingLabel: UILabel!
```

Open **ViewController.swift** and add the following code to `prepareCaptureSession()`, just after the video device input is created:

```
do {
    let audioDevice =
AVCaptureDevice.defaultDevice(withMediaType: AVMediaTypeAudio)
    let audioDeviceInput = try AVCaptureDeviceInput(device:
audioDevice)
    if session.canAddInput(audioDeviceInput) {
        session.addInput(audioDeviceInput)
    } else {
        print("Couldn't add audio device to the session")
        return
    }
} catch {
    print("Unable to create audio device input: \(error)")
    return
}
```

A live photo is a full-size photo with an accompanying video, which contains sound. This means you need to add another input to the session. As with high-resolution capture, you need to configure the output object up front to support live photos, even if you're not taking live photos by default.

Add the following code after the line where you enable high-resolution capture:

```
photoOutput.isLivePhotoCaptureEnabled =
    photoOutput.isLivePhotoCaptureSupported
DispatchQueue.main.async {
    self.livePhotoSwitch.isEnabled =
        self.photoOutput.isLivePhotoCaptureSupported
}
```

This checks to see if live photo capture is possible on the device, and if so, it adds that capability to the output. If not, the live photo switch is disabled, but left on screen to show you what you're missing.

Move to `capturePhoto()` and perform the additional configuration needed to support live photo capture. Before the delegate object is created, add the following:

```
if self.livePhotoSwitch.isOn {
    let movieFileName = UUID().uuidString
    let moviePath = (NSTemporaryDirectory() as NSString)
        .appendingPathComponent("\(movieFileName).mov")
    photoSettings.livePhotoMovieFileURL = URL(
        fileURLWithPath: moviePath)
}
```

During capture the video file will be recorded into this unique name in the temporary directory.

Switch to **PhotoCaptureDelegate.swift** and add these two new properties:

```
var capturingLivePhoto: ((Bool) -> ())? = .none
fileprivate var livePhotoMovieURL: URL? = .none
```

The first is a closure which the view controller will use to update the UI to indicate if live photo capture is happening. The second will store the URL of the movie file that accompanies the live photo.

In the `AVCapturePhotoCaptureDelegate` extension, add the following to `...willCapturePhotoForResolvedSettings...`:

```
if resolvedSettings.livePhotoMovieDimensions.width > 0
    && resolvedSettings.livePhotoMovieDimensions.height > 0 {
    capturingLivePhoto?(true)
}
```

This will call the closure, saying that another live photo capture session will begin.

Close the loop by adding this new delegate method, which you'll be happy to know keeps with the tradition of lengthy method signatures:

```swift
func capture(_ captureOutput: AVCapturePhotoOutput,
             didFinishRecordingLivePhotoMovieForEventualFileAt
    outputFileURL: URL,
             resolvedSettings: AVCaptureResolvedPhotoSettings) {
    capturingLivePhoto?(false)
}
```

This delegate method is called when the video capture is complete. As with photos, there is a further method that is called when the *processing* of the video capture is complete. Add this now:

```swift
func capture(_ captureOutput: AVCapturePhotoOutput,
             didFinishProcessingLivePhotoToMovieFileAt
outputFileURL: URL,
             duration: CMTime,
             photoDisplay photoDisplayTime: CMTime,
             resolvedSettings: AVCaptureResolvedPhotoSettings,
             error: Error?) {
    if let error = error {
        print("Error creating live photo video: \(error)")
        return
    }
    livePhotoMovieURL = outputFileURL
}
```

Add the following code to capture(_: didFinishCaptureForResolvedSettings:error:), just after you call addResource on the creation request:

```swift
if let livePhotoMovieURL = self.livePhotoMovieURL {
    let movieResourceOptions = PHAssetResourceCreationOptions()
    movieResourceOptions.shouldMoveFile = true
    creationRequest.addResource(with: .pairedVideo,
                                fileURL: livePhotoMovieURL,
    options: movieResourceOptions)
}
```

This bundles in the video data with the photo data you're already sending, making your photo live. Setting the shouldMoveFile option means that the video file will be removed from the temporary directory for you.

You're ready to take a live photo now, but first you'll add that handy capturing indicator to the view.

Switch back to **ViewController.swift** and add a new property to track the number of ongoing live photo captures:

```
fileprivate var currentLivePhotoCaptures: Int = 0
```

Then in `capturePhoto()`, where you assign all the other closures, add this new closure:

```
// Live photo UI updates
photoCaptureDelegate.capturingLivePhoto = { (currentlyCapturing)
in
    DispatchQueue.main.async { [unowned self] in
        self.currentLivePhotoCaptures += currentlyCapturing ?
1 : -1
        UIView.animate(withDuration: 0.2) {
            self.capturingLabel.isHidden =
                self.currentLivePhotoCaptures == 0
        }
    }
}
```

This increments or decrements the property and hides the label as necessary. Build and run, turn on the live photos switch and start creating memories!

Editing Live Photos

Previously, when you edited Live Photos they lost the accompanying video and became, well, Dead Photos. In iOS 10 you can apply the same range of edits to a Live Photo as you can to any photo; those edits are applied to every frame of the video as well. What's even better is that you can do this in your own apps. You're going to apply a cool core image filter to live photos taken in PhotoMe.

Open **Main.storyboard** and drag a button into the bottom of the **Preview Stack**. Set the title of the button to **Edit**.

Drag a new view controller into the storyboard, Control-drag from the edit button to the new controller and choose to create a **Present Modally** segue.

Set the main view's background color to black. Drag in a vertical stack view and drag the left, top and bottom edges out to reach the edges of the screen. Add constraints to pin those edges, and set the spacing to **20**.

Add a UIView and two buttons to the stack. Create a 3:4 aspect ratio constraint on the view, and set its class to **PHLivePhotoView** using the Identity Inspector. This class allows you to play live photos as in the Photo Library.

Set the text of the first button to **Comicify** (because that's definitely a real word) and the font size to **30**. Set the text of the second button to **Done**.

Create a new view controller subclass called **PhotoEditingViewController**. Add the following imports to the new file:

```
import Photos
import PhotosUI
```

These modules are required to handle photo assets and the live photo view.

Switch back to **Main.storyboard** and change the class of the new view controller to `PhotoEditingViewController`. Open the assistant editor and create and connect an outlet for the live photo view and actions from each button:

```
@IBOutlet weak var livePhotoView: PHLivePhotoView!

@IBAction func handleComicifyTapped(_ sender: UIButton) {
}

@IBAction func handleDoneTapped(_ sender: UIButton) {
    dismiss(animated: true)
}
```

Add a property to `PhotoEditingViewController` to hold the asset being edited:

```
var asset: PHAsset?
```

And code to load and display the live photo:

```
override func viewDidAppear(_ animated: Bool) {
    super.viewDidAppear(animated)
    if let asset = asset {
        PHImageManager.default().requestLivePhoto(for: asset,
            targetSize: livePhotoView.bounds.size,
            contentMode: .aspectFill,
            options: .none, resultHandler: { (livePhoto, info)
in
                DispatchQueue.main.async {
                    self.livePhotoView.livePhoto = livePhoto
                }
        })
    }
}
```

Switch to **ViewController.swift** and add this import to the top of the file:

```
import Photos
```

Then add a new property to hold the last photo that was taken. Add `import Photos` to the top of the file first, then:

```
fileprivate var lastAsset: PHAsset?
```

Store the value by adding this to the completion closure you create when making the capture delegate in `capturePhoto()`, right after the line `self.photoCaptureDelegates[uniqueID] = .none`:

```
self.lastAsset = asset
```

Finally, pass the asset along by adding this implementation of `prepare(for: sender:)`:

```
override func prepare(for segue: UIStoryboardSegue, sender:
Any?) {
    if let editor = segue.destination as?
PhotoEditingViewController {
        editor.asset = lastAsset
    }
}
```

Build and run, take a live photo, and tap the edit button. You'll see your live photo, and can 3D touch it to play:

In **PhotoEditingViewController.swift** add the following method:

```swift
fileprivate func comicifyImage() {
    guard let asset = asset else { return }

    // 1
    asset.requestContentEditingInput(with: .none) {
        [unowned self] (input, info) in
        guard let input = input else {
            print("error: \(info)")
            return
        }

        // 2
        guard input.mediaType == .image,
            input.mediaSubtypes.contains(.photoLive) else {
                print("This isn't a live photo")
                return
        }

        // 3
        let editingContext =
```

```
            PHLivePhotoEditingContext(livePhotoEditingInput:
  input)
        editingContext?.frameProcessor = {
            (frame, error) in
            // 4
            var image = frame.image
            image = image.applyingFilter("CIComicEffect",

withInputParameters: .none)
            return image
        }

        // 5
        editingContext?.prepareLivePhotoForPlayback(
            withTargetSize: self.livePhotoView.bounds.size,
            options: .none) {
                (livePhoto, error) in
                guard let livePhoto = livePhoto else {
                    print("Preparation error: \(error)")
                    return
                }
                self.livePhotoView.livePhoto = livePhoto
        }
    }
}
```

Here's the breakdown:

1. `requestContentEditingInput` loads the asset data from the library and gets it ready for editing.

2. Check that the photo is actually a live photo.

3. Create a live photo editing context and assign it a frame processor. This is a closure that is applied to each `PHLivePhotoFrame` in the live photo, including the full-resolution image. You can identify how far through the video you are, or if you're editing the full image, by inspecting the frame object. The closure must return a `CIImage` — returning `nil` at any point aborts the edit.

4. In your case, you apply the same `CIFilter` to each frame, which is the Comic Effect filter. You could put any combination of core image filters in here, or perform any other manipulations you can think of.

5. This call creates preview-level renderings of the live photo. When it's done, it will update the live photo view.

Build and run, take a live photo and hit that Comicify button. See, I told you it was a real word.

prepareLivePhotoForPlayback only renders a low-resolution version of the edited photo, for previewing. To edit the actual live photo and save the edits to the library, you need to do a little more work. Add the following code to comicifyImage(), at the end of the completion block for prepareLivePhotoForPlayback.

```
// 1
let output = PHContentEditingOutput(contentEditingInput: input)
// 2
output.adjustmentData = PHAdjustmentData(
    formatIdentifier: "PhotoMe",
    formatVersion: "1.0",
    data: "Comicify".data(using: .utf8)!)
// 3
editingContext?.saveLivePhoto(to: output, options: nil) {
    success, error in
    if !success {
        print("Rendering error \(error)")
        return
    }
    // 4
    PHPhotoLibrary.shared().performChanges({
        let request = PHAssetChangeRequest(for: asset)
        request.contentEditingOutput = output
        }, completionHandler: { (success, error) in
            print("Saved \(success), error \(error)")
    })
}
```

The code is placed into that completion block because it needs to wait until the preview is rendered, otherwise saving the photo cancels the preview rendering.

In a full app you'd have a separate save button for the user once they were happy with the preview. Here's the breakdown:

1. The content editing output acts as a destination for the editing operation. For live photos, it's configured using the content editing input object you requested earlier.

2. Despite the adjustment data property being optional, you *must* set it, otherwise the photo can't be saved. This information allows your edits to be reverted.

3. `saveLivePhoto(to: options:)` re-runs the editing context's frame processor, but for the full-size video and still.

4. Once rendering is complete, you save the changes to the photo library in the standard manner by creating requests inside a photo library's changes block.

Remember to call this method from `handleComicifyTapped()`:

```
comicifyImage()
```

Build and run, go through the motions and now, when you hit Comicify, you'll get a system prompt asking for permission to modify the photo:

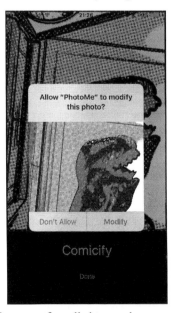

If you don't hit that Modify button after all this work, you and I can't be friends any more.

Where to go from here?

Congratulations! That was a marathon session, but you built an entire live-selfie filtering app! It's easy to imagine building on that foundation with a wider range of filters and options to come up with a really nice product.

There's more information on the new photography capabilities in WWDC16 sessions 501, 505 and 511, including RAW capture and processing. The Photos framework itself was introduced in iOS 8 and is covered in our iOS8 By Tutorials book.

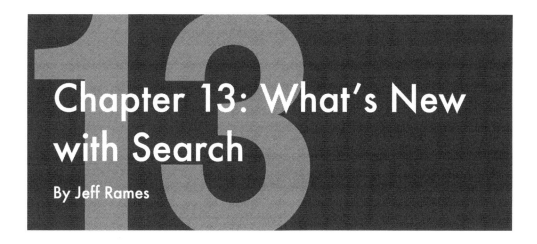

Chapter 13: What's New with Search

By Jeff Rames

Search frameworks gain some hefty new features with iOS 10. Most notable is the introduction of the Core Spotlight Search API, which brings the power of Spotlight search to your apps. For apps that already use Core Spotlight or user activity indexing, leveraging that same engine and index inside your app is easy — and powerful.

Another great new feature is the ability to continue Spotlight searches in your app. If a search yields results for your app, you can enable an annotation that launches your app and passes in the search string for further searching.

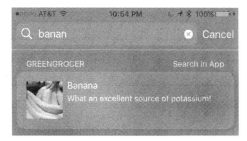

In addition, proactive suggestions have learned some exciting new tricks. By adding location data to your user activities, addresses displayed in your app can be made available throughout iOS. Features and apps such as QuickType, Siri and Maps will now have direct access to your data, while giving your app credit as the source.

All of these changes continue the trend of increasing your app's reach outside of its own little world. iOS 10 gives you more ways to entice users into launching your app — and more opportunities to remind users how useful your app can be.

If you're already indexing Core Spotlight or NSUserActivity items, these features are amazingly easy to implement in your apps. If your app deals in data, and you're not currently using these features, this is probably the time to bring your app into the 21st century and integrate these frameworks in your app.

For some background on search APIs in iOS, check out Introducing iOS 9 Search APIs here: https://videos.raywenderlich.com/courses/introducing-ios-9-search-apis/lessons/1

You can complete most of this chapter with the simulator, but you'll need a device running iOS 10 to test proactive location suggestions.

Getting started

In this chapter, you'll update an existing app called Green Grocer. It displays produce available at Ray's Fruit Emporium and employs a simple product filter. It also has a tab with contact info for the store along with a map.

In the starter folder, open **GreenGrocer.xcodeproj** and take a look around. There's quite a lot in the project, but here's a quick overview of the important files:

- **AppDelegate.swift** does two things of note already. In `application(_:didFinishLaunchingWithOptions:)` it calls `dataStore?.indexContent()` which indexes all products in Core Spotlight. `application(_:continue:restorationHandler:)` is currently set up to restore state when the user launches the app by tapping a product that Core Spotlight matched.

- **Product.swift** is the model object for the `Product` class. This represents one of the produce items central to Green Grocer.

- **SearchableExtensions.swift** contains an extension to `Product` that generates `CSSearchableItem` and `CSSearchableItemAttributeSet` objects used when indexing to Core Spotlight.

- **ProductTableViewController.swift** is the root controller in the **Products** tab. It displays a table view of produce and includes a `UISearchController` for filtering the content. Filtering happens in `filterContentForSearchText(searchText:)` which triggers each time content in the search bar changes.

- **ProductViewController.swift** is the detail controller for produce, which displays when the user selects a cell in the `ProductTableViewController`. It configures the view with data from the passed Product and creates a `NSUserActivity` to index the activity.

- **StoreViewController.swift** controls the view displayed in the **Store** tab that contains contact info for Ray's Fruit Emporium. It also contains a map view for displaying the location of the store — something you'll leverage when implementing proactive suggestions.

Green Grocer already enables Spotlight search via Core Spotlight and NSUserActivity indexing. In this chapter, you will make three modifications:

1. You'll start by implementing search continuation to feed Spotlight search queries to the search filter found in `ProductTableViewController`.

2. Next, you'll refactor the existing in-app search to use the Core Spotlight Search API.

3. Finally, you'll modify the `StoreViewController` so that it provides activity information necessary to enable location based proactive suggestions.

Enough talk — the future of Ray's Fruit Emporium depends on you! Head on in to the next section to get started.

Enabling search continuation

Spotlight search helps users quickly find what they're looking for. A user could enter the word *apple* into Spotlight and be one tap away from seeing the price on the Ray's Fruit Emporium product page. Spotlight fits that model quite well.

But what if the user's goal is a little different? If the user wanted to view all of Ray's fruit, they could search for *fruit* in Spotlight, but it would be unreasonable to expect every item to display right there. Results are limited to just a few matches per source; otherwise, responses would be unmanageably long.

This is where **search continuation** steps into the, er, spotlight. It lets Spotlight launch your app and pass the user's search query. This lets you not only display all results, but display them in your custom interface.

Open **Info.plist** and add a Boolean key named **CoreSpotlightContinuation** and set it to **YES**.

Key	Type	Value
▼ Information Property List	Dictionary	(19 items)
CoreSpotlightContinuation	Boolean	YES

This key tells Spotlight to display an annotation in the upper right of Green Grocer search results to indicate the search can be continued in-app.

This is where things gets scary. As of the initial public release of iOS 10, updating this plist does not cause the annotation to start working until you reboot the device or simulator. Feel free to bravely forge ahead without a reboot, but if **Search in App** doesn't appear in the next step, you're going to have to reboot your device after building.

Build and run, then background the app with the home button or **Shift+Command+H** in the simulator. Drag down to reveal Spotlight search and enter **apple**. Note the **Search in App** annotation that appears to the right of **GREENGROCER** in the section header:

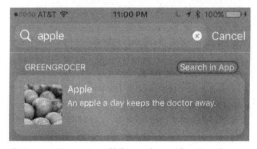

Tap **Search in App**, and Green Grocer will launch to the Products table — but it won't kick off a search.

This shouldn't come as a surprise, considering you haven't written any code to accept the query from Spotlight and act on it!

You'll take care of that next.

Implementing search continuation

Open **AppDelegate.swift** and add the following near the top of the file with the other `import`:

```
import CoreSpotlight
```

Search continuation requires some properties that are available in the framework.

Now look for `application(:_continue:restorationHandler:)` and replace the following line:

```
if let rootVC = window?.rootViewController,
```

With this:

```
if userActivity.activityType == CSQueryContinuationActionType {
  // TODO handle search continuation
} else if let rootVC = window?.rootViewController,
```

Previously, `application(:_continue:restorationHandler:)` was used solely as an entry point for restoring state after a user had selected an activity indexed in Spotlight. You've added a check for `CSQueryContinuationActionType` activities — which is what **Search in App** triggers. The prior check moves down to an `else if`, letting the processing of Spotlight result launches operate as they did before.

Now replace `// TODO handle search continuation` with the following:

```
// 1
guard let searchQuery =
  userActivity.userInfo?[CSSearchQueryString]
    as? String else {
    return false
}
// 2
guard let rootVC = window?.rootViewController,
  let tabBarViewController = rootVC as? TabBarViewController
  else {
    return false
}
tabBarViewController.selectedIndex = 0
```

```
// 3
guard let navController =
  tabBarViewController.selectedViewController as?
  UINavigationController else {
    return false
}
navController.popViewController(animated: false)
if let productTableVC = navController.topViewController as?
  ProductTableViewController {
    //4
    productTableVC.search(with: searchQuery)
    return true
}
```

Here's some detail on what happens when you hit a search continuation activity:

1. The CSSearchQueryString key in userActivity.userInfo points to the string typed into Spotlight.

   This guard unwraps and casts the searchQuery or, on failure, returns false to indicate the activity could not be processed.

2. The root view of Green Grocer is a tab bar controller.

   This guard places a reference to that controller in tabBarViewController. You then set selectedIndex to the first tab to display the product list.

3. The selected tab in tabBarViewController contains a navigation controller. You get a reference to it here, then call popViewController(animated:) with no animation to get to the root controller.

   The root is the ProductTableViewController, which productTableVC now points to.

4. search(with:) is a method in ProductTableViewController that kicks off the in-app product search using the passed parameter.

   It's called here with the searchQuery, followed by return true to indicate Green Grocer was able to handle the incoming search request.

Build and run, background the app, then search for **apple** in Spotlight. Tap the **Search in App** annotation by the Green Grocer results. This time, your new restoration handler code will trigger and you'll be brought straight to the search results!

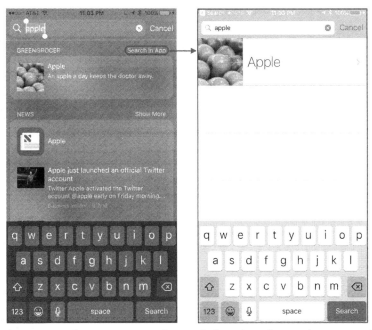

Of course, doing a search continuation for *apple* doesn't make much sense. Before you tapped **Search in App**, you already knew there would be only a single match, because Spotlight would have shown at least a few if there were more. Beyond that, the custom search result cells in Green Grocer actually provides less information than Spotlight does!

A search with a result set too large to display completely in Spotlight would be a better use case for this feature. Green Grocer includes the term "fruit" with every product it indexes in Spotlight, so that's a good one to try.

Background Green Grocer again and complete a Spotlight search for **fruit**. Only three results will display; a mere sample of what Green Grocer contains. Tap **Search in App** to see the in-app results for *fruit*.

> **Note** Keep in mind your results, especially for a generic term like fruit, may vary from those presented here. This is dependent on what you have indexed on your device, what Spotlight brings from the web, and on Spotlight's ranking algorithms. You can learn more about best practices for search ranking in the resources at the end of this chapter.

Green Grocer successfully launches and presents a search result for *fruit* — but where are all the matches?

It's clear `fruit` was included in the meta-data when indexing the produce, but the search must not be looking at this in the same way. Open **ProductTableViewController.swift** and find `filterContentForSearchText(searchText:)`. Take a look at the filter contained in this method:

```
filteredProducts = dataStore.products.filter { product in
  return
  product.name.lowercased().contains(searchText.lowercased())
}
```

`filteredProducts` acts as the data source when filtered results display. Here it's set using a `filter` on the complete `dataStore.products` array. The filter does a case-insensitive compare to identify any product names that contain the search string.

This isn't a bad way to filter the product list, but it's clear you could do better. To replicate Spotlight's results, you could index all of the associated meta-data for each product and create a more complex filter that includes that data.

But wouldn't it be nice to use Spotlight's existing index, search algorithm, and performance benefits instead of rolling your own? With iOS 10, you can! The new Core Spotlight Search API provides access to all of these features in Spotlight.

Before refactoring your code, you'll do well to walk through the following overview of Core Spotlight's features and query syntax first.

Core Spotlight Search API

Spotlight handles the indexing of your data and provides a powerful query language for use with its speedy search engine. This lets you use your own search interface — backed by the power of Spotlight.

If you've already indexed content with Core Spotlight, using the Search API means you'll have more consistency between in-app searches and those completed in Spotlight. It also protects user privacy as an app can only search its own indexed data.

To complete a search, you first create a **CSSearchQuery** that defines what and how you want to search. The initializer for `CSSearchQuery` requires two things:

- **queryString**: A formatted string that defines how you want to search. You'll learn more about how to format query strings shortly.

- **attributes**: An array of strings that correspond to names of properties in the **CSSearchableItemAttributeSet** class. The properties you include here will be returned in the result set, if available. You'd then use them to display the result or look it up in the application model.

Knowing how to format the search query string is the primary challenge in implementing Core Spotlight Search. The format of the most basic query is as follows:

```
attributeName operator value[modifiers]
```

Note these names are for illustration and not associated with the format syntax. Here's a breakdown of each component:

1. **attributeName** is one of the properties included in the `attributes` array. For example, this could be the product `title` in Green Grocer.

2. **operator** is a relational operator from the following list: ==, !=, <, <=, >, >=.

3. **value** is the literal value you're comparing against. For the title example, the value might be *fruit*.

4. **modifiers** consist of four different character values that represent modifications to how the comparison is applied. See the table below for detail on the available modifiers.

modifier	Comparison type
c	Case insensitive
d	Insensitive to diacritical marks (glyphs added to letters that are prevalent in certain languages)
w	Word based comparisons match on whole words—the word *apple* will not match for *applejack*
t	Comparisons are on tokenized values

The existing Green Grocer in-app search does a case-insensitive compare for product names that contain the search query. Assuming the user searched for *apple*, and *title* was passed as an attribute, a comparable Spotlight search query would look like this:

```
title == "*apple*"c
```

The base compare checks that the `title` attribute contains the string *apple*. The * is a simple wildcard, meaning titles that contain *apple* meet the criteria, even if they have text before or after the word. The c modifier makes the comparison case-insensitive.

A word-based search may make more sense if the user simply wants strings that contain the unique word *apple*. They may want to see Fuji Apple and Red Delicious Apple, but not Pineapple or Snapple. In such a case, you likely want to ditch the wildcard to focus only on complete matches, making it more like a true search rather than a filter.

Here's what such a search would look like:

```
title == "apple"wc
```

Here the string is *apple*, with no wildcards. The w modifier says *apple* can appear anywhere in the title string, as long as it's a standalone word. Core Spotlight indexing is optimized to handle this faster than a wildcard, and as a bonus it provides a more accurately refined result set.

Numerics, especially dates, are quite common in search queries. It's especially common to check that a value falls within a given range. For this reason, the query language provides a second query syntax for this purpose.

```
InRange(attributeName, minValue, maxValue)
```

This checks that values associated with `attributeName` fall within the range bounded by `minValue` and `maxValue`.

Dates are an obvious use case for InRange queries. For dates, the query language uses floating-point values representing seconds relative to January 1, 2001. More commonly, you'll use `$time` values to derive dates.

`$time` has properties such as `now` and `today` that represent specific times relative to when a query kicks off. It allows for calculated dates relative to the current time, such as `now(NUMBER)` where `NUMBER` represents seconds added to the current time.

These simple queries formats can be combined to create more complex searches with the familiar `&&` and `||` operators. Here's an example using both query formats:

```
title == "apple"wc && InRange(metadataModificationDate,
$time.today(-5),$time.today)
```

`metadataModificationDate` is an attribute property that indicates the last date an item's metadata was updated. This query looks for products with *apple* in the title, as before. In addition, it checks that the item has been updated within the past 5 days — a great way to search for new or updated product listings.

> **Note**: The above query example won't work in Green Grocer, because it doesn't set the `metadataModificationDate`. If you wanted to do this, you'd have to add the property when indexing data. Additionally, you'd likely only do this if the user indicated a desire to view only new or updated products, perhaps via a search flag in your UI.

A complete list of `$time` properties, along with more detail on query language in general, can be found in Apple's documentation on CSSearchQuery: apple.co/1UPjAry

With this knowledge in hand, you've got all you need to start converting Green Grocer's search to use Core Spotlight!

Migrating to Core Spotlight Search API

Open **ProductTableViewController.swift** and add the following to the other properties at the top of `ProductTableViewController`:

```
var searchQuery: CSSearchQuery?
```

You'll use this to manage the state of the `CSSearchQuery` requests you kick off.

Now look for `filterContentForSearchText(searchText:)` in the `UISearchResultsUpdating` extension. This is called when the user updates their search string. It currently uses a `filter` to identify products in the `dataStore` with names matching the search string.

It's time to throw that away in favor of Core Spotlight Search!

Start by deleting this code:

```
filteredProducts = dataStore.products.filter { product in
  return
product.name.lowercased().contains(searchText.lowercased())
}

tableView.reloadData()
```

In its place, add the following:

```
// 1
searchQuery?.cancel()

// 2
let queryString = "title=='*\(searchText)*'c"
// 3
let newQuery = CSSearchQuery(queryString: queryString,
attributes: [])
searchQuery = newQuery

// 4
//TODO: add found items handler
//TODO: add completion handler

// 5
filteredProducts.removeAll(keepingCapacity: true)
newQuery.start()
```

This sets up the bones of the search. Here's what's going on:

1. As this method gets called each time a new search should be kicked off, canceling any currently running searches is good practice. `searchQuery` will later point to the new search query.

2. This `queryString` seeks to replicate Spotlight's behavior; it looks for the user-provided `searchText` in the `title` property. The query uses a case-insensitive compare and flanks the term with wildcards, meaning the product name can have other text before or after it and still match.

3. You then create a `CSSearchQuery`, passing `newQuery` as the query string and an empty attributes array. No attributes are required in the result set; instead, you'll pull object from the database using the returned search item's unique identifier. `searchQuery` now points to the `newQuery` so that you can cancel it when you kick off another search.

4. These TODOs relate to required handlers associated with the `CSSearchQuery` operation. You'll address these shortly.

5. You use `filteredProducts` as the table view data source when a filter is in effect. Because you're kicking off a new search, you should clear out the previous results. `newQuery.start()` then starts the Spotlight query.

Right now, nothing is listening for returned search results. Fix that by replacing `//TODO: add found items handler` with:

```
newQuery.foundItemsHandler = {
  (items: [CSSearchableItem]) -> Void in
  for item in items {
    if let filteredProduct = dataStore.product(withId:
      item.uniqueIdentifier) {
      self.filteredProducts.append(filteredProduct)
    }
  }
}
```

The `foundItemsHandler` is called as batches of `CSSearchableItem` objects matching the query criteria return from Core Spotlight. This code iterates over each returned `item` and locates a Product with a matching `uniqueIdentifier` in the `dataStore`. You then add the products to `filteredProducts`, which is the table view data source when a filter is active.

Finally, there is a `completionHandler` that runs when all results are in. This is where you'd do any processing on the final results and display them.

Replace `//TODO: add completion handler` with the following:

```
newQuery.completionHandler = { [weak self] (err) -> Void in
  guard let strongSelf = self else {
    return
  }
  strongSelf.filteredProducts =
strongSelf.filteredProducts.sorted
    { return $0.name < $1.name }

  DispatchQueue.main.async {
    strongSelf.tableView.reloadData()
  }
}
```

You added the results to `filteredProducts` in the arbitrary order as returned by Core Spotlight. This code sorts them to match the order used by the unfiltered data. Code to reload the tableview is dispatched to the main queue, as this handler runs on a background thread. Build and run; test your the filter on the **Products** tab. The behavior will be identical to the previous implementation.

The example below shows a partial match for *Ap* that includes *Apple* and *Grapes*:

This query filters products in a similar manner to Spotlight, but it has a major shortcoming: It only searches the product title, whereas Spotlight checks all of the metadata. To prove this, do an in-app search for *fruit* as you did before implementing Core Spotlight Search.

The title field doesn't include *fruit*, but the `keywords` property does. Clearly, Spotlight searches more than just title. You'll have to expand your query to match.

Still in `filterContentForSearchText(searchText:)`, find the following line:

```
let queryString = "title=='*\(searchText)*'c"
```

Replace it with the following:

```
let queryString = "**=='*\(searchText)*'cd"
```

The main change here is that instead of matching on `title`, you're using `**`. This applies the comparison to all properties in the search items' attribute sets. You've also added the d modifier to ignore diacritical marks. While this has no impact with Green Grocer's current inventory, it's a good general practice to follow.

Build and run, and enter a search for **fruit**. This time, you'll see all of the produce in the result set, just as you do in Spotlight.

> **Note:** A more practical example might be a user who recalled seeing a product with "potassium" in the description. Searching on that keyword in Spotlight will show "banana" — and now you can support that with in-app search!

The search you implemented was a simple one, with the primary goal of making Green Grocer's in-app results match those out of Spotlight. However, understanding these mechanics gives you all you need to know to deploy more sophisticated searches tailored to your specific data and user's needs.

Proactive suggestions for location

Adopting search makes it easy to implement other features that use NSUserActivity, such as Handoff and contextual reminders. Adding location data to your indexed NSUserActivity objects means they can be consumed by Maps, QuickType, Siri, and more.

View the Store tab in Green Grocer; the content is related to a physical location: the address of Ray's Fruit Emporium.

Wouldn't it be great if the Emporium address appeared above recent locations when you switch to the Map view? Or what if if the address appeared as a QuickType option in Messages, so you could tell your friends where to pick up the freshest pears in town? Proactive suggestions with location based activities make all of this possible, and more. Below are a few examples.

App Switcher   QuickType   Maps   Siri

From a user's perspective, this is one of the more exciting multitasking features iOS has introduced in a long time. From a developer's perspective, it's a great way to increase awareness of your app and your brand throughout iOS. As an added bonus, it's extremely easy to implement for apps that already index NSUserActivity objects.

To enable the feature, you need to minimally set the new **thoroughfare** and **postalCode** `CSSearchableItemAttributeSet` properties for location-related activities. These are used both for display purposes and to help location services find the address. You can further improve the quality of the results by including the following optional properties:

- `namedLocation`

- `city`

- `stateOrProvince`

- `country`

For more accuracy, you should include the `latitude` and `longitude` properties as well.

Adding a few properties isn't too hard, but wouldn't it be easier if it was just one propery? If you're using MapKit, you can point your `MKMapItem` to an NSUserActivity and it will populate all the location information for you. Fortunately, Green Grocer already leverages this, so it will be a snap to set up.

Time for a quick experiment. You need to do this on a physical device, as many location features are unavailable on the simulator. If you haven't already, be sure to set your development team in the GreenGrocer target's Signing section in the General tab.

Launch Green Grocer on a physical device, navigate to the **Store** tab and take note of the store address on Mulberry Street. Switch back and forth between tabs a couple of times to make sure the NSUserActivity indexing occurs.

Now jump to the home screen and do a Spotlight search for **Mulberry Street**. Make sure to scroll through all the results, and you'll see there are no Green Grocer matches.

Take a quick look in **StoreViewController.swift** and you'll see a `MKMapItem` with the store's address, as well as a `CSSearchableItemAttributeSet` containing the `longitude` and `latitude` of the shop.

The `supportsNavigation` attribute is also set to `true`, allowing navigation from Spotlight using the coordinates. However, Spotlight currently has no knowledge of the address, so it makes sense that Mulberry Street turned up no matches.

In one single line of code, you're going to provide the `NSUserActivity` with attributes needed to enable address search and enable proactive location suggestions.

In **StoreViewController.swift** find `prepareUserActivity()`. This is called when the store view loads and creates a search eligible `NSUserActivity` for the view.

Add the following line just above the `return` at the end:

```
activity.mapItem = mapItem()
```

`mapItem()` returns an `MKMapItem` that represents the location of the store. Setting `mapItem` to that value is all that's required to unlock location suggestions. Additionally, setting the `mapItem` populates the `CSSearchableItemAttributeSet` of the activity with all of its location information, including the street name.

Although `CSSearchableItemAttributeSet` properties are now set from the `MKMapItem`, they are overridden by existing code.

Find the following line in `updateUserActivityState(_:)`:

```
let attributeSet = CSSearchableItemAttributeSet(itemContentType:
  kUTTypeContact as String)
```

This creates a new `CSSearchableItemAttributeSet` that is ultimately assigned to the new NSUserActivity, thus replacing anything `MKMapItem` provided.

Replace it with the following:

```
let attributeSet = activity.contentAttributeSet ??
  CSSearchableItemAttributeSet(itemContentType: kUTTypeContact
  as String)
```

Now, if `contentAttributeSet` is already populated — thanks to the map item — it's added to, rather than replaced.

Build and run on a device, and flip between the two tabs a few times to ensure the NSUserActivity changes are indexed. Now double-tap the home button to bring up the app switcher. You'll see a proactive suggestion appear at the bottom of the screen including Green Grocer's name and the location of Ray's Fruit Emporium.

The suggested app differs based on what you have installed, but in the example below it's offering to launch Maps with directions to the store. Tapping the banner takes you to the suggested app with your location data prepopulated. Ray's Produce is really great, but it might not be worth the 18 hour drive from Texas! :]

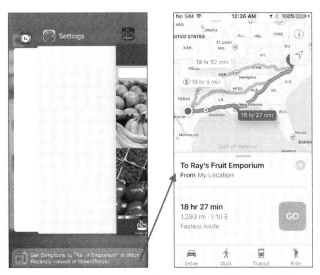

Open Messages and start typing a message that includes the words **Meet me at** and you'll see a QuickType suggestion including Ray's store. As with other proactive suggestions, your app is getting some good press here with the *From GreenGrocer* tagline.

Think back to the test in Spotlight search, where *Mulberry* pulled up zero results from Green Grocer. Repeat the search for **Mulberry**, and you'll now see a result for Ray's Fruit Emporium! This means the `MKMapItem` is successfully providing location information to the `CSSearchableItemAttributeSet`.

These are just a handful of examples of proactive suggestions. It should be pretty clear at this point that adding location data to your NSUserActivity objects is quite powerful. Not only does it streamline common user workflows, it reinforces awareness of your app throughout iOS.

Where to go from here?

In this chapter, you took an existing app with Core Spotlight and activity indexing and added some seriously cool functionality with minor effort. You enabled search continuation from Spotlight, and then refactored in-app search to use Spotlight's engine. Then with a single line of code, you enabled location based proactive suggestions to better integrate your app with iOS.

If you have an app already using Core Spotlight, the effort-to-benefit ratio should make adopting these features very compelling. Not only do they improve user experience, but they better integrate your app with iOS, giving you more opportunity to engage with the iOS ecosystem.

For more detail, check out the following resources:

- WWDC 2016 Making the Most of Search APIs apple.co/2cPwCbA

- WWDC 2016 Increase Usage of Your App With Proactive Suggestions apple.co/ 2cvOsAM

- search.developer.apple.com

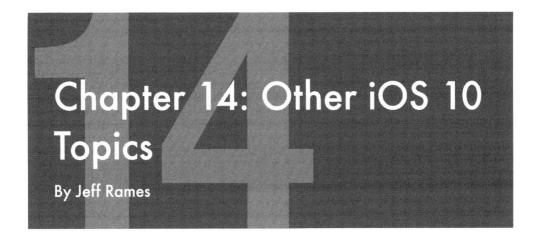

Chapter 14: Other iOS 10 Topics

By Jeff Rames

iOS 10 introduced many high profile features such as iMessage apps and SiriKit; it includes major enhancements to user notifications, Core Data, search, photography and numerous other topics that you've read about in this book.

But what you *haven't* seen are the smaller ways iOS 10 has improved. Every major framework has had notable updates, so regardless of the app you're working on, you have an opportunity to improve performance, architect better code, or delight your users with new features.

Many of these changes are too small to warrant a chapter of their own, but a few are notable enough that we felt we just had to share them with you. This chapter focuses on three bite-sized iOS 10 topics that many will find useful:

- **Data Source Prefetching**: Improves the responsiveness of your app by kicking off data processing well before a cell displays on the screen.

- **UIPreviewInteraction**: A new protocol that allows for custom interactions via 3D Touch.

- **Haptic Feedback:** An all-new feature tied to new hardware in the iPhone 7 and 7 Plus. The API provides the ability to produce several unique types of feedback.

Getting started

This chapter is designed a bit differently than others. Each topic gets its own mini chapter, including a high-level introduction with a starter project so you're ready to dive in.

This lets you go only as deep as you want on the topics that interest you. Feel free to choose one of these three options:

1. **Start to finish**. The first option is to read from start to finish as you would any other chapter. Each topic works with the same sample project.

2. **Skip ahead.** Alternatively you could skip to any section that interests you and complete it in tutorial fashion. Starter and completed projects are included for each section, so you don't need to worry about getting up to speed.

3. **Skim**. Finally you could read just the introduction of each section to get a high level understanding of these three topics. You can always return later for a deeper dive of the section.

All sections work with an app called EmojiRater that consists of a collection view displaying various emojis.

You'll give the collection view a speed boost in the section on prefetching. You'll then add the ability to rate emojis during the preview interaction section. Finally, you'll feel the result of haptic feedback in your app as the user scrolls to the top of the collection view.

Data source prefetching

In this section, you'll add data source prefetching to EmojiRater. If you haven't worked with collection views in the past, you'll want to check out our UICollectionView Tutorial series first: bit.ly/2d2njWi

The folder titled **prefetch-starter** contains the starter project for this section. Open **EmojiRater.xcodeproj** and get ready to super charge your collection view!

Data source prefetching provides a mechanism for preparing data before you need to display it. Consider an app with cells containing remotely housed images. You could drastically reduce the apparent loading delays with a prefetch that kicks off download operations.

A new data source protocol — **UICollectionViewDataSourcePrefetching** — is responsible for prefetching. The protocol defines only two methods:

- **collectionView(_:prefetchItemsAt:)**: This method is passed index paths for cells to prefetch, based on current scroll direction and speed. The items are ordered from most urgent to least, based on when the collection view anticipates needing them. Usually you will write code to kick off data operations for the items in question here.

- **collectionView(_:cancelPrefetchingForItemsAt:)**: An optional method that triggers when you should cancel prefetch operations. It receives an array of index paths for items that the collection view once anticipated, but no longer needs. This might happen if the user changes scroll directions.

For large data sources with content that is time consuming to prepare, implementing this protocol can have a dramatic impact on user experience. Of course, it isn't magic — it simply takes advantage of down time and guesses what will be needed next. If a user starts scrolling very quickly, or resources become limited, prefetch requests will slow or stop.

> **Note:** Fret not, table view users! If you are using a table view instead of a collection view, you can get similar behavior by implementing the **UITableViewDataSourcePrefetching** protocol. I recommend that you follow along here to learn the general idea behind prefetching, and then check out the API doc for table view specific syntax: apple.co/2dkSDiw

Implementing UICollectionViewDataSourcePrefetching

Take a quick peek at EmojiRater to familiarize yourself with the starter project. In this section, you'll focus on **EmojiCollectionViewController.swift**, which contains a collection view controller that displays `EmojiCollectionViewCell` objects. These cells currently just display an emoji.

The cells are configured in `collectionView(_:willDisplay:forItemAt:)`, where `loadingOperations` provide the content. `loadingOperations` is a dictionary keyed by `indexPath` with a `DataLoadOperation` value. This value is an `Operation` subclass that loads the emoji content and provides the result in `emojiRating`.

When `collectionView(_:willDisplay:forItemAt:)` is triggered, `DataLoadOperation` objects enqueue with their associated `indexPath`. Notice `collectionView(_:willDisplay:forItemAt:)` attempts to check for an existing operation before kicking one off. Currently that situation won't occur, because currently the only method that creates operations is `collectionView(_:willDisplay:forItemAt:)`.

Build and run, and scroll around the collection view at a brisk pace. You'll see a lot of place holder views containing activity indicators as cells first appear.

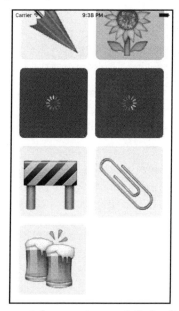

The project simulates what you might experience while loading images from a remote location, or retrieving data that requires expensive pre-processing. Open **DataStore.swift** and take a look at `DataLoadOperation` if you'd like to see how.

This is the `Operation` used for loading `EmojiRating` objects, which consist of an emoji and a rating in strong format. It simply introduces a random delay with a `usleep` before calling the completion handler.

Scrolling around isn't a user-friendly experience since the cells load so slowly. You're going to improve this by kicking off data load operations in the prefetcher.

Open **EmojiCollectionViewController.swift** and add the following extension to the bottom of the file:

```
extension EmojiCollectionViewController:
UICollectionViewDataSourcePrefetching {
  func collectionView(_ collectionView: UICollectionView,
                      prefetchItemsAt indexPaths: [IndexPath]) {
    print("Prefetch: \(indexPaths)")
  }
}
```

The `EmojiCollectionViewController` now conforms to `UICollectionViewDataSourcePrefetching` by implementing the one required method: `collectionView(_:prefetchItemsAt:)`.

When the collection view anticipates the need for specific cells, it sends this method an array of index paths representing those cells. For now, the method simply prints the passed index paths so you can get a feel for how prefetching works.

Now find `viewDidLoad()` and add the following near the top, just below the call to `super`:

```
collectionView?.prefetchDataSource = self
```

This sets `EmojiCollectionViewController` as the `prefetchDataSource` so the collection view can call the newly defined `collectionView(_:prefetchItemsAt:)` as needed.

Build and run and check the console output. Without touching anything in the collection view, you should already see something like this:

```
Prefetch: [[0, 8], [0, 9], [0, 10], [0, 11], [0, 12], [0, 13]]
```

Cells 0 through 7 present on the initial load, since the iPhone 6s simulator fits 8 cells. The collection view is smart enough to know that the user is at the top of the list, so the only place to go is down. With that in mind, the collection view requests cells 8 through 13, hoping to preload 3 rows.

Play around a bit, and you'll notice patterns to the requests made to the prefetcher. Your scroll speed affects the number of cells requested; scrolling faster requests more cells. Your scroll direction, coupled with how close you are to the start or end of the collection, also help determine which cells to prefetch.

Since the upcoming cells don't yet exist, you can't configure them. What you *can* do is tackle the time consuming part of the work: loading the data to be ready when the cells are. You'll kick off a `DataLoadOperation`; the existing architecture will check for this and load from it when it's available.

Change the contents of `collectionView(_:prefetchItemsAt:)` to the following:

```
// 1
for indexPath in indexPaths {
  // 2
  if let _ = loadingOperations[indexPath] {
    continue
  }
  // 3
  if let dataLoader = dataStore.loadEmojiRating(at:
indexPath.item) {
    loadingQueue.addOperation(dataLoader)
    loadingOperations[indexPath] = dataLoader
  }
}
```

The method now kicks off data loader operations for the upcoming data. Here's a closer look:

1. `indexPaths` is in priority order, with the most urgent item appearing first. You'll kick off load operations in that order.

2. `loadingOperations` is a dictionary of `DataLoadOperation` objects keyed by `indexPath`. `DataLoadOperation` is a custom operation that loads the emoji and its rating. This code checks to see if an operation already exists for this `indexPath`; if so, it skip the operation with `continue`.

3. `loadEmojiRating(at:)` creates a `DataLoadOperation` to fetch data for the EmojiRating corresponding to the passed `indexPath.item`. You then add the operation to the `loadingQueue` operation queue, in line with other requests. Finally, you add the new loader to `loadingOperations` using the item's `indexPath` as a key for easy lookups of operations.

You're now kicking off loaders as the prefetcher requests them. When a cell is configured, the data source checks the loaders for emojis. This should result in fewer placeholders when the user scrolls.

Build and run, and let the initial cells load. Now slowly scroll the collection view and you'll notice the majority of cells load immediately.

Usability is much better, thanks to prefetching.

User behavior can also change suddenly, making prefetched elements obsolete. Consider a user scrolling steadily through a collection, with the prefetcher happily requesting downstream items. If the user suddenly starts scrolling up instead, there are likely to be items in the prefetch queue that won't be required.

Because upstream items are now more urgent than the downstream ones already in the queue, you'd want to cancel any unnecessary requests. Calling `collectionView(_:cancelPrefetchingForItemsAt:)` with the unneeded downstream indexPaths cancels the associated operations to free up resources.

Add the following to your `UICollectionViewDataSourcePrefetching` extension:

```
func collectionView(_ collectionView:
  UICollectionView, cancelPrefetchingForItemsAt indexPaths:
  [IndexPath]) {
  for indexPath in indexPaths {
    if let dataLoader = loadingOperations[indexPath] {
      dataLoader.cancel()
      loadingOperations.removeValue(forKey: indexPath)
    }
  }
}
```

If a loading operation exists for a passed `indexPath`, this code cancels it and then deletes it from `loadingOperations`.

Build and run, then scroll around a bit. You won't notice any difference in behavior, but rest assured any unneeded operations will be canceled. Keep in mind that the algorithm is fairly conservative, so a change in direction doesn't guarantee operations will be removed — this depends on a number of factors private to Apple's algorithm.

The benefits of prefetching are evident even for a lightweight application like EmojiRater. You can imagine the impact for large collections that take a lot longer to load.

The folder titled **prefetch-final** contains the final project for this section. To learn more about Data Source Prefetching, check out the 2016 WWDC video on UICollectionView here: apple.co/2cKuW1z

UIPreviewInteraction

iOS 9 introduced 3D Touch along with an interaction you (hopefully) know and love — Peek and Pop.

The Peek (known as Preview to the API) provides a preview of a destination controller, while the Pop (Commit) navigates to the controller.

While you can control the content and quick actions displayed with Peek and Pop, you can't customize the look of the transition or how users interact with it.

In iOS 10, the all new **UIPreviewInteraction** API lets you create custom preview interactions similar in concept to Peek and Pop. A preview interaction consists of up to two interface states that can be accessed by the steadily increasing pressure of a 3D Touch. Unique haptic feedback is provided to signal the end of each state to the user.

Unlike Peek and Pop, these interactions are not limited to navigation. Preview is the first state; this is where you animate your content and interface into view. Commit is the second state; this is where you allow interaction with the content presented.

Below is an example of the two states followed by the outcome you'll implement with EmojiRater:

Preview State

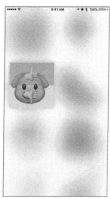
Commit State

Post Commit

The preview state slowly fades out the background, focuses on the selected cell and finally places voting controls over the emoji. In the commit state, moving your finger will toggle selection between the two thumbs. Press deeper to commit the rating; the interaction will fade away and the the cell will display the new rating.

To implement this, you need to configure an instance of UIPreviewInteractionDelegate; this is an object that receives messages from progress and state transitions.

Here's a brief overview of the protocol methods:

- **previewInteractionShouldBegin**(_:): Executes when 3D Touch kicks off a preview. This is where you would do anything required to present the preview, such as configuring an animator.

- **previewInteraction**(_:didUpdatePreviewTransition:ended:): Executes as the preview state progresses. It receives a value from 0.0 to 1.0, which represents the user's progress through the state. The ended boolean switches to true when the preview state completes and the value reaches 1.0.

- **previewInteractionDidCancel**(_:): Executes when the preview is canceled, either by the user removing their finger before the preview ends, or from an outside interruption like a phone call. The implementation must gracefully dismiss the preview when it receives this message.

- **previewInteraction**(_:didUpdateCommitTransition:ended:): Executes as the commit state progresses. It works identically to its preview counterpart and takes the same parameters. When this state ends, you must take action based on which control the user force-touched to commit.

You'll need a 3D Touch capable phone for this section, so have your iPhone 6s or newer at the ready. If you completed the prefetching section, you can continue with that project. If not, the folder titled **previewInteraction-starter** contains the starter project.

Open **EmojiRater.xcodeproj**, set your development team in the EmojiRater target, and get ready to be strangely judgmental about emojis! :]

Exploring UIPreviewInteractionDelegate

You'll start by implementing some UIPreviewInteractionDelegate methods and add a bit of logging to learn how they work.

Open **EmojiCollectionViewController.swift** and add the following to the properties at the top of EmojiCollectionViewController:

```
var previewInteraction: UIPreviewInteraction?
```

UIPreviewInteraction objects respond to 3D Touches on their associated view. You'll create one shortly.

Find viewDidLoad() where you create ratingOverlayView and add it to the controller's view. ratingOverlayView is responsible for the interaction interface; it creates a background blur and focuses on a single cell, which it then overlays with rating controls.

Find the if let that unwraps ratingOverlayView, and add the following just above the closing bracket:

```
if let collectionView = collectionView {
  previewInteraction = UIPreviewInteraction(view:
collectionView)
  // TODO - set delegate
}
```

collectionView is connected to a new UIPreviewInteraction to enable the rating interaction for cells. You've left a TODO here to set a delegate, which you'll do after configuring one.

Add the following extension at the end of the file:

```
extension EmojiCollectionViewController:
UIPreviewInteractionDelegate {
  func previewInteraction(_ previewInteraction:
    UIPreviewInteraction, didUpdatePreviewTransition
    transitionProgress: CGFloat, ended: Bool) {
    print("Preview: \(transitionProgress), ended: \(ended)")
  }

  func previewInteractionDidCancel(_ previewInteraction:
    UIPreviewInteraction) {
    print("Canceled")
  }
}
```

EmojiCollectionViewController now adopts the UIPreviewInteractionDelegate protocol and implements its two required methods. For now, you're printing some info so you can get a better understanding of how collection view calls these methods. One prints progress during the preview state, and the other indicates cancellation of preview.

Head back to viewDidLoad(), and replace the TODO - set delegate comment with:

```
previewInteraction?.delegate = self
```

Your `EmojiCollectionViewController` is now the
`UIPreviewInteractionDelegate`. 3D Touches on the `collectionView` will now
trigger the protocol methods you implemented.

Build and run on your device. 3D Touch one of the cells and increase your touch
pressure until you feel some haptic feedback. Watch the console and you'll see something
like this:

```
Preview: 0.0, ended: false
Preview: 0.0970873786407767, ended: false
Preview: 0.184466019417476, ended: false
Preview: 0.271844660194175, ended: false
Preview: 0.330097087378641, ended: false
Preview: 0.378640776699029, ended: false
Preview: 0.466019417475728, ended: false
Preview: 0.543689320388349, ended: false
Preview: 0.631067961165048, ended: false
Preview: 0.747572815533981, ended: false
Preview: 1.0, ended: true
Canceled
```

The preview state progresses from 0.0 to 1.0 as you increase pressure. When the progress
hits 1.0, `ended` is set to `true` to indicate the preview is complete. Once you remove your
finger, you'll see `"Canceled"`; this comes from `previewInteractionDidCancel(_:)`.

`UIPreviewInteractionDelegate` has two optional methods: one to signify the start of
preview, and one to track progress in the commit state. Add the following to the bottom
of the `UIPreviewInteractionDelegate` extension:

```
func previewInteractionShouldBegin(_ previewInteraction:
  UIPreviewInteraction) -> Bool {
  print("Preview should begin")
  return true
}

func previewInteraction(_ previewInteraction:
  UIPreviewInteraction, didUpdateCommitTransition
  transitionProgress: CGFloat, ended: Bool) {
  print("Commit: \(transitionProgress), ended: \(ended)")
}
```

`previewInteractionShouldBegin(_:)` triggers when the preview kicks off. You print
a commit message and return `true` to let the preview start.
`previewInteraction(:_didUpdateCommitTransition:ended:)` works much like its
preview state counterpart.

Build and run, then progress through the preview and commit states while watching the
console. You'll feel one style of haptic feedback when preview completes, and a different
style when the commit completes.

```
Preview should begin
Preview: 0.0, ended: false
Preview: 0.567567567567568, ended: false
Preview: 1.0, ended: true
Commit: 0.0, ended: false
Commit: 0.252564102564103, ended: false
Commit: 0.340009067814572, ended: false
Commit: 0.487818348221377, ended: false
Commit: 0.541819501609486, ended: false
Commit: 0.703165992497785, ended: false
Commit: 0.902372307312938, ended: false
Commit: 1.0, ended: true
```

The Preview should begin line indicates previewInteractionShouldBegin(_:) triggered as soon as the touch started. Preview progresses as before, followed by a commit in a similar fashion. When complete, the commit progress will be 1.0 and its ended property will become true.

Implementing a custom interaction

Now that you have a better feel for the flow of these delegate calls, you're just about ready to set up the custom interaction.

First, you'll build a helper method to associate the cell with an interaction. Add the following method to the bottom of the UIPreviewInteractionDelegate extension:

```swift
func cellFor(previewInteraction: UIPreviewInteraction)
  -> UICollectionViewCell? {
  if let indexPath = collectionView?
    .indexPathForItem(at: previewInteraction
      .location(in: collectionView!)),
    let cell = collectionView?.cellForItem(at: indexPath) {
    return cell
  } else {
    return nil
  }
}
```

cellFor(previewInteraction:_) takes a UIPreviewInteraction and returns the UICollectionViewCell where it originated.

The UIPreviewInteraction method location(in:) returns a CGPoint that identifies the touch position within the passed-in coordinate space. You use this to find the location of the touch in collectionView.

You pass that position to indexPathForItem(at:) to get the indexPath of the cell. You use cellForItem(at:) to obtain the cell with that indexPath. Finally, you return the cell if successful, or nil if not.

It's time to implement the interaction. Update the contents of `previewInteractionShouldBegin(_:)` to match the following:

```
// 1
guard let cell = cellFor(previewInteraction:
    previewInteraction) else {
  return false
}

// 2
ratingOverlayView?.beginPreview(forView: cell)
collectionView?.isScrollEnabled = false
return true
```

Here's what you're doing above:

1. You pass the `previewInteraction` associated with the touch that started the interaction to `cellFor(previewInteraction:_)`. If unable to retrieve the originating `cell`, you return `false` to prevent the preview from occurring.

2. `ratingOverlayView` is a full screen overlay you'll use to animate the preview control in place. `beginPreview(forView:)`, included in the starter, prepares a `UIViewPropertyAnimator` on the `ratingOverlayView` to blur the background and focus on the cell involved in the interaction. You then disable collection view scrolling to keep the focus on the interaction. Returning `true` allows the preview to proceed.

Next, you need to handle progress through the preview state. Replace the contents of `previewInteraction(_:didUpdatePreviewTransition:ended:)` with the following:

```
ratingOverlayView?.updateAppearance(forPreviewProgress:
    transitionProgress)
```

`updateAppearance(forPreviewProgress:)`, included in the starter, updates the `UIViewPropertyAnimator` object's `fractionComplete` based on the passed `transitionProgress`. This lets the animation progress in step with the preview interaction. This is a great example of how preview interaction progress indicators work seamlessly with other elements of UIKit for transitions.

Build and run, and press lightly on one of the cells. You'll see the preview state animate in, but you'll also notice something weird. Once you lift your finger, or the animation completes, it freezes in place.

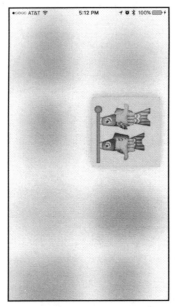

Take a quick look at the console. You'll see `Canceled` in the log — does it make sense now? You started animating in an interface based on interaction, but you didn't clean up the interface when the interaction ended.

You should be cleaning this up in `previewInteractionDidCancel(_:)`. Replace its contents with the following:

```
ratingOverlayView?.endInteraction()
collectionView?.isScrollEnabled = true
```

`endInteraction()` in `ratingOverlayView` reverses the animation to bring the view back to its prior state. You also re-enable scrolling on the collection view so that it can function as normal.

Build and run, and test the preview just up to the first tactile feedback. The controls fade in, and fade back out when you cancel the operation. That's much better!

Preview

Canceled

Something is still off, though. Push through to the second tactile feedback, then tap away — and the animation just disappears. This is because you've implemented the optional commit protocol method, but you're not doing anything with it.

Replace the contents of `previewInteraction(_:didUpdateCommitTransition:ended:)` with the following:

```
let hitPoint = previewInteraction.location(in:
ratingOverlayView!)

if ended {
  // TODO commit new rating
} else {
  ratingOverlayView?.updateAppearance(forCommitProgress:
    transitionProgress, touchLocation: hitPoint)
}
```

This determines where the user is touching `ratingOverlayView`, and stores that touch location in `hitPoint`. You'll use this to determine how the user is interacting with the control.

If the commit has ended, you need to commit the new rating and dismiss the preview. You've added a `TODO` for this action, which you'll circle back to shortly.

You call `updateAppearance(forCommitProgress:touchLocation:)` to update the interface if the commit is in progress. This method toggles highlighting of the rating views based on the `hitPoint`. This provides visual feedback to the user on what proceeding with the commit will do.

Build and run, and this time press past the preview haptic feedback and into the commit state. You'll see the rating views highlight as you move your finger up and down a cell.

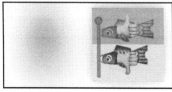

You still haven't quite reached your goal of rating those wind socks! Committing the rating doesn't do anything yet, as you need to get back to your TODO.

You'll first create a new method to handle the final commit input. Add the following method to the end of your extension:

```
func commitInteraction(_ previewInteraction:
  UIPreviewInteraction, hitPoint: CGPoint) {

  // 1
  let updatedRating = ratingOverlayView?
    .completeCommit(at: hitPoint)

  // 2
  guard let cell = cellFor(previewInteraction:
    previewInteraction) as? EmojiCollectionViewCell,
    let oldEmojiRating = cell.emojiRating else {
      return
  }

  // 3
  let newEmojiRating = EmojiRating(emoji: oldEmojiRating.emoji,
                                   rating: updatedRating!)
  dataStore.update(emojiRating: newEmojiRating)
  cell.updateAppearanceFor(newEmojiRating)
  collectionView?.isScrollEnabled = true
}
```

commitInteraction(_:hitPoint:) locates the EmojiRating associated with the item at hitPoint and updates it with the selected rating.

Taking a closer look at this code:

1. completeCommit(at:) identifies which rating appears on ratingOverlayView at the passed hitPoint and passes it back as a string (👍 or 👎). In addition, this method animates away the preview interface using the same code that previewInteractionDidCancel(_:) doeS.

2. You get oldEmojiRating from the cell identified using cellFor(previewInteraction:); if it can't be found, the guard returns early.

3. You then create newEmojiRating, passing in the old emoji and updatedRating, then save it to dataStore. You also call updateAppearanceFor(_:) to update the cell with the new rating. Finally, you re-enable scrolling.

Now you simply need to call this method when the commit is complete. In previewInteraction(_:didUpdateCommitTransition:ended:), replace the TODO commit new rating comment with the following:

```
commitInteraction(previewInteraction, hitPoint: hitPoint)
```

This calls the method you just created with the necessary parameters.

Build and run, and commit some emoji ratings by doing the following:

1. Slowly press down on a cell until you see the rating view appear and feel the first tactile feedback.

2. Select your rating, and press down harder to commit your choice until you feel the second tactile feedback.

At this point, you will see your vote show up on the cell:

Commit State   After Commit

You've now implemented both stages of a preview interaction, and acted on the results of the action. This API, along with things like UIKit animations and UIViewController transitions, provide limitless possibilities for 3D Touch initiated interactions. You'll certainly find more creative ways to rate hamburger emojis with what you've learned! :]

The folder titled **previewInteraction-final** contains the final project for this section. To learn more about UIPreviewInteraction, check out the 2016 WWDC video on 3D Touch here: apple.co/2djvSOA

Haptic feedback

The iPhone 7 and iPhone 7 Plus have a new Taptic Engine, which provides a wider range of sophisticated haptic feedback.

Haptic feedback is leveraged throughout iOS 10; new types of feedback signify different actions. For example, there's a selection feedback haptic that emits when scrolling a picker wheel.

Along with the new hardware, Apple unveiled APIs to allow developers to use the Taptic Engine in their apps. **UIFeedbackGenerator** has three concrete subclasses, each with unique haptic feedback:

- **UIImpactFeedbackGenerator** indicates an impact between two user interface elements. For example, you might use this feedback when an animation completes, snapping some object into place against a boundary.

- **UINotificationFeedbackGenerator** indicates a task has completed. For instance, uploading a message or building a new unit in a game might use this feedback. Any action that involves some type of short delay with the need for notification is a good candidate.

- **UISelectionFeedbackGenerator** indicates selection changes. For instance, scrolling through a menu might produce selection feedback each time a new item becomes selected.

Using these generators is dead simple. Below is an example of how to generate impact feedback:

```
let feedbackGenerator = UIImpactFeedbackGenerator(style: .heavy)
feedbackGenerator.impactOccurred()
```

Here you create a `UIImpactFeedbackGenerator` with a `heavy` feedback style. The style reflects the weight of objects involved in the impact. Triggering the feedback is as easy as calling `impactOccurred()`.

> **Note:** There are three `UIImpactFeedbackStyle` enum cases: `heavy`, `light` and `medium`. The style is meant to reflect the relative *weight* of objects involved in the collision. As you'd expect, heavy produces the strongest haptic feedback.

In this section, you'll trigger each of the feedback generators when the collection view in EmojiRater scrolls to the top. To experience it, you'll need an iPhone 7 or 7 Plus, and about five minutes! :]

If you completed the section on preview interactions, you can continue with that project. If not, the folder titled **haptic-starter** contains the starter project for this section.

Open **EmojiRater.xcodeproj**, set your development team for the EmojiRater target, and you're already halfway done!

Implementing UIFeedbackGenerator

Open **EmojiCollectionViewController.swift** and add the following method to the `EmojiCollectionViewController` extension indicated with a `UICollectionViewDelegate` mark:

```
override func scrollViewDidScrollToTop(_ scrollView:
UIScrollView) {
   let feedbackGenerator =
UIImpactFeedbackGenerator(style: .heavy)
   feedbackGenerator.impactOccurred()
}
```

This code overrides the `scrollViewDidScrollToTop(_:)` method found in `UIScrollViewDelegate`. The method triggers when a user taps the status bar to scroll to the top of the collection view.

You've created an instance of `UIImpactFeedbackGenerator` with the `heavy` style feedback; the impact style is appropriate in thie case, since the scrollview hitting the top of its offset results in a visual collision between the collection view content and status bar. You then call `impactOccurred()` to trigger the impact feedback.

Build and run, scroll down a bit in the collection view, and then tap the status bar to return to the top. Once scrolling finishes, you'll feel the heavy impact feedback. Feel free to experiment with `medium` and `light` `UIImpactFeedbackStyle` to note the difference.

While `UIImpactFeedbackGenerator` is appropriate for this UI interaction, you'll swap in swap in the remaining two types to see how they feel as well.

Replace the contents of `scrollViewDidScrollToTop(_:)` with the following:

```
let feedbackGenerator = UINotificationFeedbackGenerator()
feedbackGenerator.notificationOccurred(.success)
```

You create a `UINotificationFeedbackGenerator` and trigger it with `notificationOccurred()`. `success` emits feedback that indicates a task succeeded. Other options include `error` and `warning`.

Build and run, scroll down and hit the status bar. You'll experience a different haptic response, indicating success. Feel free to test again with the other two statuses to get a feel for them.

The last type is `UISelectionFeedbackGenerator`, which is not at all applicable for this interaction, but is still worth a test drive. :] Replace the contents of `scrollViewDidScrollToTop(_:)` once more with the following:

```
let feedbackGenerator = UISelectionFeedbackGenerator()
feedbackGenerator.selectionChanged()
```

`selectionChanged()` triggers `UISelectionFeedbackGenerator` to indicate a new selection event. Unlike the other `UIFeedbackGenerator` classes, it accepts no options and provides only a single type of haptic feedback.

Test it out, make a mental note of the feel. This should be familiar if you've set any timers in iOS.

`UIFeedbackGenerator` is a very simple yet important API, as it adds a compelling physical component to the user experience. Apple has started adopting haptics through their own apps, and you'd do well as an early adopter of haptics as well.

> **Note**: Keep in mind that haptic feedback is only available on the iPhone 7 and 7 Plus. Even on those devices, feedback may not occur depending on battery levels, user's settings, and app status. Haptic feedback is designed to supplement visual indicators, not replace them.

The folder titled **haptic-final** contains the final project for this section. A feedback generator is enabled by default, but the other styles are provided in comments. For more details on `UIFeedbackGenerator`, including best practices, check out the API Reference here: apple.co/2cVBAW7

Where to go from here?

iOS 10 is, by most metrics, a huge release. While it wasn't anything like the major overhaul of iOS 7, iOS 10 introduced improved and matured features throughout the SDK. Data source prefetching, preview interactions, and haptic feedback are just a few examples of the added niceties.

It's always a great idea to read through the What's New in iOS developer notes for iOS 10: apple.co/2coIGCr.

WWDC videos are also a great resource for any APIs or tools that you use in your development, and contain tidbits of information you might not find elsewhere : apple.co/1YtgQWy

There's only one thing left to do...

iOS 10 all the things!!

Conclusion

We hope this book has helped you get up to speed with the new changes in Xcode 8 and iOS 10.

If you have any questions or comments as you continue to develop for iOS 10, please stop by our forums at http://www.raywenderlich.com/forums.

Thank you again for purchasing this book. Your continued support is what makes the tutorials, books, videos, conferences and other things we do at raywenderlich.com possible—we truly appreciate it!

Wishing you all the best in your continued iOS 10 adventures,

– Sam, Jeff, and Rich

The *iOS 10 by Tutorials* team

65149840R00180

Made in the USA
Lexington, KY
02 July 2017